The Quest for Gender Equity in Leadership

The House of Prisca and Aquila

Our mission at the House of Prisca and Aquila is to produce quality books that expound accurately the word of God to empower women and men to minister together in a multicultural church. Our writers have a positive view of the Bible as God's revelation that affects both thoughts and words, so it is plenary, historically accurate, and consistent in itself; fully reliable; and authoritative as God's revelation. Because God is true, God's revelation is true, inclusive to men and women and speaking to a multicultural church, wherein all the diversity of the church is represented within the parameters of egalitarianism and inerrancy.

The word of God is what we are expounding, thereby empowering women and men to minister together in all levels of the church and home. The reason we say women and men together is because this is the model of Prisca and Aquila ministering together to another member of the church—Apollos: "Having heard Apollos, Priscilla and Aquila took him aside and more accurately expounded to him the Way of God" (Acts 18:26). True exposition, like true religion, is by no means boring—it is fascinating. Books that reveal and expound God's true nature "burn within us" as they elucidate the Scripture and apply it to our lives.

This was the experience of the disciples who heard Jesus on the road to Emmaus: "Were not our hearts burning while Jesus was talking to us on the road, while he was opening the scriptures to us?" (Luke 24:32). We are hoping to create the classics of tomorrow: significant and accessible trade and academic books that "burn within us."

Our "house" is like the home to which Prisca and Aquila no doubt brought Apollos as they took him aside. It is like the home in Emmaus where Jesus stopped to break bread and reveal his presence. It is like the house built on the rock of obedience to Jesus (Matt 7:24). Our "house," as a euphemism for our publishing team, is a home where truth is shared and Jesus's Spirit breaks bread with us, nourishing all of us with his bounty of truth.

We are delighted to work together with Wipf and Stock in this series and welcome submissions on a wide variety of topics from an egalitarian inerrantist global perspective.

For more information, visit www.houseofpriscaandaquila.com.

The Quest for Gender Equity in Leadership

Biblical Teachings on Gender Equity and Illustrations of Transformation in Africa

Edited by
KEUMJU JEWEL HYUN
and DIPHUS C. CHEMORION

Foreword by Joseph D. Galgalo

WIPF & STOCK · Eugene, Oregon

THE QUEST FOR GENDER EQUITY IN LEADERSHIP
Biblical Teachings on Gender Equity and Illustrations of Transformation in Africa

Copyright © 2016 Wipf and Stock Publishers. All rights reserved. Except for brief quotations in critical publications or reviews, no part of this book may be reproduced in any manner without prior written permission from the publisher. Write: Permissions, Wipf and Stock Publishers, 199 W. 8th Ave., Suite 3, Eugene, OR 97401.

Wipf & Stock
An Imprint of Wipf and Stock Publishers
199 W. 8th Ave., Suite 3
Eugene, OR 97401

www.wipfandstock.com

PAPERBACK ISBN: 978-1-4982-9333-4
HARDCOVER ISBN: 978-1-4982-9335-8
EBOOK ISBN: 978-1-4982-9334-1

Manufactured in the U.S.A. 08/30/16

Scripture quotations marked KJV are from the King James Version.

Scripture quotations marked NKJV are taken from the New King James Version®. Copyright © 1982 by Thomas Nelson. Used by permission. All rights reserved.

Scripture quotations marked NIV are taken from the Holy Bible, New International Version®, NIV®. Copyright © 1973, 1978, 1984, 2011 by Biblica, Inc.™ Used by permission of Zondervan. All rights reserved worldwide. www.zondervan.com The "NIV" and "New International Version" are trademarks registered in the United States Patent and Trademark Office by Biblica, Inc.™

Scripture quotations marked NLT are from the Holy Bible, New Living Translation, copyright © 1996, 2004, 2007. Used by permission of Tyndale House Publishers, Inc., Wheaton, IL 60189. All rights reserved.

Scripture quotations marked ESV are from the Holy Bible, English Standard Version. Copyright © 2001 by Crossway Bibles, a division of Good News Publishers. Used by permission.

Scripture quotations marked NASB are from the New American Standard Bible, copyright © 1960, 1962, 1963, 1968, 1971, 1972, 1973, 1975, 1977, 1995 by The Lockman Foundation. Used by permission. (www.Lockman.org)

Scripture quotations marked CEV are from the Contemporary English Version® Copyright © 1995 American Bible Society. All rights reserved.

Scripture quotations marked TLB are from The Living Bible copyright © 1971 by Tyndale House Foundation. Used by permission of Tyndale House Publishers Inc., Carol Stream, Illinois 60188. All rights reserved.

Scripture quotations marked NRSV are from the New Revised Standard Version Bible, copyright © 1989 the Division of Christian Education of the National Council of the Churches of Christ in the United States of America. Used by permission. All rights reserved.

Scripture quotations marked RSV are from the Revised Standard Version of the Bible, copyright © 1946, 1952, and 1971 the Division of Christian Education of the National Council of the Churches of Christ in the United States of America. Used by permission. All rights reserved.

Dedicated to all men and women who are committed to practicing and promoting biblical teachings on gender equity.

Contents

Contributors | xi
Foreword by Joseph D. Galgalo | xv
Acknowledgements | xix
Introduction | xxi
  —*KeumJu Jewel Hyun*

Part I: A Survey and Analyses of Gender Equity and Leadership in Africa

Chapter 1
The Cultural Basis of Gender Inequity: An *Agikuyu* Perspective on Identifying the Root Cause of the Problems in Practicing Biblical Equity | 3
  —*Sammy Githuku*

Chapter 2
Biblical Gender Equity and Women in Leadership: An Examination of the Anglican Church of Kenya | 14
  —*Lydia Mwaniki*

Part II: Reflections on Biblical Equity and Leadership

Chapter 3
Created Equal: A Fresh Look at Gender Equity in Genesis 1–3 | 31
  —*Diphus C. Chemorion*

Chapter 4
New Testament Evidence of Biblical Equity Revealed in Creation and Redemption | 42
  —*Kabiro wa Gatumu*

Chapter 5
Rereading Esther 1–2 for Equity and Women's Leadership: A Reflection on Gender and Leadership in the Old Testament | 56
—*Dorcas Chebet*

Chapter 6
Gazing at the Creation Purpose: Gender Equity at the Creation and Jesus' Esteem for Women as a Model | 65
—*KeumJu Jewel Hyun*

Chapter 7
Appreciating How the Apostle Paul Champions Women and Men in Church Leadership | 77
—*Grace May*

Chapter 8
Women Leaders in the New Testament: Biblical Equity Reflected in the Ministries of Jesus and the Apostle Paul | 96
—*Lois Semenye*

Chapter 9
Biblical Equity and the Meaning of Servant Leadership | 109
—*Aída Besançon Spencer*

Part III: Transformation in Africa as Gender Equity Is Practiced

Chapter 10
Women Leaders Rising Up: Two Case Studies in West Africa | 125
—*Martine Audéoud*

Chapter 11
Biblical Equity Practiced in the Reformed Tradition in Zimbabwe | 139
—*Rangarirai Rutoro and Ester Rutoro*

Chapter 12
Inclusive Leadership in African Instituted Churches in Nigeria | 147
—*Samuel Peni Ango*

Chapter 13
The Experience of Women Leaders in the Presbyterian Church of Nigeria | 162
—*Miracle Ajah*

Chapter 14
Practicing Biblical Equity in African Society | 180
—*John Peter Bwire*

Chapter 15
Biblical Equity within African Families | 197
  —*Judy Mbugua*

Conclusion | 208
  —*Diphus C. Chemorion and KeumJu Jewel Hyun*

Bibliography | 213
Scripture Index | 225

Contributors

Martine Audéoud is an associate professor in social sciences. She currently coordinates a doctoral program in Transformational Leadership as well as two master's programs at the Evangelical Theological Seminary of the Christian Missionary Alliance in Abidjan, Côte d'Ivoire. She also teaches graduate courses at international universities. Her academic qualifications include a PhD in School Administration and Supervision, Berne University, Switzerland; a DMin in Transformational Leadership, Bakke Graduate University, Dallas, TX, and an MEd from The Open University, UK. She is the author of *A Case for Transformational Leadership in Niamey* and a coauthor of *Être transformé pour transformer: La formation cachée de nos leaders africains*.

Samuel Peni Ango is a professor of Christian Education at the United Missionary Church of Africa Theological College, Ilorin, Nigeria. He holds a PhD in Religious Education from the Nigerian Baptist Theological Seminary, Ogbomoso, Nigeria; a Master of Arts in Christian Education from Evangelical Church Winning All Theological Seminary, Igbaja, Nigeria; and a Master of Arts in Literature from Ahmadu Bello University, Zaria, Nigeria. Dr. Ango has published numerous articles and chapter contributions in academic journals and textbooks around the world, as well as more than ten devotional books.

Miracle Ajah is a lecturer at the Department of Christian Theology, National Open University of Nigeria, Lagos; a minister of the Presbyterian Church of Nigeria; and a former rector of Hugh Goldie Lay/Theological Training Institution, Arochukwu. He obtained his Doctor of Theology in the Old Testament at Stellenbosch University, South Africa, and his Masters of Arts at Austin Presbyterian Theological Seminary, Texas, USA. He has authored many books and articles in Biblical Studies.

John Peter Bwire holds a PhD in Religious Studies specializing in Islam from Catholic University of Eastern Africa and an MA in Christian-Muslim relations from St. Paul's University, Kenya, and is a lecturer at Kenyatta University. He has written and published works on gender, human rights, and constitutionalism in Kenya; Genesis of Kadhi courts in Kenya; religious extremism; effects of global terrorism upon Kenyan Christians; women and microfinance; and Somali culture and Islamization in the Horn of Africa.

Dorcas Chebet holds a PhD in Old Testament from Stellenbosch University, South Africa, and an MTh from Protestant Theological University, Netherlands. She is a senior lecturer at the Presbyterian University of East Africa (PUEA) and serves as the head of the Department of Biblical Studies. She has authored several publications, including a chapter contribution titled, "Women and Leadership in the Reformed Church of East Africa: Addressing Gender Inequality in Africa."

Diphus C. Chemorion is the director of Postgraduate Studies and associate professor at St. Paul's University, Limuru, Kenya. He is the author of *Community Participation in Scripture Version Design: An Experiment in Translating Jonah into Sabaot* and *Introduction to Christian Worldview*. He has also co-edited *Contested Space: Ethnicity and Religion in Kenya*. He holds a Doctor of Theology in Old Testament from Stellenbosch University, Stellenbosch, South Africa, and a Master of Theology from Candle School of Theology, Emory University, Atlanta, GA.

Sammy Githuku is the dean of the Faculty of Theology, St. Paul's University, Limuru, Kenya. He holds a PhD in Old Testament Studies from the Catholic University of East Africa and an MA from McGill University, Canada. A priest in the Anglican Church of Kenya, Dr. Githuku has published a book entitled *Inculturation Biblical Hermeneutics: A Christian Integration of the Old Testament and the Agikuyu Concept of Sin* and has contributed to several academic journals.

KeumJu Jewel Hyun is founder and president of Matthew 28 Ministries, Inc., North Billerica, MA, a non-profit organization that focuses on training and developing Christian women leaders, as well as promoting and training women's economic empowerment for community transformation in Kenya. She is an adjunct professor of Theology of Work at Bakke Graduate University, Dallas, TX, and co-editor of *Some Men Are Our Heroes: Stories by Women about the Men Who Have Greatly Influenced Their Lives*. Dr. Hyun holds a Master of Arts degree in New Testament and a Doctor of Ministries degree from Gordon-Conwell Theological Seminary, South Hamilton, MA.

She also holds a Master of Science degree in Nuclear Physics from Yonsei University, Seoul, Korea.

Joseph D. Galgalo is the vice chancellor at St. Paul's University, Limuru, Kenya, as well as an associate professor of Systematic Theology. He holds a PhD in Systematic Theology from the University of Cambridge, UK. An ordained minister in the Anglican Church of Kenya, the Rev. Canon Prof. Galgalo has extensive experience in teaching and administration; he has served on the Inter-Anglican Theological and Doctrinal Commission, as well as on many boards—including World Vision Kenya as chairman and the Ecumenical Disability Advocacy Network (EDAN–WCC). His current research interests include developments in contextual theologies, especially African Christianity, and inculturation Christologies. He authored *African Christianity: The Stranger Within* and edited *Theological Education in Contemporary Africa* and *Disability, Society, and Theology: Voices from Africa*. He has also published over 15 book chapters and articles in refereed journals on various subjects, including God and disability.

Kabiro wa Gatumu is a senior lecturer in New Testament at St. Paul's University, Limuru, Kenya, and holds a PhD from Durham University, UK, and an MTh from KwaZulu-Natal University, South Africa. He is an ordained priest in the Anglican Church of Kenya. He is the author of *The Pauline Concept of Supernatural Powers: A Reading from the African Worldview* and has published several peer-reviewed journal articles and book chapters.

Grace May is an associate professor of Biblical Studies at William Carey International University in Pasadena, CA. She received her MDiv from Gordon-Conwell Theological Seminary and her ThD from Boston University School of Theology. Ordained in the Presbyterian Church (USA), she pastored at the Chinese Christian Church of New England, the First Chinese Presbyterian Church, Overseas Chinese Missions, and Emmanuel Presbyterian Church. She is a contributing author to *The Global God, Proclaiming the Scandal of the Cross, Growing Healthy Asian-American Churches*, and *Seeking Harmony: Intergenerational Theology of the Household of God*.

Judy W. Mbugua is the founder and CEO of Homecare Spiritual Fellowship, Nairobi, Kenya. She hosts a TV program entitled *Families under God* every Sunday evening and co-hosts a radio program with her son Robert every Sunday morning. She has authored several books and articles, including the soon-to-be-released *Relentless Faith*. Previously, she served as the continental coordinator for the Pan African Christian Alliance for twenty-one years. She also served as a lecturer at the Haggai Institute for Advanced Leadership.

Lydia Mwaniki is the director of Theology, Family Life, and Gender Justice in All Africa Conference of Churches, Nairobi, Kenya. She holds a PhD in New Testament from Kwazulu Natal University, South Africa, and an MTh in African Christianity from the University of Natal. Previously she served as a lecturer of New Testament studies at St. Paul's University. Dr. Mwaniki is also an Anglican priest and has authored several articles in refereed journals and books.

Ester Rutoro holds a Doctor of Philosophy in Education and specialized in Gender, Culture, and Education Management. She is a lecturer as well as the dean of Student Affairs at Morgenster Teachers' College, Zimbabwe, and is involved with the women's ministry in the Reformed Church in Zimbabwe.

Rangarirai Rutoro holds a Doctor of Theology in Practical Theology from Stellenbosch University, South Africa. He holds several positions: the principal of Murray Theological College, the chancellor of the Reformed Church University, the moderator of the Reformed Church in Zimbabwe, and the present chairman of NetACT.

Lois Mvuli Semenye received her EdD/PhD from Biola University, CA, and her MCE from Reformed Theological Seminary, Jackson, MS. She is an adjunct professor at Bridgeworld College, Karen, Kenya, the former deputy vice chancellor of Academic Affairs at International Leadership University, Nairobi, Kenya; deputy vice chancellor of Academic Affairs and ag vice chancellor at Kenya Highlands Evangelical University; and professor at Daystar University, Nairobi. Prof. Semenye has published several articles in peer-reviewed journals.

Aída Besançon Spencer is a professor of New Testament at Gordon-Conwell Theological Seminary, South Hamilton, MA. Dr. Spencer earned a Doctor of Philosophy degree in New Testament at Southern Baptist Theological Seminary and a Masters of Theology and Divinity at Princeton Theological Seminary. She has authored *Paul's Literary Style*; *Beyond the Curse: Women Called to Ministry*, a 1986 *Eternity* Book of the Year; *2 Corinthians: Daily Bible Commentary*; *1 Timothy*; and *2 Timothy and Titus* (New Covenant Commentary Series). She has also written with her husband, the Rev. Dr. William Spencer, *2 Corinthians*, Bible Study Commentary; *The Prayer Life of Jesus*; *Joy through the Night: Biblical Resources for Suffering People*; *The Goddess Revival*, a 1996 *Christianity Today* Book Award winner; *Global Voices on Biblical Equality*; *The Global God*; and *God through the Looking Glass*. Listed in *Who's Who in the World*, *Contemporary Authors*, and *Who's Who of American Women*, Dr. Spencer is an ordained Presbyterian minister.

Foreword

The question, "Where is my omelet?" can only be asked by human beings. This does not surprise us, since a human being is the only creature capable of asking questions. The strange thing is that the demand has become so "natural" that the question assumes such a sense of entitlement. The question "naturally" comes to mind without any thought that the egg belonged to the hen in the first place. What is so "natural" in a world where the "egg-eater" entertains no thought of the pain of the mother hen? What is "natural" in a world where antelopes must die for lions to live, and human empires must concentrate power in the hands of the ruler to keep the ruled in their place?

Even stranger is that a stratified society has so engendered inequality that societal disparity has become "natural." What divides one from the other spans economic and social class, gender and age, ethnicity and race, as well as religious and cultural spheres of life. This is even justified in such flamboyant catchphrases as "survival of the fittest," "eat or be eaten," "conform or die," "live by the rules," "know your place," etc.—and even philosophized in such thoughts as "But that is the way things are" or "Conformity *necessarily* guarantees order." This oddly "natural" order of things divides society at all levels of human existence. The fault lines are culturally and socially drawn, politically enforced, and in most cases, even religiously sanctioned. Rules and laws, as well as taboos and doctrines, are evolved to determine and prop up inclusion and exclusion, as well as to define identity, status, acceptance, honor, shame, roles, and rights.

Normalized inequalities, as absurd as this notion may be, have become characteristic of human existence, shaping worldviews, influencing values, and unfortunately *defining* gender relations. Such is the context within which gender inequality has become "natural." Contextualized beliefs and practices determine social structures such as patriarchal systems, which in turn shape and maintain ethical and moral ideas, societal expectations, and the application of justice or practice of equity. Justification is even sought in religious faith where culturally prismed hermeneutics buttress theological positions. In time, we are blinded and may easily fail to see obvious oppression, discrimination, and glaring inequalities at all levels of existence.

This collection of essays deals with the all-important and timely topic of gender relations and biblical equity in leadership. The essays are of varied strengths and focus, but each in its own way is of great value, bringing a helpful perspective to the volume. Different views are explored and varied conclusions drawn. Nevertheless, the question of a Christian biblical response to the concern of gender equity in leadership remains in focus.

Each writer in his or her own way explores, expounds, critiques, and challenges established views, social systems, and cultural structures vis-à-vis gender relations and arrangements, and brings these views under the searching light of relevant biblical teachings and appropriate theological considerations. Anecdotal experiences and carefully chosen case studies have been provided by some of the contributors, and in my view, add great value to the whole collection. Carefully crafted exegeses of pertinent texts are a particular strength of most of the chapters that deal with the topic of biblical equity in leadership. Where exegetically well-trodden paths have been followed, old arguments are recast in new ways. Their work is commendable and can afford the reader fresh inspiration and helpful ideas.

Having read these essays, I am convinced that, whichever way one looks at the issue of gender equity in leadership, our biggest difficulty will always remain that of reconciling varied hermeneutical and theological views. My humble submission is that the differing views can be reconciled, one way or the other, but only if we see "gender equity" first and foremost as a matter of justice. Theological and hermeneutical considerations must be approached from the perspective of justice and conclusions drawn with the question of "what is just" in mind. The world of ideal harmony (shalom) was shattered following the Fall. Masculine dominance, male superiority, and oppressive submissiveness are a product of a fallen world, and not of God's design or divine will.

As humanity contends with the effects of the curse—thorns and thistles, sweat and pain, and conflict and sorrow—God graciously journeys with us. Our basic human identity, although dented, is not lost. By virtue of a shared basic identity, man and woman are entwined as creatures made in the image of God, who are meant to become "one flesh." Man and woman must gratefully receive God's grace in order to journey together back to God's ideal world of equity. In the meantime, in matters of gender equity, as it should be in all matters of ethics and morality, the prophetic inquiry, "What does God require of you?" should be the light for our path in a fallen world of absurd "naturalness." Thankfully, by divine revelation the answer to this searching question is helpfully provided: "He has shown you, O mortal, what is good . . . to act justly and to love mercy and to walk humbly with your God" (Mic 6:8, NIV).

The Lord requires justice from us in all our dealings with one another, including in matters of gender relations. Theological soundness and hermeneutical correctness will never be free from biased conclusions, unless we first and foremost, accept one another as one—each of us, man and woman, standing in need of God's grace. Both are mercifully and equally endowed with varied talents and abilities for service in every domain of existence, including that of leadership. There is nothing in either common experience or divine revelation, which shows that men are better suited for leadership than women. Denial of equity cannot reasonably be justified on any ground, and our differences are no satisfactory basis for divisions. Our unfortunate divisions must be overcome by conscientious response to the divine call to act justly in all matters relational.

God dealt with our divisions in Christ Jesus and made us one even as we wait for the final consummation and perfection—when we shall all be one, even as the Father and the Son are one (John 17:21). We may differ with what the apostle Paul says on many different things, but not on this one—that "there is neither Jew nor Greek, there is neither bond nor free, there is neither male nor female: for ye are all one in Christ Jesus" (Gal 3:28, KJV). The clarity here should serve as a hermeneutical key to Paul's overarching intention when discerning the meaning of any of his other, seemingly obscure statements.

The crude "normalcy" or absurd "naturalness" of our fallen world must be overcome by justice—the new normalcy in Christ. In embracing the new normalcy, men and women accept the call to become "heirs together of the grace of life" (1 Pet 3:7, NKJV). Each deserves equal chance and opportunity to exercise their God-given leadership potential without hindrance and discrimination. Thankfully, in the following pages, the contributors to this book have presented brilliant and honest engagements with the subject. I need not belabor the significance of their substantial work. The reader is invited to deal "justly" with these considerable offerings.

Rev. Canon Prof. Joseph D. Galgalo
Vice Chancellor
St. Paul's University
Limuru, Kenya
January 2016

Acknowledgements

THIS BOOK IS THE fruit of the rigorous labor of many men and women who believe in the biblical teachings on gender equity and are committed to advocating these teachings.

We are grateful to all the contributors for having participated in the project and for granting us their precious time and thoughtful chapters. We truly appreciate each of their efforts. We also thank the Reverend Canon Professor Joseph D. Galgalo for his wonderful preface.

Many thanks are due to Rev. Dr. Grace May, our manuscript editor, for putting a great deal of effort into editing each chapter of the book and for collaborating with the book editors to ensure that each chapter is theologically and biblically sound, yet cohesive as a book. We also thank our copyeditor, Esmé Bieberly, for her tireless work in making the manuscript typesetting-ready. Without her work, the manuscript would have been merely a stack of printed paper. The work of these two people is thorough and impeccable; however, any residue of blemish or errors in the book remains with us, the book editors, as our responsibility.

We know it would not be possible to publish this book without the encouragement of Drs. William and Aída Spencer, co-publishers of The House of Prisca and Aquila, a series of Wipf and Stock Publishers. We also thank Matthew Wimer and his staff, especially Brian Palmer at Wipf and Stock for guiding us through the entire process of the publication of this book.

Finally, we thank the supporters of Matthew 28 Ministries for funding the project as well as our respective families for their love and support.

To God be the glory!

Introduction

—KeumJu Jewel Hyun

> *The teachings touched us women to come out of our inferiority complex and serve God.*
>
> *The conference helped me to see that I have a duty to my wife. Instead of criticizing what she does that does not satisfy me, I will be trying to initiate the things that I would like her to do. I will also support my wife giving her moral encouragement.*
>
> —Leadership conference attendees

I AM REMINDED OF a friend of mine who so dearly wanted to pursue seminary studies. She felt that her Bible knowledge had reached a limit, and she wanted to learn more systematically. The problem was that her husband would not support her desire for seminary studies. He did not see how further theological training would be useful to a woman. Thus, he was skeptical about the usefulness of seminary education and wondered what a woman was going to do with a seminary degree. His view was in keeping with the norm of what most Korean men think would be appropriate for their wives.

I had a similar experience when I had just enrolled in a program at a seminary. Being excited about my studies, another friend of mine told a pastor who happened to be around about my study plans. To her disappointment, he responded, "For what?" It did not surprise me, as I knew the pastor was not supportive of women's participation in church leadership and expected that he would not view my seminary studies positively. I do not know where he is now, but my friend is still talking about it.

These are only a couple of examples that illustrate the outcome of not understanding gender equity, as conceived at the Creation. This is a symptom and a result of redeemed people neglecting the Creation purpose and command God intended for man and woman together to carry out.

My exposure to the subject of Africa goes back many years. One Sunday evening some thirty years ago, I was in a special prayer meeting at my home church to pray for our missionaries. The pastor gave us a devotional on Matthew 28:19–20. While we were praying, suddenly a thought came to me: "What if God wants me to go to Africa? I do not want to interrupt my life at this time and go to Africa. I have a good job, my family is doing well, and I am happy with my church." Then, an unsettling fear swept through me so overwhelmingly that I was no longer able to stay there. I walked out of the church to go home in the middle of the prayer meeting. When I stopped at a stop sign a few blocks away from the church, I suddenly felt the song, "I have decided to follow Jesus . . . no turning back no turning back," ringing in my ears. The ringing sound was so loud that I could not go any further. Subsequently, I turned around, went back to church, and rejoined the prayer meeting. After that episode, I never went more than a thirty-mile radius from my home except during occasional, short travels here and there for various ministries. Then ten years ago, I was reconnected to the subject of Africa at the close of my seminary studies when I sensed that God was telling me the time had come to go to Africa, specifically Kenya. I was to minister to women all over the world—and, in particular, in Kenya—who suffer from inequity resulting from gender, religious, cultural, and traditional injustice.

Thus, we started a women's leadership training ministry in Kenya. Although our training is primarily focused on women leaders, we have intentionally invited male leaders to be trained along with female counterparts. We believe that no women's leadership training would be complete without having male leaders involved. Contrary to the common assumption that men are not concerned about the issues of gender inequity, we learned during the course of training that many male pastors and church leaders were interested in developing women leaders in their respective churches and organizations. Many senior pastors recognize that gender inequity is being practiced in the church as well as at home. They are eager to learn a correct biblical view of women and equip other men to change their view of and attitude toward women. Here is the story of one such pastor, Pastor Wangari, who did not know that his wife was created in God's image, just like himself, until he attended the leadership training. Intrigued by the biblical teachings on leadership and gender equity, he began to recognize the equality of his wife's humanity. One night he woke up and took care of their newborn baby, allowing his wife to sleep. Until then, he had thought that it was a woman's job to do all that was needed to take care of the baby. Startled by his unexpected gesture of kindness, his wife thought something was wrong with him. After the training, Pastor Wangari sensed the need for further education and enrolled in one of the most prestigious universities in

Kenya, receiving a bachelor's degree in theology. Since then, he has planted a church and is now deeply committed to developing women leaders.

Here are some examples of what male leaders said after their training on gender equity. One pastor said, "The conference was relevant to my life and ministry. I have learned the importance of women's involvement in church . . . [and] will start immediately giving [women] opportunities to preach and involve women in decision making. . . . The conference was timely for me, and it has made me a better pastor/husband/father." Another pastor expressed, "It has actually changed my life and way of thinking." Yet another pastor commented, "This will now enable me to work confidently together with women." One more pastor said, "This conference has been of great help. I am a changed person. . . . I have given only one women an eldership position, but from now on I am going to do something more. . . . The big problem was me, because I had never trusted them [women]." We also noticed, in our interactions with women throughout the training, that many women suffer from low self-esteem and have negative views of male leadership. The root of the problem can be attributed to the fact that women have been disregarded in society for so long that they were accustomed to believing what they had been told about their identity. Subsequently, this resulted in forgetting or no longer recognizing that they had been created in God's likeness. Despite poor self-image, however, many women were committed to attaining biblical and theological knowledge to become effective leaders in their respective communities.

The following stories of improved self-esteem and empowerment reflect the impact that the women attending equity training received. Naomi[1] is a worship leader of her church who constantly struggled to serve the church without alienating her non-believing husband. She helped three women from her church complete beauty school training and earn a steady income. However, Naomi sensed something lacking in herself; she wanted to be better equipped to be more effective in her service but was not sure what to do. After attending one of our leadership training conferences, she enrolled in and earned a diploma program from a Bible college. Now Naomi serves her church with confidence. Rachael came from a rural area in the western part of Kenya. She was so moved by the contextual Bible study training that, upon returning home, she immediately started leading a Bible study at her "support group" for women and men with HIV/AIDS. The response from the group was so overwhelming that Rachael wanted to learn more about

---

1. Not her real name. All names subsequently mentioned in the chapter are not real names to protect the individual's privacy.

the Bible and ministering to people. She then eventually received a diploma in counseling and became an effective leader in her community.

The ongoing feedback of transformation from our conferences compelled us to extend our teachings on biblical equity to a broader range of communities. We wanted to make resources promoting women and men ministering together to be readily available because we believe in God's vision of women and men working side by side with mutual respect at home, in the church, and in society.

That is how we undertook a project to publish this book, *The Quest for Gender Equity in Leadership*. We chose the title to communicate that God created man and woman equally in His image and commanded them both to increase and multiply and rule over the earth. However, sin brought enmity between male and female, resulting in constant animosity between the genders. Regardless of such a tragic state of affairs, we believe that gender equity can be practiced at the leadership levels among redeemed people in Christ.

We opted for the word *equity* instead of *equality* in order to communicate our primary focus on equal treatment and equal opportunity in fairness. Various dictionaries define equity as a term stating quality. Equity connotes fairness and impartiality toward all involved parties based on principles or regulation. In biblical terms, the word *equity* is used to describe uprightness and fairness: "doing what is right and just and fair" (Prov 1:3, NIV). "I the LORD, speak righteousness, I declare things that are right" (Isa 45:19, NKJV). The LORD establishes equity (Ps 99:4, NKJV); judges the world with righteousness and "the people with equity" (Ps 98:9b, NKJV); and makes "fair decisions for the exploited" (Isa 11:4, NLT). When the LORD gives wisdom, and "guards the paths of the just and protects those who are faithful to him," then people will understand what is "righteousness and justice and equity" and find the right path to go (Prov 2:8–9, NKJV, NRSV). He rebukes the leaders and rulers who detest justice and "pervert all equity" (Mic 3:9, NKJV).

The book is organized into three parts. Part I addresses the historical and cultural background of inequity being practiced in Africa. Sammy Githuku examines cultural influences on gender among the *Agikuyu* tribe, while Lydia Mwaniki explores the challenges facing women leaders in the context of the Anglican Church in Kenya. Through case studies, the two authors examine strengths and weaknesses in the African concept of equity in leadership.

The second part of the book presents a theological and biblical basis of exercising fairness and equal treatment for granting leadership opportunities to men and women in all areas of life. In this section, the authors examine a wide range of Bible passages and offer a biblical view of how equity can be practiced. Diphus Chemorion leads us in a walkthrough of the Creation and the Fall in the first few chapters of Genesis. He sees that interpreting Genesis 1–3 through cultural worldviews is one of the impediments of gender equity and corrects commonly misunderstood subjects. He reminds us that men and women equally bear the image of God; women and men are of the same rank; woman was not created to be subordinate to man; woman is not man's property, nor is woman inferior to man. Following Chemorion, Kabiro wa Gatumu presents biblical evidence that both male and female are included in God's redemption plan, contrary to other religions. The chapter is very creative in looking at gender equity through redemptive history. Dorcas Chebet gives us her reflection on gender and women leadership by rereading chapters one and two of the book of Esther. She presents different modes of women's leadership as demonstrated by Queen Vashti and Queen Esther. Jewel Hyun examines the Creation narrative and takes "interdependency" as an attribute of God's likeness of man and woman. She then presents from the Old Testament a few stories of man and woman working in partnership, explores the Gospels, and shows how Jesus treated women counterculturally in first-century Palestinian culture.

In the New Testament, Grace May shows us how the apostle Paul championed women and men in extending God's reign in the world, an example of women and men working side by side in advancing God's kingdom. Lois Semenye walks through the Gospels, as well as the writings of the apostle Paul in the New Testament and gives us a profile of some women leaders in the ministry of Jesus and Paul. Aída Spencer looks at the meaning of servant leadership in the context of equity. She gives us a profile of a woman leader in Kenya as today's servant-leader model.

Part III of the book brings good news on how gender equity is practiced in some African societies. Martine Audéoud tells us stories of two women in West Africa who rose up to become prominent leaders. Rangarirai and Ester Rutoro, a husband and wife team, write about gender issues in the Reformed tradition in Zimbabwe and how the Reformed Church reached the decision to ordain women. Samuel Ango presents his research results of the AIC in Nigeria, which agreed to advocate for women's leadership in the church. He reports that while problems still exist, a few churches have called women to assume prominent roles, including senior minister positions. Miracle Ajah reports on women's roles in the Presbyterian Church in Nigeria. He explains various terms used in discussing gender equity, such as the egalitarian view versus the complementarian view, before he introduces us to some women leaders of the Presbyterian Church of Nigeria. He concludes with a recommendation that more aggressive education for gender equity be sustained in the Presbyterian Church of Nigeria. John Bwire takes us through the past and present on how inequity against biblical teachings has been practiced in African society. He lists such elements as African traditional culture, gendered social life, cultural norms, and colonial laws as being barriers to practicing biblical equity. Bwire then leads us to the good news that, despite the barriers, some progress is being made in society. His recommendations for ways of practicing biblical equity that will transform society are quite valuable. He then concludes that biblical teachings on equity need to be promoted with "gender acceptable interpretations." Finally, Judy Mbugua ends our book with a pastoral message on how family members can live out biblical teachings on equity. She concludes that deliberate effort for renewing our minds is the best way of achieving the virtue of living out biblical equity in the family.

This book is intended for men and women throughout the globe who are engaged in Christian leadership in church, ministry, business, or family. Although the book takes African countries as the point of departure to explore the cultural and traditional influences in gender inequity and presents how some countries are progressing in alleviating the problem, the issue itself is universal and relevant for all. Thus, we aim at bringing awareness to women and men throughout the world, promoting biblical teachings on gender equity and encouraging the practice of gender equity for the purpose of advancing God's kingdom. The evil effects of gender prejudice at church, at home, and in society become an enormous hindrance to spreading the good news of Jesus Christ because it keeps women from exercising God-given gifts fully. The ill effects of gender inequity are not limited to females only; when women suffer, men suffer from the consequences as well. Therefore, both men and women are encouraged to be aware of what the Bible teaches about gender equity and actively embrace the truth in all aspects of their lives. By doing so, women may be encouraged to grow in self-esteem with the knowledge that God made them wonderfully and fearfully in His image so that they might fulfill His purpose. Likewise, male leaders will acknowledge that much work needs to be done and will help bring harmony, empowering women to strengthen their ministry contributions at home, at church, and in church. In addition, male leaders can take the initiative in their areas of responsibility and leadership to advocate for change and empower women to lead.

The authors of this book are women and men representing five countries in two continents: Kenya, Nigeria, the Ivory Coast, Zimbabwe, and the USA with diverse cultural and traditional heritages. We believe that readers from different cultures throughout the globe will benefit greatly from understanding biblical teachings on equity in leadership and the consequences of gender inequity which become hindrances to spreading the gospel throughout the world. For the same reason, we would like to point out that this book is not just for women readers only. We believe both men and women will find the book beneficial for removing the obstacles that keep women and men from fully utilizing God-given gifts for His glory's sake.

We pray and hope that this book can serve as an instrument to all who follow Christ for betterment in ministry, in society, and in family life.

PART I

A Survey and Analyses of Gender Equity and Leadership in Africa

Chapter 1

The Cultural Basis of Gender Inequity
An *Agikuyu* Perspective on Identifying the Root Cause of the Problems in Practicing Biblical Equity

—Sammy Githuku

INTRODUCTION

FIFTY YEARS AFTER KENYA got her independence, most women have not realized their full potential. They are still being held down by African traditional culture. Article 27 (8) of the Constitution of Kenya requires the government and other institutions to ensure that at least a third of the employees are women.[1] Although some significant progress has been made, the goal has yet to be achieved. Affirmative action is meant to remove the gender inequity inherent in many tribal cultures in Kenya and seeks to increase women's participation in leadership, decision-making, and economic opportunities.

Today, some resilient traditional beliefs and cultural practices still influence the inequity between men and women in many areas of life in Africa. Furthermore, many activities are still inscribed in traditional cultural structures, reinforcing the inequity between the genders and perpetuating

---

1. *The Constitution of the Republic of Kenya,* Article 27 (8).

traditional models of inequity in economic, legal, and leadership opportunities. Women, for example, are still denied access to property and justice. The aim of this chapter is to illustrate how *Agikuyu* traditional culture, worldview, and practices prescribe the continual inequity between men and women. Examples are drawn from socially constructed *Agikuyu* proverbs that have been accepted as tradition and used for years to propagate gender inequity. Let us first define some of the terms used in this chapter.

The term *African traditional religion* is used here to refer to belief systems peculiar to the *Agikuyu*, practiced before conversion to Christianity. These beliefs and practices permeated every aspect of individual and community life. The dictionary meaning of the term *equity* is used in this paper. It is the quality of being fair, unbiased, and just—to both men and women. This involves ensuring that everyone in the community has a fair opportunity to access resources, opportunities, influence, and responsibility indiscriminate of their gender. The term *gender* is used in this paper to refer to the tasks, responsibilities, conduct, and activities the *Agikuyu* believe are fitting for men and women respectively. Basically, gender plus biological differences are what distinguish men from women. The following is a synopsis of the *Agikuyu* people.

THE AGIKUYU

The *Agikuyu* is one of the Bantu-speaking ethnic groups living in Kenya.[2] The current, administrative Central Province was their original home. Presently, like all other Kenyan communities, they are found in different parts of the country. According to the 2009 census, the *Agikuyu* are estimated to be 16.9 percent of the national population. *Gikuyu* is their ethnic language and the name of their first mythological patriarch. Traditionally, the *Agikuyu* were peasant farmers who also practiced livestock keeping. The tribe is divided into ten *mihiriga* (clans). Each clan is made up of several *mbari* (subclans) that are made up several households called *nyumba*. The head of the *nyumba* is a man called *muthuri* (one who discerns). He is the ultimate authority in all family affairs and exercises great power. The wife, as opposed to *muthuri,* is known by several humbling names; the most common term is *mutumia* (one who keeps her mouth shut). This is a familiar term used to

---

[2]. The people call themselves *Agikuyu* in their mother tongue. *Gikuyu* is the proper noun of their mythological father and also their language. Users and writers from other languages, such as English and Kiswahili, refer to the people and their language as *Kikuyu*. The writer is a member of the community under study and prefers the term *Agikuyu*.

refer to a wife. *Muka* or *mundu muka* is another term, which means, "one who does not belong," because she is from another family. The wife was also known as *mundu wa nja,* a general term for the feminine gender. *Nja* is the *Agikuyu* word for "outside." The wife is, therefore, one who does not belong to "the inside." The literal meaning is "she is an outsider." The *Agikuyu* families lived in homesteads with several houses of different family members.

Historically, the *Agikuyu* did not have a written language. Information was passed on orally through folklore, songs, and proverbs. Through these proverbs, knowledge, instructions, wisdom, philosophy, values, morals, and a justice system were communicated. Through these avenues, the responsibilities of men and women were culturally determined and passed on. Women and girls were restricted to the home and the farmyard. A woman or a girl who broke these traditions was considered to be arrogant and inappropriate. She was ostracized by her group as punishment. According to Kenyatta, ostracism by the community was worse than imprisonment.[3] Religious matters, livestock, legal matters, land, and property ownership was, and still is, in the hands of the men. Similarly, a man who did not adhere to these culturally determined responsibilities was ostracized by the community.

The paragraphs below illustrate how the cultural determination of responsibilities leads to inequity between men and women. Both genders are discriminated against, making certain duties and careers off limits. The *Agikuyu* are a patriarchal society. Some of the stereotypes against men and women are simplistic generalizations and assumptions without evidence. However, the resulting negative consequences have led to serious inequities between men and women. Women, for example, are underrepresented in decision-making forums. Community bias impairs their job performance. Those who step out of their spheres of restriction encounter hostility.

THE AGIKUYU PROVERBS AND GENDER EQUITY

Proverbs reflect values, beliefs, experiences, and teachings held by members of a community. These proverbs express the *Agikuyu* worldview that will change with time. They offer great instructions and pass on community wisdom from one generation to another. However, there are some proverbs that are designed to instill a feeling of superiority in men and boys, while others inculcate in women and girls fear and inferiority. In this paper, in the interest of space, we will limit our study to proverbs that illustrate gender partiality in *Agikuyu* traditional culture.

---

3. Kenyatta, *Facing Mount Kenya*, 230.

One unique fact about African Christianity is that most adherents live in duality. That is, while they are fully Christians, they continue to observe the teachings of their respective traditional religions. Christians have not yet found teachings that can fully replace the traditional cultural teachings, which are seen as basically good and are not fully abandoned when people become Christians. John Mbiti observes that,

> Unless Christianity and Islam fully occupy the whole person as much as, if not more than, traditional religions do, most converts to these faiths will continue to revert to their old beliefs and practices for perhaps six days a week and certainly in times of emergency and crisis.[4]

Christianity has not fully occupied the whole of human activity. Most Africans still see most activities through the African worldview. The *Agikuyu*, like other communities, have continued to use proverbs as instruments to transmit their culture, social morality, beliefs, and human experience. The following proverbs convey the *Agikuyu* worldview that highlights gender norms, roles, and community expectations. This, in turn, determines what each member of the community becomes.

Traditionally, male *Agikuyu* elders were the custodians of the community law. They were the prosecutors and judges of community disputes. They were often required to keep the information they received from clients confidential. Women were discriminated against on this responsibility. The *Agikuyu* generalized that women cannot keep secrets and, therefore, cannot be trusted with confidential legal matters. This was propagated through certain proverbs, such as *Muici na mundu muka atigaga kieha akua* (He who has stolen in the company of a woman lives in fear until she dies, for a woman cannot keep a secret).[5] This proverb is demeaning to women because it assumes a woman cannot keep confidence, and it can be understood in the context of a parallel proverb equating the status of a woman to a youth: *Muici na kihii atigaga kieha akua* (He who has stolen in the company of a boy lives in fear until the boy is initiated into adulthood).[6] *Kihii* is the *Agikuyu* word for a teenage boy. It is synonymous with disobedience and bad behavior. These proverbs put a woman and a youngster on the same level. Both teenage boys and women cannot keep secrets, and, therefore, they cannot be trusted. This kind of belief about women served to maintain a particular social order dominated by men. Women cannot, therefore, be

---

4. Mbiti, *African Religions*, 3.
5. Barra, *1,000 Kikuyu Proverbs*, 58.
6. Ibid., 57.

involved in legal matters or any arena where participants are expected to treat information confidentially. This bias against their trustworthiness is further attested to by two other proverbs: *Mundu muka ndatumagwo thiri-ini* (A woman is not sent to collect debts);[7] and *Aka matiri cia ndiiri no cia nyiniko* (Women have no upright words but only crooked ones).[8]

The *Agikuyu* considered women to be flawed human beings. This was taught through the proverb *Mutumia na kionje ni undu umwe* (A woman is comparable with a physically challenged man).[9] *Kionje* is the *Agikuyu* word for a physically challenged, feeble person—or one suffering from a chronic disease.[10] Among the *Agikuyu*, a person with a disability was seen as hopeless and helpless. Physical disability was considered to be a curse, a result of witchcraft, and a divine punishment. Physically challenged individuals were discriminated against by the community. This prejudice against the physically challenged was heightened further by the following proverb: *Cionje ikumi irugitwo ni umwe uri na hinya* (Ten physically challenged people are surpassed by a single strong person).[11] In other words, one man is stronger than ten women. Such unfortunate proverbs have enormous implications on women's contributions to economics.

The *Agikuyu* did not consider the life of a woman equal to that of a man. If a man took the life of another man, the family of the deceased was compensated according to the customary law. The fine for such an offence was ten cows or one hundred sheep or goats. However, if a woman was killed, the offender was charged three cows or thirty sheep or goats.[12] By implication, a woman was considered to be of less value than a man. Under Kenyan national law, the death of a man and a woman are considered equal.

Domestic violence is another area where gender inequity surfaces. A gender-equitable man is opposed to violence against women. The *Agikuyu* warriors were not equitable men. They did not respect girls or their mothers. The belief that men and women should have equal rights and share responsibility in the community was unknown. The following examples illustrate this fact. According to L. S. B. Leakey, the *Agikuyu* girls were required to shave warriors (*anake*). It was inconceivable that a warrior would shave a girl.[13] Furthermore, during public dances, the warriors commanded

7. Ibid., 62.
8. Ibid., 2.
9. Ibid., 71.
10. Benson, *Kikuyu--English Dictionary*, 361.
11. Barra, *1,000 Kikuyu Proverbs*, 5.
12. Kenyatta, *Facing Mount Kenya*, 228.
13. Leakey, *The Southern Kikuyu Before 1903*, 742.

the girls to cut firewood for the dances. Leakey observes that orders issued by these warriors were considered more important than those of their mothers.[14] He further observes that the warriors (*anake*) had certain rights of restricted sexual intercourse (*nguiko*) with the girls against their will. If the girls refused, the *anake* bewitched the girls.[15] Women and girls had no lives of their own. Every aspect of their lives was decided by men. Girls were expected to help their mothers in the field and perform household duties. A young widow who had no adult sons was married off to her brothers-in-law. However, she was free to get other lovers if she chose to.[16] Parents had great influence on the marriages of the children. If the parents judged the girl to be lazy, regardless of the love between the young adults, the parents would not allow such a marriage to take place.[17]

Christianity teaches that both male and female are created in the image and likeness of God (Gen 1:26–27). The *Agikuyu* viewed women differently from men. They discriminated against women by associating certain untamed animals with women. Antelopes are referred to as *mburi ya atumia* (women's goats).[18] Similarly, one other proverb is aimed at creating enmity between women and cows: *Aka na ngo'mbe itiri ndugu* (women and cows are not friends).[19] Cows and goats are the two most precious properties of an Agikuyu man. They are so close to his heart that he will safeguard them with all his might. This proverb has been formulated to perpetuate the inferior status of women which denies them the right to own sheep and cows.

Naturally, human beings grow from childhood to maturity. A mature person is able to make conscious decisions. We grow to the awareness that we are responsible for our own life. The *Agikuyu* denied that a woman was capable of this development. This was taught through the proverb *uhii ni umagwo no uka ndumagwo* (The man grows up out of childhood, but a woman never comes out of womanhood).[20] According to Giovanni Barra, when a Kikuyu boy was initiated, he was no longer considered a boy. He received full rights as a man. However, a girl, even after initiation, is not entitled to new rights. A girl does not get rights even after she grows up to

---

14. Ibid., 742.
15. Kenyatta, *Facing Mount Kenya*, 159.
16. Ibid., 963.
17. Ibid., 741.
18. Benson, *Dictionary*, 276.
19. Barra, *1,000 Kikuyu Proverbs*, 7.
20. Ibid., 109.

be a woman.[21] This proverb has been formulated to perpetuate the inferior status of women.

Traditionally, the *Agikuyu* men dominated socio-economic and political leadership and organizations. Economically, the women contributed equally with men. When a girl got married, for example, she was given up to four sheep and goats for herself.[22] This was an economic addition to the family wealth. Furthermore, the woman and her daughters worked in the farm contributing to the economy of the family and the community. In spite of this contribution to the economy, women and girls could not own property or inherit land. This was the preserve of men and their sons. According to Leakey, women were inheritors of land only if they had no children.[23] Another proverb was formulated to discourage women from engaging in commerce. The *Agikuyu* had stereotypes that hindered women in their personal development. It was believed that debts stir quarrelsome emotions in women: *Haro ni ya muka uri thiri* (Quarreling is peculiar to a woman who has debts, or a woman in debt is quarrelsome).[24] Thus, by implication, a woman who takes out a bank loan to invest for personal development will naturally turn confrontational. This proverb has been structured to justify male dominance in economic matters.

Furthermore, women who engaged in duties and tasks culturally reserved for men were looked down at and ridiculed. A girl who, for example, climbed trees, competed with boys, or challenged boys was mocked. She was referred to as *Wanja kahii* (small, boyish girl) or *Wanja kihii* (big, boyish girl) depending on the size of the girl. *Kihii* is not a term of endearment when used for a girl. It is term used for dirty, uninitiated boys with detestable manners. *Wanja* is a feminine personal noun or an adjective describing a girl. When used as an adjective, the noun *nja* (outside) is combined with a prefix *wa* (of) to describe a girl who spends her time outside with boys instead of staying indoors doing domestic chores. This stereotype is a threat to gender equity and can impair girls' performance.

In the above section, we have observed some of the *Agikuyu* proverbs that propagate inequity. There are, however, a few *Agikuyu* proverbs that teach justice and fairness for all. These proverbs, probably because of the sinful nature of humankind, have not influenced the community as much as the negative proverbs. Furthermore, the few proverbs demanding equity are

---

21. Ibid., 110.
22. Ibid., 785.
23. Ibid., 883.
24. Barra, *1,000 Kikuyu Proverbs*, 20.

easily challenged by several proverbs standing for inequity. Let us consider some the proverbs that teach equity:

The *Agikuyu* proverbs that call for equity use the term *kihooto*. According to Benson, the *Agikuyu* noun *kihooto* means "a powerful plea, justice, equity, fairness, right, and proof."[25] The word *kihooto* may not be synonymous with the word *equity* in every instance, but it describes the spirit behind fair or just action. The phrase "judge the case with equity" is translated as *tua cira na kihooto*. The following sayings and proverbs demand evasive equity: a saying defining *kihooto* states, *Kihooto ni kio kioma* (Justice is firm and inflicting).[26] The belief that justice is supreme is expressed with this proverb: *Muingatwo na kihooto ndacookaga* (A person who has been prevailed with justice does not return to discuss the matter).[27] There is also a longer version of this proverb affirming the same truth: *Muingatwo na njuguma niacokaga, no muingatwo na ikihooto ndacookaga* (He who is driven away by a club appeals, but he who is driven away by justice does not return to make an appeal).[28] Lastly, the following proverb states that justice is unmovable: *Kihooto kiunaga uta mugeete* (Justice prevails over the drawn bow).[29] That is, justice can triumph over an archer who has drawn his bow against an accused person. These few proverbs confirm that equity was not totally lacking; however, its application was left in the hands of men. Justice overrides the tribal law.

BIBLICAL TEACHINGS CHALLENGE INEQUITY

The Holy Scriptures challenges the inequity justified through culture. In the Bible, both women and men are created equally in the image of God. "So God created man in His own image, in the image of God He created him; male and female He created them" (Gen 1:27, NKJV). The psalmist declares that all human beings are "fearfully and wonderfully created" (Ps 139:14, NKJV). Both women and men are created "a little lower than God and crowned . . . with glory and honor" (Ps 8:5, NLT). The *Agikuyu* proverbs we have examined above have portrayed women with inequity, contrary to the biblical teachings.

The Bible counters the stereotypes, propagated by the *Agikuyu* proverbs, that women cannot be leaders. In the Scriptures, we find women who

25. Benson, *Dictionary*, 163.
26. Wanjohi, *The Wisdom and Philosophy*, 49.
27. Barra, *1,000 Kikuyu Proverbs*, 59.
28. Benson, *Dictionary*, 188.
29. Ibid., 163.

were prophets and judges. Deborah, who lived roughly in 1200 BC, was one of the judges who ruled Israel before the monarchy was established under King Saul. She judged Israel under a palm-tree between Ramah and Bethel (Judg 4:4–5). She summoned Barak to make war against Jabin, king of Canaan. She accompanied him into the battle and gave the signal for the army to launch the attack (Judg 4:8–9). Jabin was completely routed (Jugd 4:16).

Another example of a woman leader is Huldah. She was a prophetess who lived in Jerusalem during the reign of Josiah (640–609 BC). The king and the high priest appealed to her rather than to Jeremiah who was a prophet at the time. She was consulted by the king regarding the "book of the law" discovered by the high priest Hilkiah in the temple. Her word was accepted by all as the word of Yahweh. This book became the basis of major reforms carried out by King Josiah (2 Kgs 22:14–20; 2 Chr 34:22–29).

Esther, a Jewish girl married to Ahasuerus, king of Persia, was a woman of courage, piety, and patriotism. She used her wisdom to save the Jews in Persia from a genocide planned by Haman (Esth 7:1–10). And in the New Testament, women played their part in the ministry of Jesus and Paul. Like Jesus, Paul did not have women evangelists traverse the rugged lands of Asia Minor with him, but he appreciated the support he received from women.

A gender-equitable man could be defined as a man who believes that women and men should have equal rights and opportunities, who believes that women and men share responsibility in decisions and roles in the household and community, and who is opposed to all forms of inequality. Gender equity informs programming and policies. Achievement of gender equity is central to any development. Women's contributions in today's societies are essential and indisputable. However, nowhere is their status on par with that of men. Women are a vulnerable group in all areas. Inequality is deeply rooted in social and cultural practices. The legal, economic, and social dependency of women has historically placed them in a subordinate position. Gender is a social construct that defines how men and women behave and what femininity and masculinity look like in society. Furthermore, the construct affects how society perceives women and men *de facto* and in the eyes of law.

CONCLUSION

This chapter has documented how traditional culture and practices transmitted in *Agikuyu* proverbs prescribe the inequity between men and women. These traditions are old but continue to have impact on the community. The gender bias illustrated above is harmful to both men and women because stereotypes are not always true—and having a false view of either gender is not fair.

However, much progress has been made on three fronts. Firstly, culture, customs, practices, and traditions are dynamic. Interaction with other cultures and the effects of globalization are causing considerable changes in gender dynamics.

Secondly, the spirit and letter of the new Kenyan Constitution (2010) provides an avenue and opportunity for gender equity. Article 27 on equality forbids discrimination and affirms that both genders are equal in the eyes of the law. Article 53(1)(e) provides that all children have a right to parental care and protection. These laws will go a long way to prohibit cultures and practices that are discriminatory. Courts are now obligated to apply these standards and laws while carrying out their judicial duties.

Thirdly, and probably most importantly, education and Christianity have changed many beliefs and teachings, especially in the urban centers. Christianity is a gift from God that can overcome gender inequity based on cultural, traditional beliefs and practices. According to Ed Matthews, Christ is above culture.[30] Christianity provides a unique opportunity to promote equity between both genders. There are almost no responsibilities that are catalogued in the cultural, traditional way as being the preserve of a particular gender. In Christ, there is "neither male nor female: for ye are all one in Christ Jesus" (Gal 3:28, KJV). Both men and women can perform all traditional activities without being ostracized. This promotes the participation of both women and men, as well as the rightful distribution of resources. It is my assertion that negative cultural practices thrive in an environment where women and men have unequal access to education, wealth, health, and employment as is the case in *Agikuyu* traditional culture. These social constraints, traditions, customs, and religion make equity untenable. While cultural biases and stereotypes are part of our fallen nature and undermine equity in leadership, examples of women leaders drawn from the Bible and the good news of Jesus Christ will correct these cultural biases against women. The church, on her part, will embrace good proverbs that enhance equity in leadership.

The good news has been proclaimed in Africa for more than a century now. Those who believe are witnesses that Christ is a transformer of negative culture. The struggle is far from being won. Christians should confront dehumanizing cultural, religious, economic, and political beliefs and support what is good in the culture in their society. In time, and with the

---

30. Matthews, "Relationship," 3.

increase in number of those who believe in the good news, divine ideals will enrich African culture and gender equity will flow like water.

Chapter 2

Biblical Gender Equity and Women in Leadership
An Examination of the Anglican Church of Kenya

—Lydia Mwaniki

> This church proclaims that all human beings are made in the image of God and are therefore, of equal value and dignity in the sight of God, and, while careful to provide for the special needs of different people committed to its charge, allows no discrimination in the membership and government of the Church based on grounds of racial, tribal, or gender difference.[1]

BIBLICAL GENDER EQUITY IN leadership is first mentioned in the Genesis text (1:27), which describes God as creating *ha-adam* in the "image of God"—"male and female He created them"—and then charging them equally to have dominion over the rest of God's creation as God's stewards (Gen 1:28, NKJV). While the interpretation of *Imago Dei* (image of God) continues to unfold in various dynamisms, our understanding in this paper is that both male and female equally share in all implications of being created "in the image of God . . . male and female" (Gen 1:27). The implication for us includes the ability of both male and female to image God in their moral, spiritual, and intellectual nature. They image God in their ability to actualize qualities that God has bestowed on them. The denial of the possession of gifts in women, whether these are gifts of leadership or otherwise,

---

1. *The Anglican Church of Kenya Constitution* 2002:6, Article IV.

results in a distorted perception of *Imago Dei*, which adversely impacts both men and women and ultimately leaves us with an impoverished view of God whose image is both male and female.

The gender-inclusive article IV in the Anglican Church of Kenya (ACK)[2] Constitution (2002:6) seems to suggest that the church supports gender equity in leadership with the understanding that both male and female are created in the image of God. However, the journey toward the achievement of biblical gender equity in leadership has been a long one in the ACK. While a commendable effort is being made to empower women through engaging them in leadership positions—and the church has even gone as far as ordaining them—my experience as an ordained woman in ACK has shown that women are still marginalized in various areas of the life of the church. For example, the participation of the ordained women clergy in the topmost leadership positions of bishop and archbishop in the church is still a nightmare. Why has it been so difficult to meet the constitutional mandate of gender equity in the ACK? What have been the hindrances? How far has the church gone to create gender equity, and what still remains to be done? This paper responds to these questions by examining the development toward biblical gender equity in leadership within the ACK, tracing it to gender equity in pre-colonial, colonial, and post-colonial Kenya. The paper will finally give recommendations on what the church needs to do in order to attain biblical gender equity in leadership. As a witness of this development in her capacity as an ordained priest in the ACK, the author will begin by giving her own experience as a case study.

DEVELOPMENTS OF BIBLICAL EQUITY IN THE ACK: THE JOURNEY OF THE AUTHOR AS A CASE STUDY

My first experience of the struggle of ACK to achieve gender equity in leadership came when I was still in my mother's womb. Having been brought up by her parents, Mr. and Mrs. Ishmael Nduki, who were among the first missionary converts in Kabare, Kirinyaga County, Kenya, my mother was a staunch Christian. One day in her fourth month in the second pregnancy, as she was splitting firewood, she had a strong wish which she expressed to God as a silent prayer: "God, if the baby that I am carrying in my womb is a boy, I will dedicate him to your service." However, when the baby was born five months later, she happened to be a girl. Though my mother was excited that she had delivered me safely, she was a little disappointed that God had not answered her prayer and expressed these words in her mother tongue:

---

2. Formerly, Church of the Province of Kenya (CPK).

a! anga nikamuirit u, airitu onanimagitungataga nyombaini ya Ngai?" (Alas! so it is a girl! Girls do not serve in God's house, do they?). In those days, women were not ordained to the priesthood; hence, my mother's hope of her newborn child ever serving as a priest was shattered. I was born and brought up in a Christian environment and gave my life to Christ at the age of fourteen, after which I committed myself to teaching Sunday school children and later the youth group.

My second experience of the struggle of the ACK to fulfill its biblical and constitutional mandate to realize gender equity in leadership came with my training for the ministry. In January 1987, I joined St. Andrews Bible School Kabare—later St. Andrew's College of Theology and Development in Kabare, Kenya—after having a strong conviction to serve God in a more dedicated way. In a class of about 30 men, there were six girls who were happily training to become better-equipped Sunday school and youth teachers, to do pastoral visitation, and to assist the vicar (the priest in charge) with the chalice during Holy Communion and preaching. We were not allowed to perform sacramental duties. None of us dreamt that one day women would be ordained to priesthood. Nevertheless, there was a huge gender disparity which marks my second experience of the struggle to realize gender equity in the ACK leadership. After training for three years for a certificate in theology, men were immediately made deacons and then ordained to priesthood after six months. Women were commissioned to serve in the lay ministry, first as lay readers, and after six months, as deaconesses. Sometimes we were assigned to serve under our male classmates as their juniors. It was not uncommon for the vicar to ask me to prepare tea and lunch for the council meeting, or any other meeting, hence denying me my constitutional right to attend the meeting. There was also a large discrepancy with regard to remuneration. The salary scale was based on ordination rather than on the level of education.[3] Deaconesses in my diocese (at that time, the Diocese of Mt. Kenya East) began to be ordained to priesthood in 1992, after heated debates in various diocesan synods in which some of the participants argued that both the Bible and African culture do not allow women to lead men, among other reasons which will be highlighted later in this paper.

My third and most challenging experience of the struggle of ACK to meet the biblical and constitutional mandate of biblical gender equity came when I decided to test the ACK's commitment to its constitutional clause on gender equity in leadership *by applying for the position of a diocesan bishop*. My PhD interdisciplinary study between biblical studies and gender from

---

3. Mwaniki, "The Impact," 63.

the University of Kwazulu-Natal, South Africa, had led me to examine how 1 Corinthians 11:1–16 has been interpreted and appropriated in the history of the Christian tradition. I found that this and many other such biblical texts have been used to deny women leadership positions in the entire history of the Christian tradition. Therefore, after graduating with my PhD in 2011, I felt well equipped and challenged enough to bring transformation by breaking the unconstitutional gender-biased chain of leadership. In August 2012, I made a bold step to offer myself as the *first woman* in Kenya for the advertised position of the bishop of the ACK Diocese of Kirinyaga, where the current bishop was retiring. However, due to mysterious circumstances, my nomination paper was declared "spoilt" in the nomination process so that I was denied the opportunity to appear before the interviewing panel. The experience left me with more questions than answers and remains a mystery to many people, including myself. This experience serves as an indication that the topmost leadership position of bishop (and consequently that of archbishop) in the ACK is still a male preserve. Participation of women in these offices is still an unresolved agenda in the ACK, despite the egalitarian constitutional clause. Nevertheless, my journey in the ACK reveals that the church is moving toward realization of biblical gender equity in leadership. To begin with, ordination of women to the priesthood was a bold step against a culture where women were never known to lead men. More opportunities for women continue to open with their ordination.

Why then has the journey to achieve biblical gender equity in leadership been so long in the ACK? The above case study highlights two major hindrances—African culture and the Bible—to full participation of women in leadership. In the following sections, we will look at how Anglican missionaries engaged with culture in an attempt to eliminate gender discrimination as a way of promoting equity in leadership.

DIALOGUE BETWEEN THE PRE-COLONIAL AND CHURCH MISSIONARY PERCEPTIONS OF BIBLICAL GENDER EQUITY IN LEADERSHIP IN THE COLONIAL ERA

The history of the Church Missionary Society (CMS) in Kenya, from which ACK originates, goes back to 1844 when it started its mission work at the coast. By 1910, the CMS had moved up-country and planted churches in the central part of Kenya (Kikuyuland), following the British colonial occupation of the area by punitive means.[4]

The CMS missionaries made every effort to liberate Kenyan women from cultural practices, which were oppressive to them, despite the torture and resistance with which they were met by the pre-colonial Kenyan communities. Education was one of the areas through which the missionaries empowered women, despite its gender-biased curriculum.[5] The missionaries also fought against female subordinating practices such as dowry, female circumcision, polygamy, and levirate marriages, etc. It is, however, notable that, as colonial agents of civilization, the missionaries aimed at "civilizing" African culture more than they aimed at liberating women from patriarchy. The missionaries, for instance, kept women from ordination and only introduced them to supportive roles in the church. It is also worth noting that, in the Church of England from which the missionaries had been sent, women were not ordained to the priesthood but were urged through exhortations from the pulpit to find fulfillment in their duties as wives and mothers at home.[6] In so doing, the CMS missionaries imitated the existing pre-colonial religious and political structures with regard to gender equity in leadership.

DIALOGUE BETWEEN ACK, CMS, AND PRE-COLONIAL PERCEPTIONS OF BIBLICAL GENDER EQUITY IN LEADERSHIP IN THE POST-COLONIAL ERA

A Brief History of ACK

The Anglican Church in East Africa was founded originally as the Diocese of Eastern Equatorial Africa, comprising present-day Kenya, Uganda, and central Tanzania in 1884, with James Hannington as its first bishop. This diocese was split into two, giving way to the Dioceses of Mombasa and Uganda in 1899. Mission work in Kenya, which had begun in 1844 in Mombasa, continued to grow under white missionaries, particularly with their settlement in the Kenyan highlands. In 1955, Bishops Obadiah Kariuki and Festo Olang' were consecrated as the first Kenyan bishops. With the

---

4. Temu, *British Protestant Missions*, 90–93; Smith, *The History*, 34; Mwaniki, "The Impact," 47–51.

5. For more information about the CMS missionaries in Kenya and women's education, see, among others, Presley, *Kikuyu Women*; Kanogo, "Mission Impact on Women," 165–86; KNA Mss/61/341 "CMS" 1939–1940; KNA Mss/61/348 "Kabete Girls' School" 1941–1943.

6. Gill, "The Liberated Woman," 4.

new African leadership of the church, the numerical growth of the church increased, which led to the splitting of more dioceses to this day. Currently, ACK has thirty-seven dioceses.

The Role and Status of Women in ACK

The ACK, improving on what the missionaries did to emancipate women, has shown aspects of resistance to the colonial and patriarchal perceptions of women by empowering them, especially through education and ordination to priesthood, and through encouraging women to participate in diverse ways in the church as lay people. How did the ordination of women to the priesthood come about, what roles do women play in ACK, and what challenges do they face?

Developments in the Ordination of Women to Priesthood in the ACK

Discussions about the ordination of women to the priesthood began taking place in the House of Bishops in ACK in 1980, following the recommendation of the Lambeth Conference of 1978 that the member churches could consider ordaining them.[7] Although the province agreed in principle that women could be ordained in 1980, each diocese was to be autonomous in taking up the issue. Rev. Lucia Okuthe was the first woman to be ordained to the priesthood in Kenya in 1983. The Church of England began to ordain women to the priesthood only in 1994, long after several women had been ordained in the ACK.

One of the leading dioceses that took up the issue of women's ordination was the then-Diocese of Mt. Kenya East, under the bishopric of the late Rt. Rev. Dr. David M. Gitari, who later became the archbishop of ACK. He made a remarkable impact on the whole province. His enthusiasm was, however, not shared by many, as we can see from the debates on ordination in his diocese. Bishop Gitari raised the issue of women's ordination to priesthood in four consecutive diocesan synods: 1979, 1981, 1983, and 1986. The motion lost in the first three synods because the majority of the members, who were predominantly male, opposed it.[8] The motion was finally passed

---

7. Lambeth Conference 1978:44–45, Resolution No. 20.

8. *The Diocese of Mount Kenya East*, Resolution 51/83. The motion lost by 71 votes against, 69 votes in favor. It was supported by 50 people in the House of Laity against 31, and 18 people in the House of Clergy against 40 clergy who opposed it.

in 1986.[9] The first three women were ordained in the new Diocese of Kirinyaga in 1992, after the split of the Diocese of Mt. Kenya East in 1990. By 2000, the Diocese of Kirinyaga was leading with twenty-nine ordained women, followed by the Diocese of Embu with ten ordained women. Other dioceses followed gradually, but the pace has slowed down.

Debates on Women's Ordination

It has been difficult to trace debates on women's ordination from the minutes of the provincial synods, because the discussions and arguments that took place were not recorded. What *was* recorded were the resolutions that were made (see, for example, Provincial Synod 1982 Min. 23/82 "Ordination of Women"). This makes it very difficult to trace arguments that were leveled against women's ordination, as well as reasons why the motion finally won at the provincial level. However, in our previous study, we were able to gather some of the factors in favor of and against women's ordination using both oral and written sources from the ACK Diocese of Kirinyaga.[10] We found that the arguments against were mainly historical, biblical, and cultural.

Historically, some Christians have argued that the CMS only trained and ordained men, but not women. Such an argument was based on ignorance of the fact that the CMS was an emissary of the Church of England's gender-biased tradition.

The biblical and theological arguments were built on church tradition, namely, that women were not part of the levitical priesthood in the Old Testament, that Jesus chose only male disciples, and that Pauline theology does not allow women to speak in church. Bishop Gitari rose against such views and argued that "the Bible should be taken in its social-cultural context through proper biblical hermeneutics."[11]

Cultural arguments were based on the fact that women were never leaders in traditional society and that the only women who participated in religious affairs were past child-bearing age. Some synod members were, therefore, of the opinion that deaconesses should be ordained to a diaconate ten years after completing their ordination training. Others recommended

---

9. Resolution 56/86, cited in Mwaniki, "The Impact," 63.

10. Mwaniki, "The Impact," 64–65. Due to the absence of ordination debates at the provincial level, we shall use the debates in ACK Kirinyaga Diocese as representative of some of the factors that withheld women from being ordained in the entire ACK and how these were finally overcome.

11. Gitari, oral interview, quoted in Mwaniki, "The Impact," 64.

that only married women should be ordained, while still others claimed that ordained women should remain unmarried.[12]

Other cultural factors raised included the objection that the ordination of women would empower women to lead men, which is against (Kikuyu) culture. It was interesting that the proposers of such conservative arguments had no problem with women leaders in other fields. The synod rejected these arguments as mere prejudices, born from patriarchy. Others also argued that, if ordained, women would cease to be traditional wives and mothers.[13]

A further concern was the issue of menstruation and childbirth, which, biblically and culturally, renders a woman unclean. Some opponents of ordination, therefore, declared that, if ordained, women would defile the church. Bishop Gitari argued that this is a biological condition for which women ought not to be stigmatized. After all, "both men and women come from the same blood."[14]

The 1986 diocesan synod, where the motion to ordain women was finally carried with a majority of 131 votes against 78, observed that the reasons against were more cultural than theological in nature. The synod therefore argued that "the time of preserving some of our discriminative aspects of our culture is now gone in our churches."[15]

A closer look at the ordination debates in the ACK reveals a trajectory of similar arguments against full participation of women in the church in the history of Christian tradition straight from Paul, the church fathers, the reformers, the Church of England, and the Western missionaries.[16] The debates in the ACK were patriarchally, theologically, and imperially driven. The influence of the Victorian theology of gender in the Church of England, through the missionaries, is evident in the debates, alongside Pauline theology of male headship, as well as African cultural prejudices. The ACK may, however, be strongly commended for its courageous move to ordain women, because in so doing, it resists the prescribed role and place of woman in CMS missionary congregations, as well as in pre-colonial Kenyan cultures where women were not placed in positions of decision-making where they could lead men.

12. *The Diocese of Mount Kenya East*, 1983:38.
13. Mwaniki, "The Impact," 65.
14. Gitari, oral interview, quoted in Mwaniki, "The Impact," 65.
15. Min. 18/86, 18:3, quoted in Mwaniki, "The Impact," 65.
16. Mwaniki, "God's Image."

The ACK has, therefore, achieved so much in terms of its move toward realization of gender equity in leadership. The church has offered women levels of training, equal to those of men, opportunities for further studies, and, above all, some opportunity for ordination and placement in the church hierarchy. A few ordained women are holding top decision-making positions in the church hierarchy. The Rev. Canon Rosemary Mbogo, for instance, is the provincial secretary and personal assistant to the archbishop. She is also the chair of the National Council of Churches of Kenya. In some dioceses, like the Diocese of Nairobi, there are two women archdeacons who are also canons. Women have also held the position of provost (in charge of cathedrals) in some dioceses. Rev. Winnie Munene, for example, served as the provost of St. Thomas Cathedral, Kerugoya, with great success. Besides serving in the ordained ministry, women are holding powerful positions of leadership in the lay ministry, where some are the chairs and members of the Parish Church Council (PCC), Local Church Committees (LCC), development committees, and members of the Standing Committee of Synod, as well as members of the synod.

Nevertheless, although the ACK has finally succeeded in empowering women in various ways, the church has not succeeded in eradicating the cultural, imperial, biblical, and theological factors that keep women in a subservient status. This is revealed by the slow pace of ordination of women in ACK dioceses. In order to illustrate this point, we shall refer to the ACK Diocese of Nairobi, an urban diocese where I serve as a priest. The table below assesses the number of women who have been ordained to priesthood in relation to men, since the creation of the diocese in 2002.

Table 1: *Number of men and women ordained to priesthood since the creation of the Diocese of Nairobi from 2002 to 2014*

Year	2003	2004	2005	2006	2007	2008	2009	2010	2011	2012	2013	2014	Total
Men	3	4	3	5	5	5	2	3	5	6	6	13	60
Women	1	1	0	1	0	0	0	0	4	0	1	1	9

Source: Clergy Ordained from the Creation of Nairobi Diocese Document 2015

The table shows that only nine women out of a total of sixty clergy have been ordained by the Diocese of Nairobi. The highest number of women was ordained in 2011 when four women were ordained. This was after I had presented my PhD research findings in a clergy chapter,[17] which revealed that only three women had been ordained as compared to twenty-seven men between 2002 and 2009. The bishop took the challenge seriously and announced in the same clergy chapter that both men and women who had proper theological training and who felt called to serve God in the ordained ministry could apply for ordination.

Although currently there are no debates on women's ordination, since the motion was already passed, it may be argued that some of the factors that stopped women from being ordained continue to influence the board that determines who is to be ordained. In fact, these hindering factors have unfortunately recurred afresh in various ACK synods with the debate about consecrating women clergy to the position of a bishop, as we shall see below.

DEVELOPMENTS OF BIBLICAL GENDER EQUITY IN LEADERSHIP IN THE ACK—THE DEBATE ABOUT WOMEN BISHOPS

The debates about the ordination of women to priesthood unfortunately did not address the issue of consecration of women as bishops. For a long time, ACK women have not been proactive to apply for the position of a bishop, and so there has not been much talk about it in the province. However, the debate has recently been rekindled by some developments. As indicated above in my case study, in 2012, I made a bold step to apply for the position, and then after that in 2014, the Rev. Canon Rosemary Mbogo applied for the position in Embu Diocese. Though these two applications were turned down under unclear circumstances, they served as a catalyst to revive the debate on women bishops. The other major incident which heightened the conversation was when the Church of England formally adopted legislation in November 2014 to allow women bishops after which the first Anglican bishop, the Rt. Rev. Libby Lane was consecrated in January 2015.

Various synods have met to discuss the issue in the entire province. Francis Omondi has reported the developments on this debate in various ACK dioceses and the current state is as follows:[18]

- In December 2013, the Diocese of Eldoret overwhelmingly welcomed the idea of women joining the episcopate.

---

17. A "clergy chapter" is a diocesan meeting between the bishop and the entire body of the clergy in an Anglican diocese.
18. Omondi, "Making of Women Bishops."

- In July 2014, in the Diocesan Synod of Nairobi, the motion lost marginally with priests as the majority of those who opposed the motion.
- In December 2014, the Diocesan Synod of Maseno West unanimously agreed that women be consecrated bishops. The Rt. Rev. Wasonga, the bishop of Maseno West, expressed that "ministry belongs to all who are baptized, be they men or women, and as such, no one can deny the other an opportunity to serve in whatever capacity."[19]

Proponents of the election of women to the position of bishop argue that the Lambeth of 1978 mandated the dioceses to ordain women as they chose. Those who oppose the idea argue that the decision is premature and needs more consideration. They also cite tradition and the Bible as being opposed to women's consecration as bishops. Most evangelical bishops oppose it altogether. Although dioceses may act autonomously and elect women as bishops, there are various limitations in that:

- In October 2014, the ACK's House of Bishops declared *a five-year moratorium* on the possibility of women becoming bishops. Not every Anglican wants this change, and it is an irritation to the conservatives (emphasis added).
- There are legal and constitutional issues to consider. Despite article IV, which is gender inclusive, article VI, clause 4 and 5 of the ACK Constitution make a clear demarcation between the work of a bishop and that of a priest. Clause 4 refers to bishops as exclusively male, while clause 5 recognizes that priests can be male or female.

In October 2014, the chancellors concluded that these discrepancies had no weight in denying women the opportunity to become bishops. In any case, the National Constitution in Kenya forbids discrimination on the basis of sex; hence, the church would stand to lose if a woman appealed to the civil court after being barred from the episcopate.

The issue of women in the episcopate seems like a tall order. Even in England, where a woman—Bishop Lane—has been consecrated as the first woman bishop, there was a lone protester, Rev. Paul Williamson, who objected when the Archbishop of York asked the congregation to consent to Lane's appointment. In North America, the Rt. Rev. Bill Atwood warned that the decision to elect women as bishops would damage the church.[20]

Nevertheless, there are thirty Anglican women bishops worldwide who have been consecrated in the Anglican Communion since 1989. Although

19. Ibid.
20. Omondi, "Making of Women Bishops."

there are still many dissenting voices, it is only a matter of time, just as it was in the case of the ordination of women to the priesthood.

PROPOSALS TOWARD GENDER EQUITY IN ACK CHURCH LEADERSHIP

ACK leadership needs to draw up a firm policy to ensure eradication of gender disparity in synod meetings at the diocesan level, as well as the provincial level. Perhaps such a policy would help deconstruct the patriarchal ideology of male headship. Without such deconstruction, women will continue to be subordinated by the structures of church and society.

The perception of the image of God needs to change in the ACK, where God has been imaged as male, as clearly seen from the androcentric use of the language and symbolisms for God—first in the Bible and then in the Prayer Book. Such language and symbolisms are alienating and exclusive. While it is clear that the language that human beings use for God is only metaphorical, the church has not been keen to show a clear dichotomy between the metaphorical and the literal use of metaphors for God. The metaphor for God as "Father" has, for instance, been literalized to image God as male. This literalization has constructed gender in such a way that only males can image the "male" God and consequently represent God in "his" service. Women have, therefore, been excluded from the image of the divine, as well as full service to "him." Christians need to be properly taught that no human language can define God. The masculine and feminine images of God do not make God male or female. God is Spirit.

Affirmation of the divine image in male and female. Both male and female are created in the image of God (Gen 1:27). They therefore need to be accorded equal status and opportunities to serve God in the church. We affirm with Christian feminists that, although the Bible contains Scriptures that subordinate women, God's universal intention is "to liberate, save, give, and sustain life."[21] Hence, the Bible ought to be read in liberating ways that challenge structures which create unequal power relations in order to enable human beings to have life in all its fullness (John 10:10).

Use egalitarian, biblical, hermeneutical models. The church can draw some biblical and hermeneutical models to deconstruct the relationships of domination and subordination and to reconstruct equal gender relationships. These include the Trinitarian model,[22] Jesus' treatment of women

---

21. Okure, "Reading from this Place," 52–66.

22. The Trinitarian model is fitting to bring about gender equality in the church because it deconstructs the hierarchy of subordination and allows for equal participation

model,[23] and the Contextual Bible Study (CBS) interactive, interpretive model.[24]

Enforce egalitarian church structures. While there is a need for ACK to maintain its organizational structure, it should not be a gendered structure. The church needs to live up to its own constitution which clearly states:

> This church proclaims that all human beings are made in the image of God and are, therefore, of equal value and dignity in the sight of God, and, while careful to provide for the special needs of different people committed to its charge, allows no discrimination in the membership and government of the Church based on grounds of racial, tribal, or gender difference.[25]

The church, therefore, ought to enforce policies that ensure equal gender representation in the decision-making forums at all levels of the church government.

CONCLUSION

In conclusion, the ACK has made commendable efforts to include women in leadership positions in the church, especially by ordaining them to the priesthood. Nevertheless, a lot more remains to be done in terms of addressing the pre-colonial, colonial, post-colonial, and biblical mindsets which create gender disparities in leadership, resulting in male headship and female subjection. The issue of women's consecration to the position of a bishop remains a heated debate in ACK and will take quite some time to be realized since, unfortunately, discussion on this matter has been deferred for the next five years from 2015. Prolonged gender disparities in the church are retrogressive and are of no help to the growth of the church itself, the family, or the nation at large. This chapter calls the ACK to deliberately take measures to disrupt this kind of binary opposition in order to accord both men and women leadership positions in the church based on merit rather

---

of the members based on their diverse gifts.

23. Jesus affirmed the humanity of women in the Gospels, an action that elevated women's status in a way that had a bearing on women's possible leadership roles in the church.

24. This is a community reading practice that supports the reconstruction or transformation of social relation. Its uniqueness lies in its recognition of the untrained or "ordinary" African reader as a partner in academic Bible reading. It therefore gives the trained reader a safe space to collaborate with ordinary readers, who can use their interpretive resources for their own liberation.

25. *The Anglican Church of Kenya Constitution* 2002:6, Article IV.

than sex, owing to the fact that male and female are created in the image of God (Gen 1:27).

PART II

Reflections on Biblical Equity and Leadership

Chapter 3

Created Equal
A Fresh Look at Gender Equity in Genesis 1–3

—*Diphus C. Chemorion*

INTRODUCTION

CHRISTIANS OF DIFFERENT DENOMINATIONS treasure the Bible as the inspired word of God, which is useful for teaching, rebuking, correcting, and training in righteousness (2 Tim 3:17). The Bible provides direction on how people ought to relate with God, other people, and the rest of creation. There is no aspect of human life which cannot be related to the Bible in one way or the other. But the value of the Bible can only be realized when it is properly understood and applied.

The book of Genesis is one of the best resources to consult on fundamental questions of life that human beings have asked from generation to generation. As a prologue to the rest of the Bible, Genesis tells us about the origins of the universe, human life and death, and the beginnings and spread of human civilization. Many readers easily remember the events recorded in Genesis because the book is written in a captivating literary style, characterized by narrative cycles and occasional poetry. However, some parts of the book have yielded highly contested interpretations, especially when studied in relation to emerging questions in contemporary Christian life.

Some of the most critical concerns for Christians today involve gender equity in leadership. Although the subject of gender relations has been widely discussed in various fora since the end of the nineteenth century, gender inequality persists, and the question that continues to be asked is "What is God's leadership design for men and women?" This question is asked in various contexts such as the family setting, church and religious organizations, competitive politics, and public administration.

The first three chapters of Genesis have been extensively studied in an attempt to unveil God's original sketch of leadership structure and the specific roles and responsibilities for men and women. However, owing to different approaches in interpretation, there has been no consensus on what the author of Genesis says, especially with regard to the place of women in the public domain. Whereas some people hold the view that men and women are equal and should be accorded equal opportunities in leadership, a majority of conservative biblical scholars and church leaders sustain the view that leadership is the prerogative of the male gender and women ought to be subordinate to men.

In this chapter, I argue that at creation God gave to both man and woman the leadership mandate and, therefore, no one should be denied a leadership position on the basis of gender. In order to support this argument, I take a fresh look at gender equity in Genesis with three main objectives. Firstly, I seek to demonstrate how cultural worldviews shape the interpretation of Scripture. Secondly, I explore gender misconceptions of the status of women in Genesis 1–3. Finally, I review the divine paradigm of equity in leadership in the primeval period.

CULTURAL WORLDVIEWS AND INTERPRETATION OF SCRIPTURE

One of the major challenges in biblical interpretation is how to draw a balance between what the Bible says in its cultural context on the one hand, and what the Bible means in the contemporary reader's culture on the other hand. In the process of reading the Bible, a reader's worldview provides the frame of reference for understanding the text. This means that every Bible-reading process has possibilities of generating two types of meaning—namely, the author's intended meaning, and the assumed meaning that is based on the reader's worldview. The two types of meaning may be congruent, but in some cases the reader's assumed meaning may be contrary to the intentions of the author. In order to make good sense of the Bible, a reader must pay attention to both the cultural and literary contexts of the text. However, the reader's cultural worldview may also lead to misinterpretation of the text, especially when biblical ideas are misread as being identical with what is found in the reader's local culture.

The role of cultural worldviews in shaping the meaning of Scripture cannot be underestimated. Churches perpetuate inequality by supporting the roles that society has ascribed to women and giving religious sanction to them.[1] Although women form the greatest number in church membership, their participation in church activities is limited to certain activities in the periphery. A traditionally skewed cultural reading of Genesis 1–3 has given the impression that women were by design created to be less than men in almost all aspects of life. In the following passages, I shall discuss some of the worldview misconceptions derived from Genesis 1–3, which are used to minimize the status of women in relation to men.

MISCONCEPTIONS ABOUT THE STATUS OF WOMEN IN GENESIS 1–3

Misleading interpretations of Genesis 1–3 include the following claims: that only men bear the image of God; that the gender of God is masculine; that men rank higher than women in the created order; that Adam was older than Eve; that woman was created to serve man as a helper; that woman is the property of man; that woman is weaker than man; and finally, that woman was cursed to be under man. In the following paragraphs, I shall examine each of these claims with a view to stating the correct interpretation on the position of man.

God Has a Feminine Dimension

Owing to the limitations of human language, God is often described in sexual terms though he is a spiritual being. In many cultures, the misconception of leadership as a prerogative of men is reinforced by the belief that God has a male gender. The masculine images of God are widespread in the Hebrew Bible. For example, God is a king (Ps 2; 1 Sam 8); a father (Isa 63:16); and a jealous husband (Ezek 23). This imagery is also found in the context of church worship where exclusive masculine gender references to God are seen in preaching, praying, and singing praises. As Andrew L. Whitehead observes, a gendered image of God affects attitudes to gender.[2] For people with a patriarchal mindset, the male image of God functions as

---

1. Crawford and Kinnamon, *In God's Image*, 28.
2. Whitehead, "Gender Ideology and Religion," 139–56.

a grid through which life and social structures are interpreted. Since God is perceived to be male, cultures expect that leaders must put on masculine virtues such as being brave, strong, and tough.

Bruce K. Waltke argues strongly that God represents himself by masculine names and titles, not feminine ones.[3] Waltke further contends that "God identifies himself as Father, Son, and Spirit, not Parent, Child, and Spirit, nor Mother, Daughter, and Spirit." He also points out that Jesus taught his disciples to address God as "Father" (Luke 11:2) and to baptize in the name of the Father and of the Son and of the Holy Spirit. What Waltke and like-minded scholars have forgotten or simply ignored is that God also has a feminine dimension. Apart from the masculine references, there are many cases where the same Bible presents God in feminine terms. This point can be supported by examining some aspects of Hebrew grammar, the names of God, and the imagery that is used to describe God.

In Hebrew grammar, nouns are grammatically classified as either having a masculine or a feminine gender.[4] Nouns denoting animate beings usually have a grammatical gender corresponding to the natural gender (sex), but there is otherwise no correlation between gender and meaning. Apart from a few irregular cases, the gender of Hebrew nouns is identified by the nature of the suffix. Nouns ending in *-ah*, *-et*, and *-at* are nearly always feminine. Nouns without these endings are usually masculine, though there are certain exceptions of those that are feminine without feminine suffixes. Most feminine plural endings are *-ot,* while masculine plural endings are *-im*. But, as a rule, the plural for a combined group of male and female subjects has a masculine ending *-im*. A scrutiny of the Hebrew names of God in Genesis 1–3 reveals that although God is presented in Hebrew language using masculine pronouns, there is also a feminine dimension of God.

In the first chapter of Genesis, the Hebrew name for God is *Elohim*, which is parsed as masculine plural noun. This name is commonly found among Semitic people. When used to refer to the Israelite deity, *Elohim* is viewed as masculine, and the name emphasizes the transcendence and majesty of God. However, there are several reasons why *Elohim* should not be understood as exclusively masculine. Firstly, some scholars have pointed out that *Elohim* is derived from the other name of God, *Eloah*, which has a feminine ending. This term emphasizes God's inhabitance of the heavenly sphere, focusing on his transcendence over human qualities—namely, his immortality and power. According to Swidler, *Eloah* is a very ancient female Semitic God, and her residue is retained in the Hebrew biblical usage of the

---

3. Waltke, *An Old Testament Theology,* 244.
4. Lambdin, *Introduction to Biblical Hebrew,* 3.

term *Elohim*.[5] Secondly, although *Elohim* has masculine pronouns, it is also used to refer to the goddess *Ashtoreth* of the Sidonians (1 Kgs 11:5). Thirdly, the fact that *ha-adam* (the human being), as both male and female, was created in the image of *Elohim*, logically implies that that *Elohim* has both male and female attributes.

The other Hebrew name for God that occurs in the second and third chapter of Genesis is the tetragrammaton YHWH, which is the unutterable name of the God of Israel. With the help of vowels supplied by Hebrew scribes, YHWH is commonly anglicized as *Jehovah* or *Yahweh*. The name was first revealed to Moses at the time of his call (Exod 3:14). It may be translated as "I am who I am," and it emphasizes the purity of God. This name is the personal name of God as well as the most common reference to the Israelite deity. Like other Hebrew names of God in the Old Testament, *Yahweh* is used with masculine pronouns throughout the Hebrew Bible, but it has a feminine ending.

The feminine dimension of God is also seen in the actions attributed to him in the book of Genesis as well as other parts of the Bible. A few examples can be given as follows. After Adam and Eve had sewn for themselves temporary clothes, God made for them garments of skin and clothed them, thereby acting like a seamstress (Gen 3:21). While giving his final address to the Israelites, Moses reminded the Israelites of their unfaithfulness, saying, "You were unmindful of the Rock that bore you, and you forgot the God who gave you birth" (Deut 32:18, ESV). Notice that the Hebrew words *yiladeka* and *mehoneka* are synonyms that are used to refer to the woman's act of giving birth. In Hosea 11:3–4, God presents himself as having performed a motherly role in taking care of a child, teaching her how to walk, and comforting her. Finally, in Isaiah 42:13–14 in the Hebrew Bible, God is presented like a woman saying, "But now, like a woman in childbirth, I cry out, I gasp and pant" (NIV).

From the above analysis, it is clear that there is no justification for prioritizing male leadership on account of God being of masculine gender. God is asexual and has both masculine and feminine qualities. The masculinity of God among the Israelites is a cultural construction that was muted to advance the agenda of patriarchy.

Both Men and Women Bear the Image of God

Although Genesis 1:26–27 clearly indicates that both men and women bear the image of God, it is not uncommon to encounter Christians who hold

---

5. Swidler, *Biblical Affirmations*, 35.

the view that only male human beings bear the image of God. As recorded in Genesis 1:26–27, the Hebrew term *adam* is a generic designation for human beings, encompassing both the female and male gender. God created *ha-adam* (the human being) in the image of God as a pair consisting of a man and a woman. There is, therefore, no basis in Genesis for confining the image of God to the male gender alone. Femaleness pertains to the image of God as fully as maleness, since God is neither a physical nor a sexual being. God transcends gender, and for this reason, both male and female are comprehended within the being of God. Men and women share in the image of God, and both genders were assigned the responsibility of ruling over the created world without any role distinction.[6]

Men and Women Are of the Same Rank

Cultural worldviews have modified the biblical hierarchy of relationships ranging from the Creator to the creatures. Some conservative biblical scholars claim that male leadership is normative in every culture and that the Bible accords men top positions in government hierarchy. The suggested order of authority arising from this claim is that God is on top, followed by man, then woman, and the rest of creation. However, a close examination of the hierarchy that God established in Genesis 1:26–28 shows that God is at the top, followed by human beings (male and female), and the rest of the creatures at the bottom. In the process of ordering relationships among his creatures, God put up a system of divisions and separations and assigned each creature its appropriate place. For example, he assigned the sun to rule over day and the moon to rule over night. However, in the case of man and woman, no such hierarchy was put in place before the Fall.

At the time of creation, there was no indication that man was to rule over woman or vice versa. On the contrary, man and woman were created in the image of God and given equal responsibility for having dominion over the rest of creation. The creation of woman in Genesis 2:22 also indicates that man and woman are equal in age, of the same substance, and complementary. God used dust and breath to make a human being who was initially alone. He modified him by taking a rib from which he created a woman. The resulting woman is of the same substance as the man; she is the same age also, since the rib was not remolded from the soil. But from the perspective of many cultural worldviews, it is often taken for granted that man is above woman. Culture has modified the biblical hierarchy so that the male is viewed as ruler and head, big and strong, while the female is the

---

6. Stein, "The Grammar of Social Gender," 7–26.

ruled over and tail, small and weak. The creation accounts in Genesis do not support the notion of a divinely created hierarchy based on gender. Women and men are made equally in God's image and likeness. They are equally fallen, equally redeemable, and equally participants in the new covenant. They are equally able to be filled with the Holy Spirit for life and ministry.

Eve Is of the Same Bone, Flesh, and Age as Adam

Chapter 2 of Genesis presents details of the creation of woman. It has often been claimed that woman was created from man, and, therefore, man has the priority of creation, which also implies priority in leadership. But that is not necessarily the case. The passage that quickly comes to mind is Genesis 2:18–24. In this narrative, God caused man to sleep, and in the process, formed woman from a part of the man's body known in Hebrew as *tsela*. The word *tsela* has been translated in many English versions as "rib," with the ensuing interpretation that woman was formed from a very small part of man. But the word *tsela* has several meanings, and in this context, it is more appropriate to think of it as an aspect of the personality, and not as a skeletal rib, as commonly imagined. According to R. K. Harrison, a literal bone is not intended to be understood, since the removal of the *tsela* from man was not accompanied by a corresponding extraction of flesh.[7] When the woman was brought to him, the man was filled with joy, exclaiming that he had found the "bone of my bones" and "flesh of my flesh" who would be called *ishah* (woman), for she was taken out of *ish* (man). Since the woman was created from a preexisting part of the man, it follows that the woman was not only of the same substance with the man, but also of the same age. The reason for the use of man's rib in creating the woman was to demonstrate beyond doubt the essential identity between women and men.

---

7. Harrison, *Introduction to the Old Testament*, 555–56. Harrison explains that woman was created from *tsela* (an aspect of the personality) in order to demonstrate the organic and spiritual unity of the subdivided species, which is further reflected in the play on words involving man and woman. The dramatic form of the narrative conceals the spiritual equation "man= male + female," teaching that the personality of an individual of the species Homo sapiens can only be most fully expressed when it is complemented in the opposite sex.

Woman Was Not Created to Be Subordinate to Man

According to Bruce K. Waltke, the authority of man in home and in church is rooted in the order of creation.[8] In reference to Paul's argument in 1 Corinthians 11:8–9, Waltke argues that God established a pattern of authority by creating Adam first—and then the woman to help the man. This argument is based on two unfounded assumptions that serve to advance the agenda of patriarchy. The first assumption is that a man is superior to a woman because Adam was the first one to be created. However, emphasis on priority of creation would imply that human beings are subordinate to other creatures that were created first. The second assumption is that God created woman to be man's helper, and, therefore, a wife must be subordinate to a husband. This assumption is based on a misinterpretation of God's purpose for creating woman as clarified in the following paragraph.

In Genesis 2:18, the Lord God said, "It is not good for the man to be alone; I will make a helper suitable for him" (NASB). The bone of contention in the interpretation of this verse revolves around the meaning of the Hebrew term *ezer*, which in English is inaccurately translated as "helper." When the term *helper* is used, it creates the impression that woman was created to be an assistant or subordinate who is inferior to man.[9] Patriarchal communities use the cultural notion of "helper" to justify male dominance over women. However, it should be noted that the Hebrew term *ezer* carries the connotation of superiority, mutuality, or equality. This term is also used to describe God as one who rescues his people from danger. For example, in Exodus 18:4, one of Moses' sons was named Eliezer because Moses said, "My father's God was my [*ezer*] helper; he saved me from the sword of Pharaoh" (NIV). Similarly, in Deuteronomy 33:7, Moses prayed to God concerning Judah, saying, "Hear, LORD, the cry of Judah; bring him to his people. With his own hands he defends his cause. Oh be his [*ezer*] help against his foes!" In the context of Genesis 2:18–24, the term *ezer* suggests that Adam was experiencing some inadequacy which could only be addressed through the creation of a woman for him. This means that God designed human beings in such a way that one remains incomplete until a suitable companion is found. In other words, humanity is complete only in the sense of having both male and female genders complementing one another. Therefore, instead of understanding the role of woman as that of a subordinate assistant to man, we ought to appreciate women as companions to their male counterparts.

---

8. Waltke, *An Old Testament Theology*, 242.
9. Trible, *God and the Rhetoric*, 90.

Woman Is Not Man's Property

In Genesis 2, God brought all the things he had created to see how man would name them. The man identified all the creatures and gave them their names, and whatever he named them became their name. The context of Genesis 2:18–24 is concerned with addressing the loneliness of Adam, and for this reason, we can conclude that he named the animals as part of the process of identifying a suitable companion. The naming of animals also suggests the man's ownership and exercise of control over them. However, the man did not name Eve in the same way he named the animals. When the woman was formed and brought to him, the man was filled with joy. He quickly identified her as "bone of my bones" and "flesh of my flesh" and went ahead to claim that she would be called woman because she was taken out of man. This is simply a poetic affirmation of expressing joy at the finding of the helper. It does nothing to imply that Adam is naming Eve as part of his property.

Woman Is Not Weaker than Man

Women have generally been perceived as the weaker sex. The narrative of the Fall in Genesis 3 is one of the passages that is used to understand women as weak. The question that needs to be reexamined is "Why did the serpent approach Eve?" While the serpent could have picked Eve as a prey for temptation because she was the weaker of the two,[10] it is also possible that he picked on her because she was the stronger of the two. The tempter did not follow any chain of command. Either of the two could have been approached first. It is possible that being clever, the serpent may have known that the greatest resistance was to be found in Eve, so that if he succeeded with her, Adam would be no problem. Eve put up some resistance, but Adam just fell. It is not correct to apportion blame to the woman as the cause of the Fall because both the woman and the man were equally responsible for the sin. The dynamics of temptation do not support the existence of a hierarchical relationship between Adam and Eve prior to the Fall. It should be remembered that God held each of them equally responsible. Adam failed God as an individual as did Eve and the serpent.

---

10. See Keil and Delitzsch, *Commentary on the Old Testament*, 94. In their exposition of Genesis 3:1–8, Keil and Delitzsch argue that the craftiness of the serpent was evidenced by the fact that "it was to the weaker woman that it turned."

Women Were Not Cursed to Be under Men

Contrary to some cultural misunderstandings, no curse was pronounced on woman. She was not reproached for taking leadership roles (Gen 3:16). The context of consequences needs to be read carefully. God had been the primary source of their lives. Having dismissed him through rebellion, they became subject to the secondary sources of life, each to his own primeval element. Adam became subject to the soil *adamah* from which he had been taken. Eve became subject to Adam from whom she had been taken. Adam's toil would make him a slave to the ground that would eventually engulf his life. Eve's life would now be ruled by the slave; she would become the slave of the slave of the earth. It is not true that the Fall endorsed male dominance over women. "He will rule over you" (Gen 3:16) is not an expression of God's will, just as God did not intend for man to die. The statement acknowledges the emergence of a disaster resulting from the sin against which God had forewarned Adam. According to John Stott, the primeval sexual equality was distorted by the Fall. God's word to the woman was, "Your desire will be for your husband, and he will rule over you" (NIV). Thus, the sexes would experience a measure of alienation from one another. Instead of equality and complementarity with one another, one would rule over the other. The domination of women by men is due to the Fall, not Creation. But due to Christ's forgiveness, it is no longer justifiable to view women as condemned to suffer the consequences of the Fall in the Garden of Eden. Women's equality with men was restored by the redemption that is in Jesus Christ.

PARADIGMS OF LEADERSHIP IN THE PRIMEVAL PERIOD

Simply defined, leadership is the ability of the leader to impress his/her vision on those being led and to induce obedience, respect, loyalty, and cooperation. Good leaders should be able to influence others to achieve group goals. Leadership, therefore, is a process of facilitating the group toward attaining certain goals. Leadership can only be in group context. No one can be called a leader without those whom he or she leads. The quality of leadership is measured in terms of the relationship between the leader and followers and, most importantly, in terms of whether or not the goals are achieved. Leadership is a process of guiding the group toward the attainment of goals. The criteria for leadership are not pegged on traits such as height or gender; rather, it is based on the ability to interact with followers.

The principle of equity in leadership recognizes that leadership does not carry a gender tag. Both men and women can exercise leadership.

In the context of Genesis 1–3, the appointing authority for both Adam and Eve is God. God gave to both Adam and Eve the mandate of being leaders to the rest of creation. They were given the task of taking care of the garden and ruling over all the birds of the air, the animals of the land, and the fish of the sea. In the words of the psalmist, all creation is to glorify the works of God. As leaders, Adam and Eve were expected to direct other creatures to the worship of God.

CONCLUSION

Cultural constructions of gender in Africa continue to paint a negative image of the place of women in society. There are many cases where women who venture into careers that are culturally thought to belong to men are viewed with mixed feelings. In many communities, the roles of women are confined to the domestic domain. Through socialization at home and in school, young people learn that women are homemakers while men are breadwinners. Educated women are socialized to take on lighter professions like teaching, catering, nursing, and secretarial positions, while their male counterparts are encouraged to pursue more challenging careers such as medicine, architecture, engineering, and computer science. Men have equally been denied certain roles on the basis of cultural expectations. In many African cultures, it is considered inappropriate for men to remain at home taking care of children and doing house chores while their wives are working outside of the home. Men who venture into secretarial, nursing, and catering careers, which are traditionally associated with women, are often viewed with suspicion.

It is regrettable that the interpretation of Genesis 1–3 through cultural worldviews is one of the impediments of gender equity among Christians. In this chapter, I have argued that inequality between men and women was not part of God's design in the creation of human beings. Both man and woman bear the image of God, and they also share a common privilege of ruling over the rest of creation. It must be emphasized that patriarchal structures are not divinely ordained, and they should never be used as yardsticks for measuring what God expects of humanity. It is a shame that discrimination against women continues even in societies where principles of equity have been adopted as policy. Given that injustice against either gender is perpetuated through culture, the church must rise to the occasion and declare Christ as above culture.

Chapter 4

New Testament Evidence of Biblical Equity Revealed in Creation and Redemption

—*Kabiro wa Gatumu*

INTRODUCTION

MUCH HAS BEEN WRITTEN in academic books, journals, and online about the creation and redemption of humanity. The general view, especially in Christianity, is that men and women are sinners, and they cannot redeem themselves. God alone redeems them—but on an equal footing, since he created them in his own image and likeness (Gen 1:26–27). Interesting remarks on the creation and redemption of humanity, however, have been made throughout the centuries. This chapter contributes to the debate by exacting New Testament evidence of biblical equity in creation and redemption, which implies that women and men can lead alongside each other. Even so, women have been treated as subordinate to men not only in African families, church, and society, but also in the world's socio-political, economic, and religious-cultural systems. The alleged subordination of women has been used to deny them leadership opportunities in African families, church, and society.

This chapter's main purpose therefore is to show that equity in the creation and redemption of women and men allows them to lead side by side. Firstly, it explains its hermeneutical framework and assumption. Secondly, it evaluates views on the creation and redemption of men and women in diverse religious traditions. Thirdly, it analyzes views on creation and redemption in the history of Christianity. Fourthly, it evaluates Jesus and Paul's teachings on the creation and redemption of men and women, and finally, it provides a conclusion and recommendations.

HERMENEUTICAL FRAMEWORK AND HYPOTHESIS

Christian egalitarianism guides the hermeneutical framework. The evidence of the New Testament points to equity in the creation and redemption of men and women. Equity is understood as the quality of being fair and reasonable in a way that gives equal treatment to everyone, and, in particular, in the African context, equality in leadership. Contrary to Christian egalitarianism, however, which believes people are equal before God in their personhood, the practice in Africa is that women are almost entirely excluded in the leadership of the family, church, and society.

Christian egalitarianism upholds that people are equal before God in their personhood and that God calls women and men to play roles and to perform ministries in family, church, and society regardless of class, gender, or race. It also means that men and women have *equal* opportunities and responsibilities to use their gifts, leadership skills, and talents without limitations or privileges based on gender. This is because the Bible teaches on the equality of women and men despite their race or ethnic group, economic status, or age. The chapter's hermeneutical hypothesis is that New Testament teachings, especially in the examples of Jesus and Paul, point to the equity of men and women in creation and redemption, which justifies women's occupation of leadership positions.

CREATION AND REDEMPTION IN SOME SELECTED WORLD RELIGIOUS TRADITIONS

The discussion on the creation and redemption of humanity also takes central stage in other religious traditions of the world. There is a clear division among some religions with regard to the redemption of men and women. Some maintain that it is only men and not women who can be saved, and others hold that, since men and women were created equal, redemption belongs to all humanity. In Jainism, an Indian religion, adherents are divided with regard to the redemption of women. The *Svetambaras* hold that women's spiritual abilities cause them to attain redemption. However, the *Digambaras* believe that women are obviously inferior to men, so they cannot achieve salvation, which is only meant for men. In addition, they cannot attain salvation since their souls do not manifest pure transformation. While some Jain religious texts reveal the possibility of women's salvation, others show that women cannot experience redemption since they have a polluted body due to their menstruation cycle.

In the Hindu tradition, as some epics show, women attain salvation by being obedient to their husbands. Obedient wives who served their husbands like gods could attain salvation when they died. Similarly, women who demonstrated the power to work miracles received salvation. However, many women have rejected the view that service to and worship of one's husband is a path to salvation, which is only open to men. The perspective that several women have attained salvation, not by worshiping their husbands as gods, but by approaching God directly and attaining union with him, has been advanced. Additionally, women have been empowered through singing and dancing which is said to provide alternative avenues for the salvation of women.[1]

Islam believes that men and women are held responsible for their actions. Islam, therefore, rejects the idea that any person, male or female, receives redemption through an intermediary. Nevertheless, despite its general claim to promote the equality of men and women, Islam teaches that Eve was created as Adam's subordinate. While the equality of men and women is clearly explained in the Quran, the *hadith* depicts women as having been created from man and for man. Regardless of Islam's liberating view on gender redemption, the male superiority over the female is clear. The *hadith* texts that deal with married women describe a virtuous woman as one who pleases and obeys her husband at all times. This implies that Islam assumes that a woman cannot please God except by pleasing her husband. Hence, a wife who is inferior to her husband in creation attains redemption from hell only when the husband is pleased with her. Accordingly, the prayers of a wife whose husband remains unhappy with her cannot be heard. This means that a husband is the key to paradise or to hell for a wife; women, therefore, are reduced to puppets since men arbitrate what happens to them physically and spiritually. Consequently, men and women, having been created equal by God and standing equal before him, have become unequal in Islamic societies.[2] As a general rule, women do not

---

1. See Leslie, "Some Traditional Indian Views," 70–80; Jaini, *Gender and Salvation*, 9–5, 114; Sharma and Young, *Feminism and World Religions*, 36–50.

2. See Hassan, "The Issue," 35–60; Hassan, "Feminism in Islam," 261–69.

hold leadership positions, and there is no woman who has ever served as an Islamic religious leader such as a Kadhi or Seikh.

In African religion, salvation is "this worldly" because religion is both anthropocentric and life affirming. Salvation is about protection, restoration, preservation, and survival, as well as prolonging human, societal, and environmental life in this world. As a result, salvation is about rescue from the physical and immediate dangers threatening an individual and, more frequently, the community. The risks from which an individual or community are saved include all that threatens continued existence, good health, safety, and general prosperity. Salvation, therefore, is not an abstract idea, for it is retold in terms of what has happened and what is likely to be encountered as people go through life. Subsequently, redemption is about safeguarding and sustaining a community's or an individual's life and welfare, and making possible the ultimate fulfillment of individual and communal destiny. Redemption is also holistic as it embraces all aspects of life. It refers to conditions that preserve or restore the harmony of creation so that life's sequence may go on without interruption, enabling people to have space to be human and experience life more abundantly. Yet redemption is always linked to meeting the demands of ancestors, gaining protection from evil forces of destruction, preserving cosmic social order and harmony, and restoring ruined relationships.

Redemption is not only for men, but also for women. Women are agents of salvation—not only because they have power to give life, but also because they sustain life during hard and cruel times. Women also play leading roles as priestesses, prophets, and healers. Some African myths and proverbs depict them favorably, but others describe them unkindly and repulsively. The latter may have contributed to the oppression of women in the family, church, and society. In fact, women's subordination runs through African religion and culture. While women are in the majority in church and society, they are still largely absent in leadership. In some churches, the ordination of women to priesthood and their consecration and enthronement as bishops are controversial issues. Practically speaking, the oppression and marginalization of women make their redemption a tall order, because they are struggling against a culturally endorsed patriarchal system that not only abuses women, but also demeans them and justifies their abject poverty and social oppression. This continues despite African Christians holding to the Bible as the supreme pillar of their faith and practice. This is the same Bible wherein women like Miriam, Deborah, Ruth, Esther, Mary Magdalene, Dorcas, Phoebe, Priscilla, and many others served as leaders and played key roles in both the socio-political and religio-cultural affairs of their people.

Following the biblical tradition, women leaders have risen up in African Instituted Churches (AICs). Politician-cum-preacher Margret Wanjiru is the founder and bishop of Jesus Is Alive Ministry (JIAM) in Nairobi, Kenya. Wairimu Nelson is the founder and official leader of Faith Evangelistic Ministry (FEM), which enjoys international fame. Women are slowly being accepted as leaders of their own ministries, and there have been women's groups and movements, such as the Mothers' Union, Women's Guild, Women's Desk, Catholic Women's Association,[3] as well as many others, that have holistically shaped the welfare of African people.

Nevertheless, male-dominated leadership in the family, church, and society has weakened the impact of women's leadership and suppressed their gifts. It appears that the African Church and African culture have formed a coalition to restrain and frighten women away from leadership. Despite the constitutional consent on gender inclusivity in leadership, in some African countries, especially Kenya, there is still skepticism toward women's leadership and doubt about the vital role they can play in the affairs and welfare of the community.

In some Jewish literature, it is clear that women were involved in and contributed to the redemption of the nation. Judaism holds that the redemption of Jewish people from Egypt was through the agency of righteous women who never despaired of God's redemption. Rabbi Naftali Silberberg notes that, while men were dejected and had lost heart and the desire to procreate because they did not want to subject their children to the hardships of slavery, women were optimistic and confident that the day when they would be redeemed was coming soon, and they would sing a song of thanks with the tambourines they had prepared. Accordingly, they seduced their husbands in the fields and raised a generation of children who witnessed God's miraculous redemption.[4] Judaism, therefore, accords redemptive powers to the midwives who saved the boy Pharaoh had destined to death; these women feature in the story of bondage and redemption and made possible the departure of the Jews from Egypt. Modern Jews hold that, as it was through women's faith that ancient Jews were redeemed, it will also be through righteous women and their unwavering belief in the redemption that modern Jews will be redeemed.[5]

---

3. Mothers' Union is a women's movement in the Anglican Church while the Women's Guild is a women's movement in the Presbyterian Church of East Africa. The Women's Desk and Catholic Women's Association are women's movements, respectively, in the Methodist Church in Kenya and the Roman Catholic Church.

4. See Talmud Sotah 11b, as well as Rashi on Exodus 15:20 from the *Mechilta*. Silberberg, "The Woman's Role."

5. See Rashi on Exodus 15:20 from the *Mechilta*; Leila Leah Bronner, *From Eve to*

Martin Buber and Schalom Ben-Chorin provide some data that helps us to understand why redemption in Judaism includes women. Buber shows that in Judaism the redemption of the world is synonymous with perfecting creation. Judaism regards redemption as the foundation of unity, a unity that is irrefutable and is achieved in all the changeable variety of the world. In addition, Judaism considers redemption as similar to God's kingdom in its fulfillment. According to Ben-Chorin, Judaism is deeply aware of the unredeemed nature of the world and recognizes the non-redemption of the Jewish community amidst an unredeemed world. The concept of the redeemed soul in the midst of an unredeemed world is totally alien to Judaism and remote to its adherents. Redemption means redemption from all evil of body and soul, evil in creation, and evil in civilization. In between creation and redemption, Judaism only knows the revelation of the will of God. In the unredeemed world, Judaism is receptive to the revelation of the Torah on Sinai, which was given through Moses, and which guides men and women into the way of redemption.[6]

The fact that Judaism envisages a redemption that is open to all people regardless of gender is evident in Hebrew Scripture, which has no gender bias. Nevertheless, ethnocentric and patriarchal frameworks were taken for granted. For that reason, some of its trends portray women as subordinate to men. Women were not honored in places of worship due to the role Eve played at the Fall (Gen 3). In the synagogue, women sat separately to stop them from distracting men. This was built on a tradition that depicted Eve, who is regarded as the prototype of all women, as a temptress. As such, a woman's voice in religious fellowship was not to be heard, and she was not to be seen because she would tempt and distract men away from higher worship. Judaism desires to confine, calm, and control women as polluters and sexual temptresses. Finally, in a famous Jewish prayer, a man gave thanks to God for not creating him a woman among other categories of people, such as slaves and Gentiles.

Rabbinic Judaism depicts the woman as the cause of the Fall. The Creation story (Gen 2) and the story of the Fall (Gen 3) have been used to portray women as dependent and subordinate entities with no right to achieve their personal will since they are part of man. So the attitude to women is based on the Creation and Fall narratives, which are used to cement gender distinction in order to explain and justify the subordinate position of women. Hence, there is a belief in Judaism inclined toward the subordination of women. In fact, even the anticipated national vindication

---

Esther, xviii; Silberberg "The Woman's Role."

6. See Moltmann, "Israel's No."

is shaped and construed in flourishing male leadership. This means that, while women's role in redemption is highly celebrated, their leadership role alongside men is not totally appreciated.[7]

A common thread that emerges from most religions is that cultural values, norms, beliefs, and customs have transmitted major obstacles to the success of women's aspiration to leadership positions, which has been bequeathed to and imbibed by the majority of Christian churches in Africa. This may have prompted some in African Christianity to develop a theology and practice of subordinating women. It is obvious that African Christianity has resonated with Judaism through the Old Testament, with Islam due to its increasing growth in Africa, and with the never-say-die aspects of African traditional religion. In practice, the African Church seems to be propagating the gospel of women's inability to attain redemption outside the male.

CREATION AND REDEMPTION IN THE HISTORY OF CHRISTIANITY

Genesis 1:26–28 clearly states that God created both male and female in his image and in his likeness. While this certainly presupposes equity in creation, Christians have expressed differing views with regard to women's humanity. Tertullian held that women are the gateway to hell. John Chrysostom believed that women are a necessary evil, a natural temptation, a desirable calamity, a domestic peril, a deadly fascination, and a painted ill. Valentius Acidalius appealed to the *Bible* to conclude that *women do not have a soul and do not belong to the human race*. Also, during a break between sessions at the Synod of Mâcon, one bishop is alleged to have expressed his views that women do not have souls. However, other bishops rejected his view, citing Genesis 1:26–27 that God created them both, male and female in his own image and likeness. While some people claimed that women have no soul, Samuel Butler held that their souls are very small. Thomas Aquinas also held that women were defective men, imperfect in both body and soul, and were conceived either due to a defective sperm or because a damp wind was blowing at the time of conception.[8]

---

7. See Cohen, *Everyman's Talmud*, 159; Baskin, *Midrashic Women*, 30; George Alder, "Give Thanks," 166; Ginzberg, *The Legend of the Jews*, 1, 67; Cohen, *Everyman's*, 159–60, 179; Paul Héger, *Women in the Bible*, 4; Dvora E. Weisberg, "Women and Torah Studies," 4–63.

8. See King, *Extra MoJo!*, 16; " Christianity and Women's Rights," *Universal Declaration of Human Rights*; Nolan, "Do Women Have Souls?"

By selectively quoting biblical texts and a few references to other works, the author of one anonymous tract attempted to prove that women have no souls. Though being little better than higher animals, they will have no afterlife, that author argued.[9] Some Christian thinkers from the time of the early church to the time of the Reformation may have failed to accept women's redemption and leadership potential. They deemed women as having been created subordinate to men, arguing that this had biblical support. It is likely that the subjugation of women in Judaism through the activities of Eve at the Garden of Eden trickled down into the Christian tradition to make sense of women's redemption through men. Like Judaism, some Christians use Genesis 2&3 to blame women for the Fall. The perception is that women were not only created subordinate to men by God's design, but also took the lead in disobeying God, causing the Fall and the advent of evil in the world. So, as much as women bear God's image as well as the spiritual nature capable of redemption, they are physically, morally, and mentally inferior. Consequently, they lack that part of the image of God related to dominion. This implies that the redemption of women is possible, but only when they voluntarily accept subordination to male leadership.

Reformers such as Martin Luther and Calvin believed in the subordination of women to men by favoring a patriarchal model of redemption. But other Christian leaders during the Reformation period rediscovered the authentic paradigm of redemption. They based redemption on the egalitarian view of original creation in which gender subordination was explained as an manifestation of sin and the Fall, but not as God's will. They described redemption as the restoration of the original equality of men and women in the image and likeness of God. Modern feminist theologians who hold this view rightly aver that the subordination of women is a social construction that is deeply unjust and contrary to the true potential of men and women. Redemption, therefore, transforms women holistically, allowing them to regain their true nature and giving them the ability to co-lead with men as teachers and prophets in church, as well as the justification and authority to co-lead with men in family and society.

The view that women have no souls and thus no ability to attain redemption, and by extension, to lead, is certainly misguided and must not be entertained among Christians. The redemption of humanity and of the world is grounded on the birth, death, and resurrection of Jesus Christ. Christianity stands or falls on its faith that, through Christ, the redemption that God bestows on humanity was accomplished. Both male and female are

---

9. *Disputatio Nova Contra mulieres, qua probatur eas hominess non esse* (A new argument against women, in which it is demonstrated that they are not human beings) was first published in 1595. See Hart, *Treatise on the Question*.

candidates of redemption, and their redemption amounts to the redemption of all that God created. If men lead for the reason that they are created in the image and likeness of God and redeemed through Jesus Christ, then women, also created in the image and likeness of God and redeemed through Jesus Christ, can lead alongside men in the family, church, and society. Consequently, it is obvious that any teaching on the subordination of women founded on creation and redemption is confusing as to the way in which God relates with human beings. It is contrary to the well-established Christian belief in one God, the Creator and Redeemer of humanity. The subordinationist view affirms women's equal share in redemption, but denies that they can hold positions of authority and leadership in the church or society. This is contrary to the evidence of the New Testament, to which we now turn.

THE NEW TESTAMENT'S EVIDENCE ON THE CREATION AND REDEMPTION OF HUMANITY

The doctrine of creation takes central stage when dealing with the identities of men and women from a biblical perspective. Male and female have their identities and respective responsibilities because both were created in the image and likeness of God. In the New Testament, redemption points to a new creation in which men and women can be renewed to the measure and the fullness of the justice, equity, and sanctity which God approves. This is because redemption points to God's original, sanctifying action in creation. Therefore, Christianity's universal and inclusive claim on redemption in Christ, which changed gender relations, has its foundation in creation. So whatever the Bible teaches about men and women must be articulated from the vantage point that God created them. Redemption followed the Fall with far-reaching ramifications for all of God's creation. It is therefore impossible to analyze the New Testament's teachings on the redemption of male and female without considering the fact that God created them, both male and female, in his image and likeness.

As noted above, the New Testament explains the new creation as coming through redemption in Christ. However, the New Testament teaching on creation and redemption is built on Old Testament teachings that unquestionably depict God as the Creator of the universe and everything in it. But in the New Testament, the world that God created is hostile to divine intentions, and humanity is more at home in the world than with God. As such, all human beings, male and female, need to be reconciled to God on an equal basis.

In the New Testament, Jesus Christ is the sole agent of redemption of both men and women. He did not share the general demeaning attitude toward women in his time. His teachings laid the foundation for a change of attitudes in all areas of human relationships, including redemption and leadership. The New Testament evidence indicates that Jesus came to redeem women and men. The signs of the kingdom, which include the healings and exorcism miracles that Jesus performed, were directed to both male and female. Jesus' interaction with the Canaanite woman illustrates the woman's redemption (Matt 15:21–28). Also, women are among those who hear, understand, and fulfill the teachings of Jesus (Luke 10:39–42). Jesus' feeding miracles point to the redemption of men and women, because the feeding narratives presuppose the restoration of Israel (Mark 6:35–44) and, thereby, the entire human race. Jesus' blood was shed as a ransom for many so that his death could bring about redemption to humanity. This, therefore, means that Jesus brought redemption to both male and female. Mary Magdalene was a sinful woman, and Zacchaeus was a sinful man, but both repented and received redemption (Luke 7:36–50; 19:1–10). Those who received healing from Jesus were men and women who could not otherwise be fully constituted as the people of God due to their conditions. Nevertheless, Jesus broke cultural and religious barriers to ensure that every person, whether a leper or an outcast, could belong to God's family through redemption. Jesus objected to ethnic and gender groupings and regarded his followers as a united, new family that must abhor and conquer ethnic and gender divisions (John 17:20–23). People who in the past had little or no hope for God's favor congregated together into a new community as God's beloved people.

Texts outside the New Testament also record that Jesus brought redemption to both male and female on equal footing. The Gospel of the Egyptian and the Gospel of Thomas provide some answers that Jesus had given to a question as to when the kingdom would come and whether the disciples would enter it. In both texts, Jesus says that the redemption would come when male and female become one so that male shall not be male and female shall not be female.[10] Hence, while Jesus was restoring the original order of things as they were during Creation, he was also replacing them with a new creation, in which men and women stand equal in all socio-political and religio-cultural interactions, including leadership.

Paul makes it very clear that the redemption of humanity is not based on gender; hence, gender distinctions have no bearing on salvation (Gal 3:28). In that case, both male and female have equal access to God through

---

10. See Schneemelcher, "The Gospel of the Egyptians," 168–69; Schneemelcher, "The Gospel of Thomas," 298.

Christ and consequently share in every sense in the body of Christ. This means that men and women are equally saved by Christ and equally included in the redemption that Christ won for humanity; that equity in redemption promotes a social reality where values are transformed. As such, responding to the message of redemption is synonymous with admitting transformation of gender relations between men and women. This is because a radical ethic of equality among Christ's followers made division of humanity in terms of class, gender, ethnic, or religious status null and void. Like Jesus, Paul affirms the equality of women and men in redemption. He seems to imply that redemption not only creates a new world, but also brings a new order of relationships. Redemption replaces subordination of women with freedom, mutuality, and equality. It is not an overstatement, therefore, to affirm that the Bible has the most inclusive teaching on equity of men and women in creation and in redemption (Gen 1:26–28; 2:23; 5:1–2; 1 Cor 11:11–12; Gal 3:13, 28; 5:1). It indicates that both male and female have equal opportunities of leadership in the family, church, and society.

However, some Pauline texts have been interpreted to demonstrate that Paul contradicts his position that the redemption of humanity in Jesus Christ is not based on gender; hence, gender distinctions have no bearing on salvation. For instance, some Christians consider 1 Timothy 2:12–15 as supporting the conditional redemption of women.[11] This passage has received various hypothetical interpretations that have led to contradictory views about the redemption of women. Some have rightly argued that Paul did not prohibit women from holding positions of spiritual authority in the church, especially when the text is read within the context of its production. Most likely, we will see that there is a play on words occurring when the background within which this text was produced is understood. This epistle was written at a time when Timothy was at Ephesus, the capital city of magic in Asia Minor and the home of the goddess Artemis. Artemis was not only the goddess of magic, but also of hunting, wilderness, wild animals, and childbirth.[12] The Ephesian women prayed to Artemis so that they would be saved during childbirth. *Soteria* is the Greek word for salvation, and closely resembles one of the many names of Artemis—*Soteira*.[13] Therefore, it is overwhelmingly probable that Paul was referring to this goddess by saying that the Ephesian women, who had converted from the cult of Artemis or

---

11. The view of 1 Timothy is also present in the Gospel of the Egyptian and in the Gospel of Thomas, and this may imply that it was an opinion among the people of the New Testament era.

12. Pausanias, *Description of Greece*, 2. 29. 1; 2. 3.5; 2. 30. 74; 3. 4.6.9.39.2; Philostratus the Elder, *Imagines*, 1. 28.

13. Philostratus the Elder, *Imagines*, 1.40.2, 1.44.4.

Soteira, ought to trust Christ for their deliverance during childbirth instead of looking upon the pagan goddess. Paul seems to have been working against the false goddess *Soteira*. This is more convincing given that Paul tried to dissuade the Ephesians from following Artemis (Acts 19:23–27). The text does not consign women's redemption to childbearing. Paul, therefore, does not contradict his position that God justifies men and women on the same footing, and he does not show partiality in the redemption of male and female. Paul maintains a strong biblical equity in creation and redemption for both male and female, which justifies the inclusion of women in leadership positions alongside men.

The limitation of women was not Paul's universal position, because he acknowledged that women have prophetic gifts and are involved in the ministry of the church (Rom 16:1–15; 1 Cor 11:5; Phil 4:2–3). The ostensible limitations on women in the New Testament are not based on redemption, but on contextual circumstances during the New Testament era, wherein women were never treated as full persons. Paul challenged the contemporary view on women by noting that in Christ there is neither male nor female (Gal 3:28); thus, he neutralized gender and offered a gender-inclusive promise of redemption through Christ. This is not to pretend ignorance of the argument that Paul was a misogynist due to his remarks in 1 Corinthians and 1 Timothy regarding the relations between Christian women and men and their roles in the church. Even so, when we look at the entire Pauline corpus with regard to this subject, the accusation that Paul was a misogynist cannot be sustained. In Corinth and Ephesus, he was concerned with orderliness in the church, and it is from this background that he gave his advice. Moreover, the fact that he had women among his ministry associates rules out the charge.

Paul also noted that marriage is the natural procedure between men and women, and there is no indication in his teaching on marriage that wives were subordinate to their husbands. Some scholars have taken his use of the Genesis creation account (1 Cor 11:8–9) as an exhibition of his acceptance of a hierarchical relationship wherein man is dominant. However, the problem with this view is that the Genesis narrative does not require such an interpretation. When comparing 1 Corinthians 11:8–9 with Ephesians 5:31, it is clear that Paul did not recognize a gender-based hierarchy. In contrast, he shows that male and female complement each other because man and woman are dependent on each other "in the Lord" (1 Cor 11:11–12). Thus, all that Paul says about women should be taken into account when evaluating his views on gender relations. It is obvious that, in the Pauline epistles, man's standing before God is not different from that of the woman. Both men and women need salvation in the same way and on the same terms.

The New Testament teaches that, through faith in Christ, men and women become children of God, one in Christ, and heirs to the blessings of salvation without reference to racial, social, or gender distinctions (John 1:12–13; Rom 8:14–17; 2 Cor 5:17; Gal 3:26–28). In fact, Paul would not have envisaged anyone who had not experienced redemption as being "in Christ," the phrase with which he expressed redemption. This phrase refers to the individual's participation in the life, death, and resurrection of Christ; moreover, the individual must become part of the community of others rooted in the same experience. For Paul, the expression "in Christ" strengthens the boundaries separating those who are redeemed from those on the outside—and links redemption with the existence of the community of believers.

Paul envisaged redemption as devoid of marriage in the last days, when complete realization of redemption in Christ will be achieved and gender hierarchy dissolved. Even so, it is vital to recall the New Testament's tension of "now" and "not yet." Redemption in the present time means that believers experience the benefits of future redemption in the earthly life. Gender hierarchy, therefore, is not necessary in the present-day church because God uses both male and female in leadership and other ministry performed in and by the church. So while Paul seems to be emphasizing that the completion of redemption for both male and female is a future reality, it is also imminent in the present time and can be realized without difficulty. In fact, redemption is about entering into a new status of spiritual equality. It is also concerned with the restoration of the spiritual state through Christ that not only looks forward to the heavenly redeemed state free of marriages, but also the empowering of women to disconnect themselves from subordination in the family, church, and society, especially in the occupation of leadership positions at all levels.

When interpreting the New Testament's evidence of biblical equity as revealed in creation and redemption, emphasis should be placed on how Jesus included women in his healing and exorcism miracles. Emphasis should also be placed on Paul's liberating texts, especially Galatians 3:28, rather than on the seeming limitations placed on women, as seen in 1 Timothy and other passages, which need to be interpreted within their context of production. Jesus and Paul definitely taught on redemption, liberty, and equality between male and female.

CONCLUSION AND RECOMMENDATIONS

The above discussion suggests that both men and women are in need of redemption since they are equally under the power of sin. Redemption is the remedy of restoring creation from the distortion bequeathed to it via the Fall and sin of men and women. The teachings of Jesus and Paul validate such a conclusion since a central theme in their teaching is inclusivity. In the teachings of Jesus and Paul, gender equity is an intrinsic and not an accidental value; hence, their teachings represent redemption as equality not only of membership, but also of participation. Both men and women are members of the body of Christ, who participate and are involved in leading the family, church, and society. Yet in African families, church, and society, women's leadership so far is below the expectations of the New Testament. Though women are the majority in church and society, they are under-represented in structures of leadership.

What is missing in African families, church, and society is a greater application of the truth that men and women are equal before God. Therefore, the African churches ought to appropriate the theme of inclusivity and create a new social reality that replaces gender prejudice with gender equity. Since the New Testament teaches on equity in creation and redemption, both male and female should hold equal leadership positions in the family, church, and society. It is important, therefore, to allow African women to play the leading role they have always played. It is recommended that women should be restored in leadership to lead alongside men as it was in some teachings of African religion and as the teachings of Jesus and Paul indicate. The Kenyan Constitution forbids more than two-thirds gender majority in all state and county appointments in leadership positions. This should be accepted and applied not only in Kenyan churches, but also in all African churches where gender inequality in leadership is deplorable. This must not delay any longer if the constitution of some African countries, such as Kenya, has provided more expansive leadership opportunities for women than ever before. Even though their numbers in leadership positions remain low, women have the ability and skills to exercise leadership from the positions of power and authority to which only men have had access. The church and society in Africa has no option but to include women in leadership positions due to the evidence of equity in creation and redemption that the New Testament offers, especially in the teachings of Jesus and Paul.

Chapter 5

Rereading Esther 1–2 for Equity and Women's Leadership

A Reflection on Gender and Leadership in the Old Testament

—Dorcas Chebet

MANY OLD TESTAMENT COMMENTATORS have shown that there are a number of women in the Old Testament, named and unnamed, among whom are prominent queens, prophets,[1] and leaders. However, it still is evident, even in the twenty-first century, that some Old Testament interpreters have continued to devote much of their writings to the leadership roles and positions of male characters. Very little seems to be written on the noble leadership roles and positions that most women played and held in the Old Testament. According to some Old Testament interpreters, before and during biblical times, the roles of women were almost always severely restricted because most biblical stories mainly focused on "important events and important people (men)." The perception that leadership is the preserve of men continues to thrive. In this chapter, I reread Esther 1—2 to show that the unquestioned, male-centered presentation of Old Testament narratives calls for a reinterpretation that aims at bridging the inequalities between men and women in leadership.

---

1. Some commentators and public theology, too, identify women prophets as "prophetesses." However, this chapter adopts and uses the word "prophets" for both men and women as used in Judges 4:4, NIV.

INTRODUCTION

Gender discrimination continues to be underscored as the main barrier that hinders many African women from key leadership positions both in church and society. Kimani Njogu and Elizabeth Orchardson-Mazrui have argued, "Gender is a social construct which asserts that the expectations, capabilities, and responsibilities of men and women are not always biologically determined."[2] As a social construction, cultural aspects that foster gender imbalance continue to create assumptions that sanction gender discrimination, hence barring women from leadership positions. It is within this context that patriarchal ideologies embedded in societal structures continue to sanction and engender leadership roles in society in such a way that they persist in being understood as biologically determined. That is why men continue to enjoy being in key leadership positions, even determining sensitive decisions that directly affect women. Women, on the other hand, get very limited opportunities, if any at all, to question or criticize decisions that sometimes prevent their lives from flourishing.

The lack of representation in key leadership positions has caused many African women to continue to grapple with low social status and inequitable social relationships. In fact, "powerlessness (lack of voice) contributes to women's vulnerability, curtailing their freedom to decide on matters that directly affect them."[3] These experiences find expression in social exclusion and dependency. This continues to cause many African women to struggle with issues, such as an unequal and diminished capacity to participate in society or to develop meaningful connections at an equal level with other members of the society.[4] In Kenya, for example, "It is men who hold most and key positions of power in the institutions of family, religion, politics, and the workplace."[5] Within such a context, one asks, is it possible for women's leadership roles to be recognized, let alone allow women's leadership potential to flourish?

GENDER AND WOMEN'S LEADERSHIP ROLES

According to Njogu and Orchardson-Mazrui, "It is not just through socialization that inequalities are planted. Glaring gaps in policy, legal frameworks, and investment opportunities make it difficult for women to

---

2. Njogu and Orchardson-Mazrui, "Gender Inequality."
3. Sesay, *Don't Sleep*, 24.
4. Ibid.
5. Kamau, *Researching AIDS*, 11.

perform to their full potential in social, economic, political, and [leadership positions]."[6] All these factors combine to build a social construct that encourages African women to believe that leadership positions belong to men, while men are socialized to create and recreate laws that will continue to establish men in key leadership positions and give them power to continue to "rule" over women.[7] When one reads the Old Testament portrayal of women by narrators communicating their own agenda within a prescribed patriarchal context, such a context then becomes a breeding ground that serves to sanction the subordination of women. This is because the portrayal of women as "behind men" continues to be understood as God-ordained, hence preventing women from striving to take up leadership positions.

In Africa, women are key storytellers. Women have used stories to show that they are not inferior and silent subordinates whose only rightful position is in the private sphere. We often see this when women in Kenya, for example, use poems to find their voice in contexts that constantly silence them using gender-based violence. Thus, a rereading of Esther 1 and 2 will combine with African women's perspective of storytelling to retell stories of the important leadership roles played by women in the Bible, underscoring the importance of redressing an imbalance in the presentation of Old Testament narratives. It will become evident that gender equality is the key to the empowerment of both men and women for leadership positions in church and society.

In this way, it becomes possible for biblical readers to see how important it is for women to reread biblical texts for themselves, by themselves, and with themselves in order to retell women's stories from women's vantage points. Many African women interpreters of the Bible have, in fact, shown that one reason African women continue to be marginalized and prevented from ascending into leadership positions is because the Bible continues to be read to them by "the other." It is only by encouraging African women to reread the Bible by themselves and for themselves—and to retell their own stories—that many of them will stop observing from a distance and become actively involved in championing gender equity. Then women can reclaim their rightful space in leadership,[8] and then it will ultimately be possible for

---

6. Njogu and Orchardson-Mazrui, "Gender Inequality."

7. "It is because of patriarchal ideologies that Kenyan society, for example, organizes its affairs to cater for and sustain male supremacy over women" ("Gender Inequality," 112). Sadly, even women who have triumphed against the odds to emerge at the top leadership positions continue to struggle to prove that what men can do, "women too" can do better.

8. Phiri, *Women*, 145.

African women to overcome gender barriers and feel empowered to fight for leadership positions both in the church and society.[9]

A SYNTHETIC ANALYSIS OF ESTHER 1—2

The book of Esther is set within the context of the display of power, wealth, resistance, submission, defiance, and loyalty. In Esther 1:5–11, for example, King Ahasuerus is portrayed as displaying his power and wealth in terms of possessions. In the process of displaying his royal power, he seeks to show off his wife Queen Vashti alongside his other property.[10] The extreme display of power is seen when Queen Vashti is to be brought to the king "naked" so that the totality of her beauty can be displayed to "the whole world" (Esther 1:11).[11] From the way the narrator tells the story, it is possible to see that it is the leadership position of Ahasuerus as king that allows him to display his power as he pleases.[12] On the other hand, we also see that the leadership position of Vashti as queen gives her the power to say no to the king's demand—after all, they are at the same level (Esth 1:12). Their crowns (the king's crown and the queen's crown) put Queen Vashti at the same level as King Ahasuerus—a leadership level that gives Queen Vashti the power to resist an injustice.

Even though the leadership position of Queen Vashti gives her the power to say no to an injustice, the dilemma here is that her action puts her and "all" women in trouble. When King Ahasuerus learns of Vashti's disobedience, he becomes very angry and seeks advice from the men at his banquet on how he should deal with his wife. The advice given to the king is that Queen Vashti should be replaced by another woman who is better than she so that this action can serve as a warning to the rest of the women lest they also disobey their husbands (see Esth 1:19). Among some African communities, the advice to marry a second wife as a way of disciplining the first wife is very common. In the action of King Ahasuerus, and in many African countries as we may see, power imbalances cause women to be victims of cultural traditions which directly limit their advancement.

---

9. Sesay, "Female Bodies," 36.

10. Hertig, "Introduction," 17.

11. Some interpreters of this story (a position held in this essay) believe that Queen Vashti had been summoned to appear before the crowd in the nude. See Pitts, *Queen Vashti*, 21.

12. In fact, it seems that in this story, King Ahasuerus is not even portrayed as wearing a crown, yet his leadership position as a king gives him the power to "make" and "destroy"; see Craig, *Reading Esther*, 107.

In fact, the dethronement of Queen Vashti automatically indicates that there is a leadership vacuum—a matter that caused the king to issue an order without hesitation that would allow for the leadership vacuum to be filled.[13] Unfortunately, from the way the narrator tells this particular story, the bold action of Queen Vashti only served as an opportunity to give a detailed account of an extreme display of the power of male dominance over women. In the story, we see how the king used his power and leadership position to pass a verdict that impacts directly on the vulnerable in society—women. A beauty contest was organized where the virginity of hundreds of women was tested by the king. We see this in the following words: "In the evening she went in; then in the morning she came back to the second harem in custody of Shaashgaz, the king's eunuch, who was in charge of the concubines" (Esth 2:14, NRSV). When the young women were brought into the harem, they were put in the custody of Hegai, a *eunuch* who was in charge of virgins. After spending a night with the king, in the morning the young virgin—turned concubine—came back to the second harem in the custody of Shaashgaz, the king's *eunuch* who was in charge of the concubines.

In this narrative, the narrator skillfully informs the readers that the young women came in to the harem under the label "young virgins," and they were put in custody of Hegai, who was a eunuch. He was "harmless"; after all, he is a eunuch. After spending a night with the king, they were transferred to a different place under the custody of a different man—Shaashgaz, who was also a eunuch—and the young virgins then acquired a new label: "concubines." Sadly, even when it was evident that the king possibly had sexual intercourse with the hundreds of "young virgins" in the process of testing a suitable woman who would take the place of Queen Vashti, the narrator does not tell the readers what happened to the hundreds of women whose virginity was tested by the king.[14]

Readers are only left to guess their fate by being informed that after the young virgin went to the king in the evening, she would then go to the second harem under the custody of Shaashgaz, who was in charge of concubines. The point here is that the narrator only allows the readers to see how the leadership position of King Ahasuerus gives him the opportunity to display the power of male dominance over women's sexuality; after all, the societal structures only allowed for men to be in leadership positions, while

---

13. According to Craig, the two crown scenes in this story are linked by common features: first, the woman who wears the crown is the one who pleases the king; second, she can be uncrowned without being granted an opportunity to appeal if she displeases the king (*Reading Esther*, 108).

14. One can only imagine what the outcome would be if "virgin testing" happened in this era of HIV/AIDS.

women were just objects of sexual desire. On the other hand, we see here that because women were not in leadership, they became passive recipients of the extreme display of the power of male leadership.

Since it was a man who is in leadership, the rest of the men, high and low, enjoyed the fruits of the decisions made by King Ahasuerus. "This advice pleased the king and the officials, and the king did as Memucan proposed; he sent letters to all the royal provinces, to every province in its own script and to every people in its own language, declaring that every man should be master in his own house" (Esth 1:21–22, NRSV). In the king's command, it is possible to see that the dominance of the leadership of men was translated even into vernacular languages so that the recipients of male dominance felt the totality of the extreme power of men. It is within such a context that gender inequality directly makes it difficult for women to perform to their fullest potential in social, economic, and political spheres. Thus, the empowerment of both men and women into leadership positions at an equal level is a major tool in bridging inequalities, preventing violence, and fostering the self-esteem and well-being of both men and women.

The display of the king's power to create and recreate laws with or without the approval of the ones affected by the laws is a clear indicator of gender imbalance. The words, "If it pleases the king, let a royal order go out from him, and let it be written among the laws of the Persians and the Medes so that it may not be altered . . ." (Esth 1:19) clearly indicate that there were no laws in place that would be used to punish Queen Vashti for refusing to be forcefully displayed before people naked.[15] Suppose this story is retold in such a way that the readers can see the defiance of Queen Vashti in a positive light. The leadership position of Queen Vashti as a queen gave her an opportunity to allow for injustices against women to be named, exposed, and criticized. A rereading of Queen Vashti's story then gives both men and women a motivation to view each other as equally created in God's image and, therefore, having the power to be in leadership at an equal level.

While we encounter the display of male power and the defiance of Queen Vashti in Esther 1, in chapter 2, we see Queen Esther being portrayed as submissive and using the power of her beauty to win the attention of the king. In many African communities, boys and girls are socialized to believe that women are physically weak, while men are sexually weak. Thus, for a man to continue making women submissive, or in their "rightful" position in the domestic sphere, men should exert extra physical power. This will then serve to impart fear into women so that. out of fear, women

---

15. According to Craig, in *Reading Esther*, a reader who reads this story has ample opportunity to discover that with or without the crown, the king's leadership position gives him absolute power to create and recreate laws.

cannot dare demand their rightful leadership positions in society. On the other hand, for a woman to get what she wants from a man, she will use her sexuality. After all, men are sexually weak; they cannot resist women's sexual advances. Is this the strategy that the narrator of Esther 2 seems to project to the readers? We do not know. What we can see, though, is that it is the leadership position of Queen Esther and her crown that serves as a tool to safeguard and preserve the lives of the Jews.

A rereading of Esther 1 and 2 will, therefore, show that a significant feature of the existence of power in societies is often encountered in structures that exist and operate on the basis of the objectification of power—authority, law, force, its internalization (loyalty, duty, fear of sanction)—and the accumulation of the means required to wield it (money, resources, and technology).[16] Thus, if power and leadership is strategically positioned at the disposal of one gender, this then becomes a breeding ground for inequality.

REREADING ESTHER 1—2 FOR GENDER EQUITY AND WOMEN'S LEADERSHIP

Even though some contemporary biblical scholars continue to devote much of their writing to "important events and people," it is clear from the exposition of the above Old Testament passages that the Bible does not justify the subordination of women. However, the patriarchal contexts in which most African women read biblical texts continue to make it very difficult for African women to strive to be in leadership positions or to allow their leadership potential to flourish. We can see in the above discussion that even though the Old Testament narratives come to us from a patriarchal context that continues to be understood as preventing women from becoming leaders, several women triumphed against the odds to emerge in top leadership positions. Examples of women in the Old Testament who have triumphed against the odds include Tamar, Deborah, Queen Vashti, and Queen Esther.

A rereading of Esther 1—2, therefore, from the vantage point of African women as storytellers, enables them to retell biblical stories in such a way that the leadership roles of both men and women can be appreciated at an equal level. Queen Vashti has the audacity and power to turn down the king's command that demands that she display her nude beauty before a multitude. This is because the queen is at the same level with the king. She is empowered to say, "No!" This can be interpreted to mean that it is important to also give voice to women at all government and private institutions so that women can participate at an equal level with men in public dialogue

16. Ibid., 17.

and decision-making to influence decisions that determine the future of both men and women.

Additionally, the story of Queen Vashti as narrated from the context of the story of Queen Esther can be understood as an attempt to subordinate and possibly silence the voices of women who are in leadership.[17] On the other hand, the same narrative speaks about Queen Esther with such great admiration. This shows that, even though patriarchy was restrictive of the leadership voice of women, the "contradictory" narration of the story of Queen Esther suggests a much less rigid attitude toward women's leadership positions in the Old Testament. In fact, the determination to replace Queen Vashti draws the reader's attention to the importance of the different leadership roles played by both men and women in diverse and dynamic ways.

We can see in the story of Queen Vashti that, even though she is punished for refusing the king's command that demands that she display her nude body in public, there is no suggestion in her story that her leadership was in itself wrong or unacceptable. In fact, the anger of the king and the his advisors against the action of Queen Vashti can be seen as a general statement that Queen Vashti only behaved badly. By the same token, Esther's beauty is emphasized, to possibly imply that women have no leadership skills unless they use their beauty to get the attention of men who will in turn act on their behalf. Queen Esther's brains and skill should not be downplayed or ignored. Contemporary men and women can see here that there are no uniform skills of leadership. Different situations call for diverse and dynamic leadership skills.

OBSERVATIONS AND RECOMMENDATIONS

It is important to note that women are more prone to male aggression where women are economically empowered, yet have no leadership representation. However, from the story of Queen Vashti, we can see that the aggression of men does not necessarily lead to the passiveness of women. Women are gifted in using different means to display displeasure. Some use resistance; others use submissiveness. The purpose of this chapter is to highlight various ways to promote biblical equity in leadership—not to discuss the different ways that women express displeasure.

In order to reconstruct structures which empower both men and women for leadership, it is important to underscore factors that contribute to male dominance in the Old Testament during the reinterpretation

---

17. To understand how some Old Testament narratives are told, see Seidman, "The Erotic," 109.

of biblical stories.[18] This can be done by highlighting the cultural setting that characterizes the way Old Testament narratives are narrated. The way narratives are told can have the potential to empower or disempower both men and women. Access to education, development skills, economic opportunities, and participation in decision-making is key to the empowerment of both men and women for leadership positions. Last, but not least, mutual dialogue gives both men and women an occasion to negotiate for equal leadership opportunities. Conversely, that means that when one gender is silenced, there is no room for dialogue.

CONCLUSION

Structures that bar women from entering into leadership positions are socially constructed through the lens of engendered social positioning and the presentation of the stories of women. This means that it is still possible to deconstruct these structures and to reconstruct structures that empower women to take up their rightful leadership positions in society. One way of doing this is by retelling biblical stories in ways such that both men and women's leadership positions can be appreciated at an equal level. Even though some Old Testament interpreters deliberately continue to devote much of their writing to "important events and people," there are still many opportunities for retelling biblical stories in such a way that the leadership potential of both men and women can be appreciated.

---

18. See, for example, Pressler, "Deuteronomy," 93.

Chapter 6

Gazing at the Creation Purpose
Gender Equity at the Creation and Jesus' Esteem for Women as a Model

—KeumJu Jewel Hyun

INTERDEPENDENCY OF MAN AND WOMAN IN THE LIKENESS OF GOD

THE BEGINNING CHAPTERS OF Genesis show God's creation of the universe and human beings. The triune God created male and female in his image and likeness: "Let us make man[1] in our image, in our likeness" (Gen 1:26a). Being made in the image of God can be interpreted in various ways, as we study the many attributes of God's character. However, this chapter focuses on one aspect of what it means to be made in the image of God. The word *us* in the verse indicates the three persons of the triune God working in partnership. It speaks to the diversity of one God in trinity working together in unity creating human beings. The triune God in three persons is the Father, the Son, and the Holy Spirit. The diversity of the Trinity is that the Father is neither the Son (John 8:16) nor the Holy Spirit (John 14:26); the Son is neither the Father (John 8:16) nor the Holy Spirit (Acts 10:38); the Holy Spirit is neither the Father (John 14:26) nor the Son (Acts 10:38).

---

1. Refer to chapter 3 of this book, where the meaning of the word *man* in Genesis 1:26 is fully explained.

Yet, the three persons form unity through diversity and have shared authority; each member of the Trinity has his own personality and expresses his own will, working independently. Each person of the triune God is equal[2] to each other and has the same essence of the nature of God, being holy, omnipotent, omnipresent, and omniscient in eternity. The three persons in one God have shared the responsibility in harmony and interdependency. Hence, God created man and woman in his likeness to be interdependent and to have shared responsibilities to "be fruitful and increase in number; fill the earth and subdue it. Rule over the fish in the sea and the birds in the sky and over every living creature that moves on the ground" (Gen 1:26–28, NIV). They both bear the image of God (v. 27), and God was pleased with his creation of man and woman. Thus, the equality and interdependency of man and woman and their responsibility to God originated from the very beginning of the creation.

In fulfilling his purpose, God created man first (Gen 2:7) and put him in the garden; the man was commanded to freely enjoy everything in the garden, except that he was not to eat the fruit from one of the trees (Gen 2:16–17). In the creation account in Genesis 2, we see that God saw that Adam was lonely and that it was not good for him to be alone. Adam needed a helper like himself, a human being. God created woman out of his rib. Adam was insufficient by himself and needed someone to depend on to fulfill God's purpose. Thus, Eve was the solution to Adam's need for help. She was a helper God saw as "fit" for him, equal and corresponding (Gen 2:18–25). Eve was to be his helper for God's purpose in order to fulfill what God intended them to do.

Adam and Eve became one flesh, husband and wife. Being a helper to her husband did not indicate any inferiority in Eve; she was not beneath Adam. She was his equal to have dominion over the creation and was superior to all the rest of the creation. Eve did not simply exist for Adam alone. Adam and Eve both had more than husband and wife roles to perform for God. They were interdependent in ruling the creation together as partners. In the Old Testament, *helper* did not mean "subordinate." In fact, *helper* is used to refer to God, who is our "helper."[3] Thus, Eve serves as Adam's helper

---

2. Jesus called God his own Father, and the Jews tried to kill him because Jesus was making "himself equal with God" (John 5:18, NIV).

3. Here is a sampling of Scripture references describing God as one who helps, as our helper. When the Israelites were in slavery in Egypt, "They cried to the LORD for help, and the LORD sent Moses and Aaron" (Exod 2:23; 1 Sam 12:8). Moses told the Israelites that they were saved by the LORD, their "shield and helper" (Deut 33:29). King David cried, "Listen to my cry for help, my King and my God" (Ps 5:2), and "Come quickly to help me, O Lord my Savior" (Ps 38:22); "Surely God is my help; the Lord is the one who sustains me" (54:4), and God is "the helper of the fatherless" (Ps 10:14b).

in order to help fulfill the creation mandate to subdue the earth and procreate. They served side by side, both dependent on God. The insufficiency of Adam by himself became complete with the creation of Eve, and it is their interdependency that makes them able to carry out what God commanded them.

FROM INTERDEPENDENCE TO INDEPENDENCE AND HIERARCHY

Having disobeyed God in the Fall, both man and woman faced the consequences of their sin. The Fall of humankind brought a distortion to their relationships with God, with each other, and with the world. God said to the woman that she would desire to control her husband, but that her husband would rule over her (Gen 3:16). As a result, the husband had authority over his wife, and the wife became subordinate to her husband. The interdependency of man and woman devolved into independence and hierarchy in human relationships. The insistence on the "headship" of man at home, at church, and society crept in. Thus, with the introduction of sin into the relationship between man and woman, inequity was introduced. At the same time, with God's promise that the woman's offspring would crush the serpent's head (Gen 3:15), God's redemptive history was ushered in.

PARTNERSHIP EXAMPLES IN THE OLD TESTAMENT

In spite of the broken relationships between human beings, God's redemptive plan continued working through men and women. In the following, we will examine some passages in the Old Testament and present a few stories of man and woman working in partnership to obey God and bring glory to him.

Daughters of Zelophehad and Moses (Num 26:33; 27:1–11; 36:1–12; Josh 17:3–6; 1 Chr 7:15)

Zelophehad, who was from the clans of Manasseh, had no sons but five daughters. Their names were Mahlah, Noah, Hoglah, Milcah, and Tirzah.

Also, in Isaiah, God told the Israelites, "'For I am the LORD, your God, who takes hold of your right hand and says to you, Do not fear; I will help you. Do not be afraid, O worm Jacob, O little Israel, for I myself will help you,' declares the LORD, your Redeemer, the Holy One of Israel" (Isa 41:13–14).

When their father died, they realized that they would not be able to inherit the land that belonged to their father because, according to the regulations, only sons would inherit the land. Instead of accepting this, the daughters appealed to Moses, Eleazar the priest, and the leaders of the whole community and requested that they should be permitted to inherit their father's land. Moses sought God's revelation on the request. God responded to Moses to implement the daughters' proposal. As a result, a broader regulation was made that when there are no sons, daughters shall have inheritance rights, followed by other male relatives. From this story, we learn that the daughters sought to express their concerns through proper channels. They approached the leaders, and Moses did not dismiss their request just because it came from women. Instead, he took the request seriously enough to seek God's guidance. God validated Zelophehad's daughters' request and instructed Moses, "You must certainly give them property as an inheritance among their father's relatives and give their father's inheritance to them" (Num 27:7, NIV). The daughters' inquiry about their inheritance resulted in a policy change: "Say to the Israelites, 'If a man dies and leaves no son, give his inheritance to his daughter'" (Num 27:8, NIV). Moses, the priest, and other leaders did not impose their authority and power over the daughters, who were the weaker party. Women and men—the daughters, Moses, the priest, and the leaders—worked together, seeking God's way to resolve the matter. By resolving the issue according to the will of God, justice was exercised, and both parties honored God.

Naaman and the Servant Girl (2 Kgs 5:1–14)

Naaman was a mighty warrior and commander of the army of Syria. He was a prominent and well-respected man who enjoyed high favor from the king of Syria for the great victories he brought to Syria. Although he was a strong, fearless warrior, he suffered from leprosy. During this time, the Syrians had taken captive a young girl from Israel on one of their attacks and gave her to Naaman's wife as her slave. Knowing about the healing power of the prophet Elisha, one day the slave girl told her mistress, "I wish my master would go to see the prophet in Samaria. He would heal him of his leprosy" (2 Kgs 5:3, NLT). So Naaman wrote a letter to the king of Syria and received permission to go to Samaria to be healed by the prophet Elisha. To Naaman's surprise, however, Elisha did not heal him the way he expected, as he was told to wash himself seven times in the Jordan River. Naaman was angry: "'I thought he would certainly come out to meet me!' he said. 'I expected him to wave his hand over the leprosy and call on the name of the LORD his God and heal me!'" (2 Kgs 5:11, NLT). Eventually, through the persuasion of his officers, Naaman followed what Elisha told him to do, and his leprosy was healed. Naaman credited his healing to and accepted the God of Israel as the only "God in all the world" (2 Kgs 5:15b).

What do we learn from the story? Although the slave girl was young enough to be called "a little girl," she was forced to do household chores. She was snatched away from her parents and her homeland, and she was brought to a foreign land. Nevertheless, she became a channel through which God's healing was brought to the army commander of an enemy country. Instead of being filled with hate or living in fear, she extended her compassion toward the person who did wrong to her and shared her faith in what God can do through his servant, the prophet. In the same way, although it might have been from desperation, Naaman did not dismiss his wife's suggestion, nor did he consider the slave girl as an insignificant person. Whatever the reason may have been, Naaman valued the slave girl's suggestion and took it seriously; thus, he went to Israel. As a result, the man who did not know God acknowledged and praised the LORD: "Now I know that there is no God in all the world except in Israel" (2 Kgs 5:15, NIV). This is a story of salvation and of man and woman working with mutual respect, bringing glory to God. Since Naaman did not disregard the girl's suggestion, he came to know the true and living God; the slave girl became an instrument for revealing God's power and compassion. In God's realm, her life was not in vain as she demonstrated her faith in God while doing her assigned work as a slave in captivity against her will. Mutual respect between the girl and the commander brought glory to God.

Huldah and King Josiah (2 Kgs 22:2; 2 Chr 34)

During the reign of King Josiah, while repairing the Temple of Solomon, workmen discovered an old scroll, a "Book of the Law." King Josiah charged his high priest, his chief of staff, and his attendant to find out more about the book and its contents. The high priest Hilkiah and the officials went to the home of Huldah the prophetess for her explanation of the book. She was the wife of Shallum living in Jerusalem. Upon their arrival at Huldah's house, she prophesied (2 Kgs 22:23–28). Prophets Jeremiah, Zephaniah, and Nahum all lived in the same area in Jerusalem at the time, yet Huldah was chosen. There is no indication that the king gave any instructions to seek the counsel of male prophets nor that the high priest felt so obliged. They acknowledged the validity of Huldah's prophecy even though she was a woman. In a patriarchal society, it was quite remarkable that the male leaders—the king, the high priest, and the workers—would accept what Huldah, a female prophetess, told them. King Josiah wanted the word of God, valued Huldah's interpretation, and acted upon it. Again, the Bible recognized the value of a woman exercising her gift to prophesy and bringing glory to God.

WOMEN IN THE MINISTRY OF JESUS AND THE APOSTLES[4]

Having explored some passages in the Old Testament on men and women working together in partnership, in this section we shift our focus to Jesus' positive attitude toward women as a model for gender equity. Then we will examine a few passages to see how the apostles Peter and Paul, modeling after Jesus, worked with women in partnership in their respective ministries.

Jesus as a Role Model for Empowering Women

Jesus empowered women and acknowledged their personhood in a culture where women were considered to be men's property, were identified only as mothers or wives, and had no voice of their own. All the Gospels show that many women followed Jesus. Luke (8:1–3) writes that a large number of women followed Jesus, along with the twelve disciples, in his tour through cities and villages. These women listened to Jesus' preaching, ate with Jesus, supported his ministry financially (Matt. 27:55–56; Mark 15:40–41), and witnessed his teaching everywhere. In contrast to the culture of the first century in Palestine, Jesus interacted with many women, valued women, had women disciples, and recognized them as persons.

A Samaritan Woman. On his way to the Galilean region from Judea, Jesus stopped at Samaritan village of Sychar. While resting at Jacob's well, he encountered a woman who came to fetch water. He started a conversation with her in a culture where Jewish men did not talk with Samaritans, much less with a woman. During the conversation, Jesus identified himself, gave the woman a new life, quenching her thirsty soul by offering water that gives eternal life, and restored the woman's dignity, as she was so despised that she could only fetch water at noontime when no one else was around. Realizing that she was talking with the Messiah, the woman hurried to the village, leaving her water jar behind, and testified to Jesus' identity as Messiah to

---

4. A portion in this section is from an unpublished dissertation; see KeumJu Hyun, "Mobilizing Women."

the people in her village. Her testimony caused the people to leave the town to see Jesus (John 4:1–42). Thus, she became the earliest woman evangelist.

Martha. Martha, the sister of Mary and Lazarus, had her priorities mixed up when she was busy preparing dinner for Jesus and his disciples. Being wrapped up with busyness, she complained to Jesus, asking him to tell her sister Mary to help her. Jesus told her that Mary had chosen the better thing as she was listening to Jesus' teaching (Luke 10:38–42). We encounter Martha again later when Jesus was going to her home to raise her brother Lazarus from the dead (John 11:11). Hearing that Jesus was coming, Martha went out to meet him and said that her brother would not have died had he been there sooner. Correcting her misunderstanding, Jesus revealed his identity to her as "the resurrection and the life. The one who believes in me will live, even though they die; and whoever lives by believing in me will never die" (John 11:25–26, NIV). Then Jesus asked her if she believed what he had just said. Martha replied, "I have always believed you are the Messiah, the Son of God, the one who has come into the world from God" (John 11:27, NLT). Martha not only believed what Jesus had said but also affirmed his identity as the Son of God. Some scholars consider her statement as theologically significant as Peter's confession at Caesarea Philippi. Here we see Martha's spiritual growth through Jesus' interactions with her, as she transforms from a woman busy only with her work in the kitchen to a woman of theological insight into Jesus' identity.

Mary, sister of Lazarus and Martha. Jesus was at the home of Martha, Mary, and Lazarus on his last journey to Jerusalem. Dinner was prepared in his honor, and Martha served. Then Mary brought a large jar of expensive, pure nard oil and anointed Jesus' feet. Judas Iscariot complained that her deed was waste of money when the perfume, worth a year's salary, could have been sold to help the poor (John 12:1–6). Jesus, however, defended Mary and told the people around to leave her alone, saying she anointed him in preparation "for the day of my burial. You will always have the poor among you, but you will not always have me" (John 11:8b, NIV). One wonders how Mary knew of Jesus' imminent burial. We know that she was diligent in listening to Jesus when he taught at her home (Luke 10:39). Mary learned from Jesus' teachings and gained theological insight that Jesus' earthly ministry also involved death (Matt 26:6–13; Mark 14:3–9; John 12:1–8). She was able to gain such knowledge only because Jesus allowed Mary the entitlement to learn when the rabbis limited rabbinic teachings to men.

These three women are only a few examples of the women whose dignity Jesus elevated, whose personhood he restored, and whose effectiveness he empowered during his earthly ministry at a time when culture and tradition treated women unfavorably.

Women Co-Workers in the Ministry of the Apostle Peter

Jesus restored not only women's dignity, but he also reinstated Peter's discipleship. Peter denied Jesus, his own master, three times during Jesus' trial, he ran away at his crucifixion, and he did not believe his resurrection at first when women came from the tomb and told him about it. However, upon a dialogue with the resurrected Jesus along the shore of the Sea of Galilee, he was recommissioned to feed Jesus' "lambs/sheep" (John 21:15–19). After Jesus' ascension, Peter became a strong leader, carrying on Jesus' ministry, and many women were his co-workers. The book of Acts describes women's roles in spreading the gospel in the earliest churches from Jerusalem (1:14; 5:14; 12:12–17) to Samaria (8:12), Joppa (9:36–42) and Philippi (16:11–15) to Thessalonica (17:4), Berea (17:12), Athens (17:34), Corinth (18:1–3), and Ephesus (18:19–26).

Under Peter's leadership in Jerusalem, Mary, the mother of Jesus, along with other women and men devoted themselves to prayer (Acts 1:14). Multitudes of men and women were converted and actively participated in the ministry with Peter (Acts 5:14–16). The house of Mary, the mother of John Mark, was a gathering place for prayer. A servant girl named Rhoda came to answer when Peter was at the door upon his release from prison (Acts 12:12). This detail indicates that Mary's house might have been an important meeting place in Peter's ministry if he went there after his release; it is significant, too, that the new community of believers included even a slave girl. Moreover, the fact that Mary would hold such a meeting during the time of Saul's severe persecution of believers in Jerusalem signifies her strong commitment to the Christian community. When the gospel reached Samaria, many women believed the good news and were baptized (Acts 8:12). In Joppa, Tabitha, also called Dorcas (in Greek meaning, "being able to see clearly"), became a believer because of Peter's ministry. She was known for always doing good work full of kindness for others and ministering to the poor (Acts 9:36–42). When she died, Peter raised her from the dead and many began to believe. Dorcas was the first woman called a "disciple."

Women Co-Workers in the Ministry of the Apostle Paul

When Paul and his team reached Philippi, they preached the gospel to a group of women at the riverside. Lydia, a merchant of expensive purple fabric from the city of Thyatira, was among them. She was the first convert of Paul's ministry and the first woman identified by her occupation. After Lydia and her household were baptized, her house became the center of the Christian community in Paul's ministry in Philippi (Acts 16:11-15, 40). Euodia and Syntyche were also Paul's co-workers in the church at Philippi (Phil. 4:2-3). In Thessalonica, as well as in Berea, many "important women" were converted and joined Paul and Silas in ministry (Acts 17:4, 12); a woman named Damaris and a number of others joined Paul in Athens (17:34). Apphia in Colossae and her husband Philemon had a house church at their home. The apostle Paul mentions that he received much joy and encouragement from their hospitality. (Philem. 1:2).

The tentmakers Priscilla and her husband Aquila met Paul for the first time in Corinth and joined his ministry when they left Rome after Claudius' edict to leave. Priscilla and her husband established the Corinthian church with Paul (Acts 18), and they "more accurately" taught Apollos, a male evangelist who knew Scripture well (Acts 18:1-3; 18:24-28; 1 Cor 1:12). In the last chapter of Romans, Paul mentions ten women and nineteen men in his greetings to the Christians in Rome. Priscilla was one of the ten women mentioned. Paul mentions that she, along with her husband, risked her life for his ministry and affirms that all the Gentile churches are grateful to them. Although it is not known exactly how Priscilla ministered to the church, Bible teaching was probably one way. Ben Witherington summarizes Priscilla's role:

> Her significance is not confined to the fact that it is intimated she is more important or more prominent than her husband, or that she was one of Paul's co-laborers in and for the Gospel. Priscilla is presented as a teacher, and not just a teacher of other women or some nameless converts, but as someone adept enough to give Apollos, a leading male evangelist (Acts 18:24-8; 1 Cor 1:12, 3:4-6), a "more accurate" instruction.[5]

Phoebe was a deacon of the church in Cenchrea, a twin city of Corinth, and a trusted co-worker of Paul (Rom. 16:1-3). She delivered his letter to the Christians in Rome. Paul was indebted to her services and asked the Roman church to welcome her and support her needs as a means of showing gratitude on his behalf. Nympha in Laodicea (Col 4:15) and other female

---

5 Witherington III, *Women in the Earliest Churches*, 156.

co-workers mentioned in Romans 16 are all leaders who contributed to spreading the gospel and expanding Christianity alongside Paul.

Many women, like Lydia, Priscilla, Euodia and Syntyche, Apphia, Nympha, and Phoebe were leaders in their respective congregations. Mary, Rufus' mother, women in large numbers, and many prominent women joined the church from the time of its infancy. In the culture, whether in the Judaic or pagan world, women did not have prominence and dignity, yet women played an important role in the early expansion of Christianity because they were given opportunities to serve as leaders.

We contend that these few examples in the New Testament teach us that the positive treatment of Jesus toward women have set a precedent for practicing gender equity, and that the apostles Peter and Paul emulated Jesus, embracing women working in partnership in their respective ministries. They allowed women to assume leadership roles, recognized their social status, and renewed dignity within their ministries. Thus, Peter, Paul, and all the women who participated in their ministries were interdependent, working together.

Today, cultures in many parts of the world are not much different from that of Greco-Roman days. Jesus' presence in women's lives elevated their identity and transformed their lives, enabling them to play key roles in spreading the gospel. The apostles Paul and Peter are representative male leaders who modeled Jesus, enabling women to participate in their ministries and working in partnership to transform communities.

CONCLUSION

We began this chapter with the story of Creation with man and woman created in the likeness of the triune God. The sin of their disobedience resulted in broken relationships with each other, with God, and with the rest of creation. The image of human beings, who were created in the image of God, has been distorted; thus, man and woman brought about the loss of their interdependency in fulfilling God's creation purpose.

We have looked at some examples in the Old Testament where men and women can be seen working in partnership despite the consequences of the Fall: Moses and the daughters of Zelophehad, Naaman and a slave girl from Israel, and King Josiah and the prophetess Huldah.

In the New Testament, Jesus treated women favorably and the apostles Peter and Paul had many co-workers. Today, just like those women in the time of Jesus and in the early church, many women, despite the prevalent gender inequity, are committed to following Jesus and making a great impact in the church and in their communities, regardless of their official positions. We end this chapter with the story of a woman and a man, who as co-heirs of Christ, began transforming their community.

Jemaah[6] is a successful businesswoman with a big heart in a town outside of Nairobi, Kenya. Although she and her construction business owner husband are quite wealthy, Jemaah has been concerned about the poverty-stricken women in the villages surrounding her neighborhood. The women's daily chore required them to walk miles to fetch water for their families. Jemaah had some ideas as to how she might help those women. However, she was not sure if she had any leadership traits. That was when she heard about a woman's leadership training program offered at a nearby university. Upon completing the program, she gained confidence in her leadership abilities, mobilized the women in the neighboring villages, and started a weekly Bible study. She also helped the women start a group savings account from which, eventually, they bought a water tank for the community. As a result, they no longer had to walk miles to fetch water every day. As the group became stable, Jemaah encouraged the women to plan to start their own business that would help them develop a steady stream of income. The women started a utensils and dinnerware catering business. Women in the village who lacked a purpose in life now have a productive means of contributing to the community. Jemaah also helped women in another village to start a poultry business—buying day-old chicks and selling them a couple of months later in the market. Being a beneficiary of leadership training and gender equity, Jemaah rediscovered her identity and self-worth, and her gifts in organizing and starting microenterprises made a big difference to the lives of many families in her neighborhood communities.

Observing how Jemaah was helping others, her neighbor pastor, Muri, became interested in Jemaah's business skills. As the pastor of a small local church, which was not able to give him full financial support, he needed some supplementary income and asked Jemaah to teach him how to start a poultry business. He started with one chick, and when the chicken grew and started laying eggs, he sold the eggs to his neighbors. With the proceeds of the sales, he purchased a calf and more chickens. He is now a major supplier to his neighbors, not only of eggs, but also of chickens and cow's milk. Pastor Muri and his wife are happy serving their church without having to depend on the church for their financial needs. A woman was successful, and a man, recognizing her ability, learned from her; in the process, both became transformational agents in the community.

---

6. Not her real name. All names subsequently mentioned in the chapter are not real name to protect the individual's privacy.

When men and women understand what the Bible says about gender equity and exercise those teachings with mutual respect and co-dependence, we will see lives change and communities transform.

Chapter 7

Appreciating How the Apostle Paul Champions Women and Men in Church Leadership

—Grace May

PAUL THE APOSTLE UNABASHEDLY advocates for his sisters in the church. Yet despite his ardent support for women leading in the church, time and time again he is assailed as a misogynist whose teaching is, at worst sexist, and, at best, irrelevant for today. Wrestling with Paul's so-called "texts of terror,"[1] however, need not yield such deleterious conclusions. Contrary to popular opinion, Paul's adherence to gender equity aligns with the gospel of freedom that he champions and preaches. Paul's epistles show his commitment to recognizing the authority of his female colleagues and seeing his sisters flourish in exercising their gifts in the extension of God's reign. The intent of the following chapter is to examine Paul's principle of inclusion (Gal 3:2–28), his practice of integration (Rom 16:1–15), and his pastoral instruction (1 Tim 2:11–15; 1 Cor 11:2–16; 14:34–35). By demonstrating biblical equity at work in the early church, the hope is that the body of Christ around the world may be inspired to lead in a commensurate way and that God's Spirit will fall afresh on brothers and sisters partnering in ministry for God's glory.

1. Paul's Principle of Inclusion (Galatians 3:27–28)

---

1. The term refers to difficult texts about women in the Bible and is derived from Phyllis Trible's book *Texts of Terror*.

> As many of you as were baptized into Christ have clothed yourselves with Christ. There is no longer Jew or Greek, there is no longer slave or free, there is no longer male and female; for all of you are one in Christ Jesus (Gal 3:27–28).[2]

Paul understands Christian baptism as a sign of our entrance and inclusion into the body of Christ. Whatever a person's background or family of origin, baptism into Christ gives the believer a new name. We are all called Christians, united by the blood of Christ and adopted into God's family. Christ, however, desired not only to heal the sick and forgive sinners but to rehabilitate and integrate lepers, prostitutes, tax collectors, and Pharisees back into society. Paul as an ambassador of Christ gave his life to the ministry of reconciliation, reconciling people to Christ and to one another (2 Cor 5:18–20).

A telltale sign that Christ's redemptive work is taking root in our individual lives and communities is witnessing the tearing down of the middle wall of partition between ethnic and racial groups, economically and culturally diverse groups, and different genders. Paul adamantly states there is no "Jew or Greek," no "slave or free," and no "male and female," with the last category preserving the language of creation. In Genesis 1:27, "God created humankind in his image, in the image of God he created him; male and female he created them." The most intimate human relationship designed by God should not be divided. Made from the same flesh, man and woman in creation were one, and it was only the intrusion of sin in the world that separated them and destroyed their unity. According to Galatians 3:28, however, "in Christ Jesus," God has come to restore the oneness between man and woman and between people of different races and classes. The greatness of the cross lies in its power to redeem and reconcile humanity, not through force or coercion, but through Christ's love.

2. Paul's Practice of Integration (Romans 16:1–15)

> I commend to you our sister Phoebe, a deacon[e] of the church at Cenchreae, so that you may welcome her in the Lord as is fitting for the saints, and help her in whatever she may require from you, for she has been a benefactor of many and of myself as well.
>
> [e]Or minister

(Romans 16:1–2)

---

[2]. All Scripture references are quoted from the New Revised Standard Version (NRSV) unless otherwise noted.

Paul's authority came from God, who gave him the ability to practice what he preached. Paul practiced integration. Reading through the salutations at the end of Paul's letter to the Romans, Paul lists his female colleagues, a total of ten, along with eighteen male co-workers. At the very top of the list, Paul calls Phoebe a *diakonos* (Rom 16:1), which can be translated "minister," as is the case when referring to male colleagues such as Paul (2 Cor 3:6), Timothy (1 Tim 4:6), Epaphroditus (Phil 2:25; Col 1:7), and Tychichus (Col 4:7; Eph 6:21). The New American Standard Version renders the word as "helper," and the Living Bible calls Phoebe "a dear Christian woman," both translations obfuscating her identity as a leader. By introducing Phoebe as the *diakonos* or minister of "the church at Cenchreae," Paul's sentence structure suggests that she is an officer of the church (see, e.g., Phil 1:1; 1 Tim 3:8, 12). Paul specifically calls her a *prostatis*,[3] which means "chief," "leader," and literally "one who is set over others."[4] Of all the people mentioned in Paul's epistles, Phoebe uniquely enjoys the commendation of being "a leader of many and even of myself" (16:2).[5]

> Greet Prisca and Aquila, who work with me in Christ Jesus, and who risked their necks for my life, to whom not only I give thanks, but also all the churches of the Gentiles. Greet also the church in their house. (Romans 16:3–5a)

Long before clergy couples appeared in the contemporary church, the New Testament records Prisca and Aquila ministering together (Rom 16:3). Although in Graeco-Roman families it was customary to mention the man's name first as head of the household,[6] in four out of the six instances, the Bible specifically places Prisca or Priscilla's[7] name in front of her husband's (Acts 18:18; 18:26; Rom 16:3; 2 Tim 4:19). Even in referring to the church that met in "their house," Paul names her first (Rom 16:3). Most notably,

---

3. Elizabeth A. McCabe provides a helpful survey in "A Reexamination of Phoebe," 99–116. Lidell and Scott's *Greek-English Lexicon* defines *prostatis* as "leader," "chief," "president or presiding officer, one who stands before." The verb form *proistemi* appears in Romans 12:8; 1 Thessalonians 5:12; 1 Timothy 3:4–5, 12; 5:17; and Titus 3:8, 14. Romans 12:8 identifies *proistemi* as the gift of *leadership*, and 1 Timothy 5:17 speaks of the elders who *rule* [*hoi proestōtes*] as deserving of double honor (see http://www.sbl-site.org/publications/article.aspx?ArticleId=830). Justin Martyr used the term to refer to the one who presides at communion (see, e.g., *First Apology*, 65).

4. Thayer's *Greek-English Lexicon*, s.v., "prostatis."

5. Aída B. Spencer's translation concludes that the best definition for *prostatis* is leader or ruler. See *Beyond the Curse*, 115–16.

6. See, e.g., Rom 16:11 (Narcissus), Philemon 2 (Philemon), and 1 Corinthians 16:19 (Aquila).

7. Priscilla is the diminutive of Prisca.

Prisca's name appears in the place of prominence when expounding "the Way of God more accurately" to Apollos, a preacher well-versed in the Scriptures (Acts 18:26). The priority given to Prisca's name suggests that she may have taken the lead in teaching doctrinal and biblical truth.[8]

> Greet Mary, who has worked very hard among you. Greet Adronicus and Junia, my relatives who were in prison with me; they are prominent among the apostles, and they were in Christ before I was. . . . Greet those workers in the Lord, Tryphaena and Tryphosa. Greet the beloved Persis, who has worked hard in the Lord. (Romans 16:6–7, 12)

In Paul's greetings, the four women—Mary (16:6), Tryphaena, Tryphosa, and Persis (16:12)—earn the distinction of being honored for their hard work.[9] Paul uses a verb to describe their labor in the Lord that he applies to himself in the work of the gospel (e.g., 1 Cor 15:10; Phil 2:16; Col 1:29; 1 Tim 4:10). Furthermore, Junia's name stands out as the only female apostle listed in the Church of Rome. Andronicus is most likely her husband, and the plural form "apostles" (16:7) indicates that each of them in their own right is an apostle. Narrowly construed, that would make them eyewitnesses to Jesus Christ, or broadly construed, church planters or pioneer missionaries. While recent scholarship has debated whether Junia is a woman's name, her gender went uncontested through the first millennium.[10] In the fourth century, the early church father Chrysostom, who was no proponent of women's leadership in the church, extolled her position:

> Even to be an apostle is great, but also to be prominent among them. . . . Glory be! How great the wisdom of this woman that she was even deemed worthy of the apostle's title.[11]

> Greet Rufus, chosen in the Lord; and greet his mother—a mother to me also . . . Greet Philogus, Julia, Nereus and his sister, and Olympas, and all the saints who are with them. (Romans 16:13, 15)

---

8. Alternatively, Craig S. Keener posits that Prisca may have come from a higher social class, which in antiquity would have caused her name to be placed first. See his commentary on *Romans*, 185.

9. Griffiths, "Romans."

10. While Junian is the accusative form of the feminine name Junia, some have argued that Junian is another form of a man's name, Junias. There is, however, no evidence in the literature of the first century that such a man's name existed, but copious references to the woman's name Junia do exist.

11. Chrysostom, *Homily on Romans 16*. Translation as quoted from Eldon Jay Epp in *Junia*, 79.

Paul goes on to cite women such as Julia (16:15) and Nereus' sister (16:15), whom Paul does not refer to by name, but still makes a point of acknowledging. In fact, to this day, in many cultures it is more respectful to refer to a woman not by name but by her position in the family, especially if she is an older woman. Consider Rufus' mother, whom Paul regarded as "a mother to me also" (Rom 16:13). Indeed, Rufus' mother may have provided for the apostle's well-being, mending his clothes or making sure he left with food in his stomach and money in his pocket. Or perhaps she prayed earnestly for him and held prayer vigils on his behalf during his missionary journeys, especially during times of persecution. No matter how seasoned a minister is, no one ever outgrows the need for support. In short, Paul was intentional in recognizing his female colleagues, who constituted over half of his leadership team in Rome. How extraordinary it would be if our churches today reflected a similar degree of equity in our pastoral and leadership staff.[12]

3a. Paul's Pastoral Instruction to the Church in Ephesus (1 Timothy 2:11–15)

Paul benefitted profoundly from his female colleagues and did not hesitate to acknowledge their contributions, even though society gave them little to no room to exercise a public voice. Paul noted their devotion to Christ, spiritual gifts, intellectual acumen, and sacrifice. From Philippi, where he planted the first church in Europe in Lydia's home; to Corinth, where Chloe's home served as a house church; to Ephesus, where he left Priscilla and Aquila to teach Apollos (Acts 18:26), Paul upheld his sisters as leaders in the early churches, for he perceived how essential they were to the expansion of God's reign on earth. Two epistles that demonstrate the extent of Paul's commitment to the gospel of equality include his letter to Timothy and his letter to the church in Corinth.

In Paul's personal letter to his spiritual son, Timothy, a young pastor in Ephesus, Paul repeatedly speaks to the issue of orthodoxy or correct doctrine. Almost one quarter of his letter either addresses the importance of the truth or attacks heresy that is rife in the church.[13] He opposes false doctrine, arguments about genealogies, myths, and meaningless talk (see, e.g.,

---

12. I was introduced to the word *equity* in my trip to Kenya in 2006. In contrast to the principle of equality, which insists that all things being equal, individuals should receive the same pay, equity may decide in favor of giving the individual with a larger family a higher salary. Paul may have been applying the principle of equity in his conscious decision to recognize more female than male colleagues, despite the fact that he must have surely had far more male colleagues in the Church of Rome.

13. Kroeger and Kroeger, *I Suffer Not*, 45.

1 Tim 1:4, 6–7). For Timothy has inherited not only a spiritually immature church, but a church steeped in the surrounding culture of goddess worship.

For millennia, the goddesses of Asia Minor attracted a large following: Cybele, the Anatolian mother goddess, whose full-breasted carving stands on a mountain overlooking Ephesus;[14] Isis, the Egyptian lunar goddess who gave birth without a man and who resembled Artemis in so many ways that she was even called Artemis-Isis;[15] and finally, Artemis herself whose devotees from throughout the Empire flocked to Ephesus to worship at her temple, to this day regarded as one of the seven wonders of the world.[16] In other parts of the Empire, Artemis (or Diana in Roman mythology), the goddess of the moon and forest, was frequently depicted as a huntress with bow and arrows in a knee-length tunic. In Ephesus, however, she was often sculpted with a chest full of breasts and was best known and adored as a mother goddess, promising fertility to her adherents. The economy of the city thrived on the business generated by her temple, which housed the treasury and contributed to making Asia Minor the richest province in the Empire. No wonder the metal smiths cried for two hours "Great is Artemis of the Ephesians!" (Acts 19:28) in protest against Paul, because his preaching threatened to close down the idol industry, as residents turned from worshipping Artemis to worshipping Christ.

In addition to the religious femme fatales of antiquity, the heretical tenets of proto-Gnosticism were taking root in Ephesus. While it would take another century before full-blown Gnosticism appeared on the scene, Gnostic seeds were already spreading in the first century.[17] Gnosticism valued the spiritual but denigrated the physical, viewing *gnosis* ("knowledge" in Greek) as the ultimate good and enlightenment as the means of salvation and escape from the physical world.

Gnostics boast different versions of the origins of the world. The church father Irenaeus, born in 130 AD in Smyrna, near Ephesus, recorded the belief that prior to Adam, others consorted with Eve and they gave birth to angels. One story even boasted that she bore Yahweh, the God of Israel.[18]

---

14. Kroeger, 106–7. For a concise, audio-visual overview of the heresies rampant in Ephesus, see *The Untold Story of Ephesus*.

15. Kroeger, 108–109.

16. Ibid., 52–4.

17. The *Nag Hammadi* is the earliest collection of codices of Gnostic writings. Elaine Pagels writes that while the earliest papyri date back to the fourth century, Professor Helmut Koester of Harvard University posits that the *Gospel of Thomas*, compiled c. 140, may include traditions "possibly as early as the second half of the first century (50–100)." See the *Introduction to the Nag Hammadi*, edited by James Robinson, 3.

18. Kroeger, 120.

Reminiscent of the goddess Isis, Eve is cast as "the first virgin, the one who without a husband bore her first offspring. It is she who served as her own midwife."[19] "On the Origin of the World" continues,

> When Eve saw her male counterpart prostrate, she had pity upon him, and she said, "Adam! Become alive! Arise upon the earth!" Immediately her word became accomplished fact. For Adam, having arisen, suddenly opened his eyes. When he saw her, he said, "You shall be called 'Mother of the Living.' For it is you who have given me life."[20]

Reversing the biblical chronology, the common theme in each of these retellings of creation is that Eve preceded Adam and gave birth to him. Gnostics view Eve's impartation of knowledge to Adam positively, distorting the biblical understanding of the Fall. One Gnostic tale even describes the female spiritual principle in Adam escaping to take up residence in the serpent. Thus, in a final twist, the serpent becomes the hero for his impartation of knowledge which is the highest goal of Gnosticism.

> Let a woman learn in silence with full submission. (1 Timothy 2:11)

Within the local church, Paul wants to set the record straight that he will not tolerate false teaching or the promiscuous lifestyles and obscene rituals that they give rise to. In a concerted effort to dismantle the heresies of his day from the worship of the serpent to proto-Gnosticism, he teaches correct doctrine and raises up godly leaders who will disseminate the truth. The clear clarion call of 1 Timothy 2:11 is "Let a woman learn!" It is in fact the only command[21] in 1 Timothy 2:11–15. Women are to learn. Paul insists on biblical literacy, despite the fact that most women throughout the Hellenistic and Jewish world at his time were illiterate and had never received a formal education, because only after they learned could they teach, a criteria for both men and women in the church.

Verse 11 continues by qualifying the manner in which women are to learn. The NRSV, NIV, and KJV all translate the word *hesuchia* as "silence," leading a twenty-first-century reader to believe that Paul was prohibiting speech of any kind. Yet when the same Greek word appears elsewhere in the New Testament, the word is translated "quietly" or "quiet." Consider the following verses (with the word *hesuchia* translated in italics):

19. "On the Origin," 114:4–6.
20. Ibid., 115:36—116:1–7.
21. The verb "learn" (*manthaneto*) is in the imperative, which carries the force of a command.

- 1 Thessalonians 4:11–12

    But we urge you brothers and sisters . . . to aspire to live *quietly*, to mind your own affairs, and to work with your own hands.

- 2 Thessalonians 3:12

    Now such persons we command and exhort in the Lord Jesus Christ to do their work *quietly* and to earn their own living.

- 1 Timothy 2:1–2

    I urge that . . . prayers . . . be made for everyone, for kings and all who are in high positions, so that we may lead a *quiet* and peaceable life in all godliness and simplicity.

Clearly, in the above instances, Paul is not enjoining total and complete silence. Why then is the same word translated "silence" in 1 Timothy? The only difference is that in 1 Timothy 2:11, only sentences away from 1 Timothy 2:2, the subject is women. Paul's point is not to muzzle women, but to encourage them to "learn by being quiet and paying attention" (CEV). Given the earlier context, where Paul enjoins brothers to desist from praying in the congregation when they are angry and arguing (2:8), similarly Paul asks sisters to conduct themselves quietly, contributing to a peaceful, and not a chaotic, environment in which to learn (2:10).

A further amplification of the word *hesuchia* is provided by the word *hupotage*, often translated "submission." In Ephesus, where heresy was rife and orthodox teaching sorely needed, Paul was most likely pleading for full submission to the revealed truth of God. Cultivating a mindset conducive to learning starts with developing a spirit of quietness and submission. To combat the disorder in the Ephesian church and the distortions of the biblical account, is it surprising that Paul would appeal to complete acceptance of scriptural authority over human authority?

Nevertheless, most readers, informed by current debates about gender, presume that the "submission" in 1 Timothy 2 is about women's submission to men and miss altogether the radical nature of Paul's demand for women to learn the Scriptures in a day when few avenues of education were open to women. Paul wanted women as well as men "rightly dividing the word of truth" (2 Tim 2:15, KJV)[22] to keep people from being led astray and to develop the discerning mind that allows believers to mature and ultimately

---

22. In the Greek, the verb translated "to divide" (*orthotomeo*) is a civil engineering term and means to cut a straight line from one point to another without deviation. Elliott, "'Rightly Dividing'"; http://www.teachingtheword.org/apps/articles/?articleid=66757&columnid=6211.

teach others. To achieve such an outcome requires nothing less than a strong foundation in the Scriptures.

Even with a positive reading of "Let a woman learn," however, the verse that follows seems to categorically prohibit women from holding any kind of authority over men.

> I permit no woman to teach or to have authority over a man; she is to keep silent. (1 Timothy 2:12)

Verse 12 reads, "I permit no woman to teach or *authentein* a man" (2:12). Although the word in italics is typically translated in English Bibles as "authority," it is crucial to realize that the word *authentein* appears uniquely in 1 Timothy 2 and nowhere else in the New Testament. When the Bible speaks of authority over one hundred other times in the New Testament, the Greek word *exousia* is employed. The deliberate choice of the word *authentein* then, at the very minimum, suggests that Paul intends to communicate a meaning distinct from what he usually has in mind when he speaks of legitimate authority.

Since the word *authentein* only appears once in the New Testament, it is helpful to turn to literature outside of the Bible to learn more about the meaning of the word. Writing in the same time period as the apostle Paul, the Jewish historian Josephus (37–100 CE) used the term twice to mean "perpetrator of a crime" and "perpetrators of a slaughter." The word could also refer to ritual and symbolic killings common in the mystery cults that ranged from castration to dramatic renditions of death.[23] While the aforementioned definitions may seem fanciful and far removed from the context of 1 Timothy 2, they illuminate some of the forces that Timothy and his church had to contend with. In the Temple of Artemis in Ephesus, which was dominated by priestesses, men castrated themselves to qualify as priests, while Amazons, the legendary founders of Ephesus, were known as "man-slayers," who killed members of the opposite sex. At least these different shades of meaning point to a negative usage of *authentein* in the extrabiblical literature of Paul's day.[24]

Since the New Testament was written, the Vulgate, a Latin version of the Bible dating from the second to fourth centuries, translates *authentein* as "to domineer" (*dominari* in Latin). Linda Belleville speaks unequivocally of a "virtually unbroken tradition" from the earliest translations through the present that translates *authentein* as "to dominate."[25] Even the King James

---

23. Kroeger, 99–100.
24. Hubner, "Translating *Authenteo*," 19.
25. Belleville, "Teaching and Usurping," 209.

Version translates the verb negatively: "to usurp authority." If, however, it is never right to usurp power, then why are women singled out? Precisely because, like Eve, the women of Ephesus were the ones being deceived and spreading heresy in the church.[26] Let us be careful, however, not to jump to the conclusion that the prohibition to teach was due to an intrinsic female weakness; rather, it was due to a lack of training in orthodoxy. Moreover, the implication is that once the problem is corrected, then women should not be barred from teaching. Consistent with Paul's teaching elsewhere, the Holy Spirit distributes and allocates a variety of spiritual gifts for the purpose of edifying the body (Rom 12:6–8; 1 Cor 12:4–11). Therefore, if a woman's gift is teaching and she is biblically equipped, she should be given opportunities to exercise her gift.

Finally, in this author's opinion, Catherine Kroeger persuasively argues for a meaning of *authentein* that best fits the literary and cultural context of 1 Timothy 2:11, and that is "to claim to be the author."[27] For hundreds of years, *authentein* connoted authorship. Polybius (150 BCE) called a culprit the "[*authentes*] author of the deed."[28] Alexander the Rhetorician explained, "In a deliberative council, the listeners are responsible to take action [*authentes*]; for they decide what they themselves should do and not do."[29] In the fourth century, Basil asked, "Was he [the accuser] merely following someone else's lead or did he himself instigate the outrage or even profess himself to be its author [*authentein*]?"[30] Finally, Stephanus' *Thesaurus Linguae Graeca* explains that when *authentein* is followed by a genitive, the word means "to represent oneself as the author, originator, or source of something."[31]

Greek grammar lends yet a further insight. In the pastoral epistles, Paul often paired together two related infinitives, such as "to teach" and "to profess one is the author," for clarity or emphasis (see, e.g., 1 Tim 1:3–4; 4:11; 6:3). In some cases, the second infinitive even supplies the content of the first. Consider the English sentence, "I forbid a woman to teach or to discuss sports with a man." Athletics is the *subject* of woman's teaching. Similarly, one way to read 1 Timothy 2:12 is "I do not permit a woman to teach or to claim that she is the author of man." The subject would then

---

26. Spencer, "'Eve at Ephesus,'" 220.
27. Kroeger, *I Suffer Not*, 99–104.
28. Polybius, 12.14.3; 22.14.2, as quoted in Kroeger, 99.
29. Rhetor, *On the Origins of Rhetoric*, as quoted in Kroeger, 100.
30. Basil, *Epistle* 51.1, *Patrologia Cursus*, 54.788z, as quoted in Kroeger, 103.
31. Stephanus, *Thesaurus Graeca Lingaue*, as quoted in Kroeger, 102.

be the authorship of man, which is the precise problem raised by proto-Gnostics who claim that Eve, not Adam, was the first human being.

Far from prohibiting women from teaching or wielding authority in the church, Paul wants to correct a heresy and insist that women learn so that they might aspire to teach and one day impart the sound teaching of Scripture. Unfortunately, the misinterpretation of the particular passage at hand has created a great loss for so many churches which to this day deny women the right to teach or preach. Instead of using the passage to challenge women's calling, the same passage could propel women to study God's word and exhort men in the church to support their sisters the way that Paul has, by affirming their ability to understand God's word and advocating for further training.

Once when I was in downtown Nairobi, I heard a sister, endowed with the gift of teaching, leading Bible Study Fellowship (BSF), a worldwide movement to engage God's people in a deeper study of the word. It was heartening to see her, standing in the pulpit, confidently presiding over a large group of women. Assuming that God's authority lies in the Scriptures and the Holy Spirit, who resides in the teacher as well as every believer's heart, then I wonder if she had been teaching a group of men and women, would the message have been any less effective?

3b. Paul's Pastoral Instruction to the Church in Corinth (1 Corinthians 11:2–16)

> I commend you because you remember me in everything and maintain the traditions just as I handed them on to you. . . . Any man who prays and prophesies with something on his head disgraces his head, but any woman who prays or prophesies with her head unveiled disgraces her head. . . (1 Corinthians 11:2, 4–5)

> Now in the following instructions I do not commend you . . .When you come together, it is not really to eat the Lord's supper. For when the time comes to eat, each of you goes ahead with your own supper, and one goes hungry and another becomes drunk. (1 Corinthians 11:17, 20–21)

Readers of Paul's epistle to the Corinthians do not generally remember many positive traits about the church, but the apostle does commend his brothers and sisters for "maintain[ing] the traditions just as [he] handed them on" to this urban congregation (1 Cor 11:1). Following the same sentence construction in the same chapter, Paul does not commend the Corinthian Christians for their behavior around the Lord's Table (1 Cor

11:17–22). It stands to reason that if Paul's explanation for his displeasure follows in the latter case, then the explanation for his pleasure follows in the former. In the latter case, Paul reprimands the Corinthian church for the disrespect shown to poorer members of the congregation at the agape meal; whereas in the former case, Paul praises the leadership exercised by both brothers and sisters in public worship (1 Cor 11:4–5). Men and women are praying and prophesying. In an age when the vast majority of women were uneducated and not permitted to participate in civic affairs, the church may have been the very first arena, outside the home, where women were encouraged to exercise their God-given authority to speak and pray publicly—not in the agora or the halls of government, but in the local gathering of believers. What an affirmation of women's gifts and voices in the church that stood in bold relief to the values espoused by the larger culture where women's abilities and contributions were greatly curtailed. The full inclusion of women in the body of Christ pays a high compliment to the Creator of all and the genius behind the church.

At the same time, while women enjoyed a newfound freedom to speak and lead in public, Paul wanted to demonstrate that the ultimate purpose of every relationship is to glorify God. In 1 Corinthians 11:3, Paul deftly argues for human interdependency, rooted in God:

> Christ is the *kephale* of every man, and man is the *kephale* of woman, and God is the *kephale* of Christ [translation mine].

It is important to note that Paul deliberately breaks any attempt to promote a chain of command or to establish a hierarchy within the Godhead. Paul does not start with God, then continue with Christ, followed by man and then woman. Instead Paul insists on bracketing the male-female relationship between the Creation (where Christ, the Word, gives life to man) and the Incarnation (the unique point in history where Christ can be said to be born of God).[32]

Understanding the word *kephale* as "source," as in the source of a stream or of life, is key to unlocking Paul's logic of relationships in 1 Corinthians 12. In the Creation, Christ is the source of life for Adam and every man subsequent to him. In the Creation, man is uniquely the source of woman as she is taken from his side. Finally in the Incarnation, God is the source of Christ. Furthermore, in each of the relationships, there is an expectation of one party rendering honor or glory to the other. In the first set of relationships, man is the reflection of God and is expected to bring honor to God. In the second, woman is the reflection of man, who cries

---

32. Payne, *Man and Woman*, 136.

"bone of my bones and flesh of my flesh" (Gen 2:23), and she is expected to bring her husband honor. In the third, Christ is the exact image of God (Col 1:15) and is expected to bring God honor. These parallel relationships do not speak to inferiority or superiority but to honor and respect.[33] By the same token, Paul's teaching in no way undermines God's commitment to honor his Son and the husband's commitment to honor his wife. By focusing, however, on the source of honor in each relationship, Paul is building up to the means God has given men and women, respectively, to honor God in public worship.

Paul's primary concern in 1 Corinthians 11 is for propriety in worship. In verse 4, Paul asserts that "any man who prays or prophesies with something on his head disgraces his head." Now one may be inclined to think of different coverings Jews and Greeks might don in worship, but the text reveals a more basic or essential concern. There is something, literally, hanging down from or over the head[34] of the man, but what is it? While the direct object is not explicitly revealed in verse 4, it is his "hair." Throughout the Empire, where promiscuity and aberrant lifestyles ran high, especially in Corinth,[35] it was fashionable for homosexuals to wear their hair long as a means of soliciting other men. Men found themselves imitating the Greek god of wine, Dionysius, who was known for debauchery and indulgence and was often portrayed with long hair.

Orgies, drunken revelries, and cross-dressing were par for the course in the highly sensuous center of Corinth, a city like modern-day Bangkok. In contradistinction, Paul was asking believers to comport themselves in a way that would not confuse or cause others to stumble. He wanted members of Christ's body to live out their baptismal vows by putting off the old life and putting on the new life. Walking worthily of their calling entailed that men wear their hair like men, not effeminately, for the sake of the gospel.

Based on the same principle, when women leaders pray and prophesy in the church, Paul requests that they wear their hair long so that they do not present an unnecessary distraction when leading in worship, because "any woman who prays or prophesies with her head unveiled disgraces her head" (1 Cor 11:5). The word *veil*, as such, never appears. Instead, the Greek word that is used repeatedly in the passage is translated *covered* and *uncovered*.

---

33. To suggest an inherent superiority or inferiority in any relationship within the Godhead is to be guilty of subordinationism, a belief which was deemed heretical at the Council of Constantinople (AD 381).

34. Payne, *Man and Woman*, 141; *kata* with the genitive, "lit., hanging down from the head" (Bauer and Danker's *Greek-English Lexicon*, 511 A.1.a), or "over" the head of men leading in worship.

35. The verb "corinthianize" means to lead a promiscuous lifestyle.

Unfortunately, the mistranslation conceals the key to understanding the passage in 1 Corinthians 11:15, which plainly states "her hair is given to her for a covering." Paul is not insisting that women wear a veil, shawl, or any other headdress, but simply that they wear their hair long.

> For if a woman will not veil [*lit.*, cover] herself, then she should cut off her hair; but if it is disgraceful for a woman to have her hair cut off or to be shaved, she should wear a veil [*lit.*, let her be covered]. (1 Corinthians 11:6)

The further implication that Paul draws is that if a woman were to wear her head "uncovered," that is, loose and flowing or dangling, then she might as well advertise herself as a woman with a "shaved" head, the punishment for an adulteress in various ancient cultures.[36] In the cultures of Paul's day, it was uncouth for women to wear their hair loose. Respectable Hellenistic women tended to wear their hair in a coiffure, whereas honorable Jewish women typically covered their hair. Indeed, it was shameful for a Jewish women to be seen in public with "unbound" hair (Ketubah 7:6).[37]

The world of art allows us a window into the significance of long, loose hair among a particular group of Greco-Roman women. *Maeneds* were female devotees of Dionysius. Like their male counterparts, they were often depicted wearing vine leaves and carrying a thyrsus. *Maeneds* were even known to go into the woods, climb trees, tear apart animals with their bare hands, and eat the flesh raw. In the cult of Dionysius, *maeneds* customarily let their hair down and prophesied by working themselves into a frenzy, dancing wildly, and shaking their "disheveled hair."[38] Their long, loose hair symbolized sexual license.

Is it any wonder that the apostle wanted to counsel both the men and women in Corinth to distinguish themselves from the sex-crazed society around them? The cult practices of the day disdained traditional marriage vows, exalted sexual promiscuity, and encouraged ecstatic religious experiences. As a pastor, Paul did not draw back from addressing the sexual addictions and the consequent struggle with legalism and license in the Corinthian Church. Instead, he offered practical guidance on how to lead well in the body of Christ while laying out the groundwork for a robust theology of mutual respect for men and women.

---

36. Payne, *Man and Woman*, 171–72.

37. See *Mishnah Ketubot 7*.

38. Livy 39.13.12, as quoted in Payne, *Man and Woman*, 162. See also Catherine and Richard Kroeger's article "Pandemonium and Silence" for more details about the madness extolled in pagan worship.

> For a man ought not to have his head veiled, since he is the image and reflection of God; but woman is the reflection of man. Indeed, man was not made from woman, but woman from man. Neither was man created for the sake of woman, but woman for the sake of man. (1 Corinthians 11:7–9)

As Paul elaborates on his reason for men not wearing long hair, he begins with a theological argument that seems to diminish women or at least leave them out of the equation. He argues that man should not wear anything over his physical head because he is "the image and reflection of God," and woman is "the reflection of man."[39] Far from overlooking the fact that woman, too, is made in the image of God or overturning Genesis 1:27, which affirms that "God created humankind in his image . . . male and female he created them," Paul instead has another target in mind. The apostle wants to correct the self-image of his Corinthian brothers and underscore that they are made in the image of God. Therefore, to respect their God-given identity as men, they should not coif their hair in imitation of a pagan god or of women.

To support his argument, Paul recounts the story of Creation: "Indeed, man was not made from woman, but woman from man. Neither was man created for the sake of woman, but woman for the sake of man" (1 Cor 11:8–9). Paul is not siding with men to give them the upper hand in marriage or ministry. In truth, he may have just been putting things in perspective in a church where women exercised their gifts (hence the instructions on how to pray and prophesy) and may have also flaunted their newfound freedom in Christ to the humiliation of their husbands.

> For this reason a woman ought to have a symbol of authority on her head,[i] because of the angels. Nevertheless, in the Lord woman is not independent of man or man independent of woman. For just as woman came from man, so man comes through woman; but all things come from God.
>
> ([i]for this reason have freedom of choice regarding her head)
>
> (1 Corinthians 11:10–12)

After all is said and done, however, Paul still insists that women retain the right to decide for themselves whether they will wear their hair long when leading in worship. The alternative translation provided in a footnote in the New Revised Standard Version, "For this reason a woman ought to have freedom of choice regarding her head" (1 Cor 11:10), is far more compelling than the rendering that a woman must have "a symbol of authority

---

39. The word *doxa* can also be translated "glory."

on her head." To begin with, the word *symbol* does not appear in the Greek. Presumably, English translations have chosen to supply it because of the biased assumption that a man must logically have authority over a woman and that Paul could not possibly have thought otherwise. What such an assumption fails to take into account, however, is that in the over one hundred occurrences of *exousia* (the Greek word translated "authority") in the New Testament, *exousia* is never once used passively. The authority unequivocally resides with the subject of the sentence, who is responsible for its exercise. In light of the overwhelming evidence of Scripture, then, it stands to reason that in verse 10, *the woman* is the person responsible for making her own decision.

To further support the interpretation that it is the woman who holds authority, Paul begins with the strong adversative, "nevertheless" (1 Cor 11:12). Like a consummate counselor, he is urging women leaders in the church to hold in balance that "in the Lord woman is not independent of man or man independent of woman." If, on the other hand, as some have suggested, power was being exercised over her in verse 10, then in verse 11, we would expect a directive to the man to offset his authority over the woman. But this is not the case; "man" is not the first word to follow "nevertheless." Paul wants to affirm woman's self-determination as to her public comportment, and at the same time, to check any sense of entitlement to unbridled power. In short, Paul is asking women who may have bought into an over-realized eschatology not to flaunt their freedom but to consider their husband's needs and feelings in bringing glory to God. On the other hand, man must not entertain the false notion that he is somehow superior to woman but must appreciate his dependence and relationship to woman in bringing glory to God. In teaching mutual respect, Paul is careful to go back and forth between the two parties. From the standpoint of Creation, woman came from man, but in biology and every subsequent birth, man came through woman. Then building up to his climax, Paul brings everything back to its source: "For just as woman came from man, so man comes through woman; but all things come from God" (1 Cor 11:12). The whole thrust of Paul's argument is that woman and man owe their gifts, their prerogatives, their relationship, and their very being to God, the source of all that is good and worth having.

Finally, Paul provides a couple of other reasons to encourage women to wear their hair properly when they are leading in the congregation. Paul appeals to God's ministering "angels" (1 Cor 11:10), who are present in the worshipping assembly. In other words, if respect for oneself and marriage is not enough, perhaps the divine presence of angels can provide the necessary incentive.

> Judge for yourselves; is it proper for a woman to pray to God with her head unveiled [*lit.*, uncovered]? Does not nature itself teach you that if a man wears long hair, it is degrading to him, but if a woman has long hair, it is her glory? For her hair is given to her for a covering. But if anyone is disposed to be contentious—we have no such custom, nor do the churches of God. (1 Corinthians 11:13–16)

Then Paul calls on "nature" (1 Cor 11:14) as his witness. Does not the fact that most men wear their hair short and most women wear their hair long prove that men and women in the church should do the same? Actually, the line of argument is not so much an appeal to natural law as it is to the convention of the day. To seal his case, Paul concludes by saying that he knows of "no such custom nor do the churches of God" that would promote men to have long hair and women to wear their hair loose (1 Cor 11:16).[40] It is remarkable that Paul reasons with the Corinthians when he could have demanded adherence to his instructions by apostolic fiat. Instead, Paul chooses to lead by example. To brothers and sisters who are driven by worldly notions of power, he shows a better way, the way of love (1 Cor 13), which preserves the Corinthian church's freedom while encouraging them to grow in fidelity to one another.

In the same epistle, however, Paul then writes,

> Women should be silent in the churches. For they are not permitted to speak, but should be subordinate, as the law also says. If there is anything they desire to know, let them ask their husbands at home. For it is shameful for a woman to speak in church. (1 Corinthians 14:34–35)

The two verses in 1 Corinthians 14 sound jarring and dissonant after the disclaimer that in 1 Corinthians 11 Paul was in no way dismissing women's involvement in leading worship but rather instructing them as to the proper comportment when praying and prophesying in public. Why should "women be silent in the churches" (v. 33)?[41] The reason given is because "the law" teaches subordination (v.33). But nowhere in the Old Testament are women ever commanded to be silent in religious gatherings. On the contrary, Psalm 68:11 (ESV) explicitly identifies women as proclaiming the

---

40. Payne, *Man and Woman*, 203–209.

41. In 1 Corinthians 14:30, the Greek word *sigao* can be properly translated "silent" or "to cease from speaking" as distinguished from *hesuchia*, the word used in 1 Timothy 2:11–12. Craig Keener argues that *sigao* can also simply refer to a qualified silence and quiet demeanor becoming of wives. See *Paul, Women and Wives*, 85.

good news: "The Lord gives the word; the women who announce the news are a great host."

Then what is "the law" being referred to? Could Paul be redressing an issue that the Corinthians have brought up, a presumption about the law that they have mistakenly made? Or is it possible that "the law" is an allusion to a practice in Jewish and Hellenistic mainstream society, which did not as a rule permit women to speak in public, and Paul is asking Christian women not to totally overturn this, but to bear with it while exercising their God-given rights in ways that do not alienate their spouses? In point of fact, women in the Hellenistic world were defined by their relationship to men. Wives were responsible for producing male heirs and were in charge of the home, although a man ultimately held the reins over even his wife's life. Concubines sold their bodies to provide men with sex on demand. Hetaerae were high-class courtesans who provided intellectual stimulation and physical companionship for men and were the only class of women that were educated. Consequently, telling women to ask their questions at home may have been a helpful measure to encourage wives to show respect toward their husbands,[42] whereas interrupting worship would have proved shameful to their husbands. Moreover, the practice could help women to develop inquiring minds, giving them a forum to learn in their own homes.[43]

In the first century, way ahead of his time, Paul was a proponent of women in ministries, spreading the good news of equality throughout the Empire. He modeled and supported equitable practices. He led the way for establishing a new kind of community where all were empowered to lead in God's church. He even risked being misunderstood not only in his day but through the current age. Will activists and pastors alike reexamine Paul's writings to see how we can lead and serve better together?

In the spring of 2010, a Catholic monastery in Limuru near the Rift Valley of Kenya served as the host site for a Matthew 28 Ministries women's conference. While done without fanfare or media coverage, the moment may have been historic. For four days, a group of women were being served by their brothers, perhaps for the first time in their lives. The brothers, dressed in white robes, were responsible for the cooking and cleaning, changing the linens, sweeping and maintaining the grounds, and even serving tea and biscuits. Their sisters, on the other hand, that is, the women

---

42. See Keener, *Paul, Women and Wives*, 80–85, for a more extended argument for the importance of women asking questions at home so as not to be disruptive against the backdrop of Jewish and Hellenistic culture.

43. The United Nations set as Goal 2 Target 2.A of Millenium Goals for 2015 and Beyond "[to] ensure that, by 2015, children everywhere, boys and girls alike, will be able to complete a full course of primary schooling."

gathered for the conference, were meeting for sessions on biblical equity and justice, discussing weighty matters of the church and planning ways to strategize and implement what they had learned in their church fellowships and denominations.

For some of the brothers and sisters involved, the moment may have gone unnoticed, as if this were a typical day in the lives of Kenyan men and women, while for others the realization that this kind of service was a unique occurrence came either during or after the conference. But wouldn't it be wonderful if such experiences were the norm rather than the exception? Not that men always need to serve women or women always need to serve men, but that in God's kingdom we are given the choice, and neither society nor tradition dictates what we must do. It was a transformative moment to see these brothers working quietly behind the scenes supporting their sisters who were strategizing ways to embody Paul's principle of inclusion and his practice of integration in their respective churches.

May the Lord continue to add daily such profound and practical instances of the church advancing God's reign.

Chapter 8

Women Leaders in the New Testament
Biblical Equity Reflected in the Ministries of Jesus and the Apostle Paul

—Lois Semenye

INTRODUCTION

THE DEBATE WHETHER WOMEN should be in church ministries has continued for many decades without a consensus among Christians. Some have argued that none of the twelve disciples Jesus called were women, thereby setting the precedent that women cannot be in the ministry. But this argument does not take into account that Jesus also had many women among his larger circle of disciples. Some uphold the teaching where Paul states that women should not teach men nor speak in the church (1 Cor 14:34–35), forgetting that Paul had stated earlier that women can also pray and prophesy during church service (1 Cor 11:5). Apparently, people interpret scriptures to suit their own conviction. It would be morally wrong for God to have included women leaders in the Bible if he did not allow women to teach and prophesy. Indeed, God could have decreed that church ministries were inherently for men and then not included any women leaders in the Bible. Instead, God has endowed all people with spiritual gifts and not denied women any of these gifts. The Bible has shown that all people are equal, and no one is superior to the other. We read in Galatians 3:28, "There is no longer Jew or Gentile, slave or free, male and female. For you are all one in Christ Jesus" (NLT). In the Bible, many women were greatly used of God, including prophets, warriors, teachers, pastors, apostles, and evangelists.

This chapter profiles some of the women leaders in the New Testament with the intention of helping Africans to spread the equity of men and women in churches. Klaus Fiedler observed that many evangelicals in Malawi did not allow women's participation in churches. With that in mind, he wrote a paper "with its Evangelical assumptions" in hopes of "offer[ing] a way to increase participation of women in the life of the church without becoming unfaithful to scripture and the Evangelical interpretation of it."[1] Many Christians throughout Africa, including this author, share such sentiments.

The purpose of this chapter is to help the churches in Africa examine how both Jesus and Paul worked with women who were leaders in their ministries. Many of our denominations in Africa have not allowed women to take any leadership positions in the churches except leading other women or children. On the other hand, in the Bible, we see women playing a variety of leadership roles: prophesying, evangelizing, teaching, pastoring, administering, and doing diaconal work. In the Presbyterian Church of East Africa and the Anglican Church of Kenya, women have been ordained as pastors, but as of yet no woman has been appointed as a moderator or bishop in these respective denominations.

WOMEN LEADERS' PROFILES

Women leaders in the New Testament have served in the following categories of leadership: apostle, deaconess, prophetess, evangelist, pastor-teacher, and administrators.

Apostles

Apostles were the church leaders who were sent initially by Jesus to pioneer new ministries. In Galatians 1:1, we read, "This letter is from Paul, an apostle. I was not appointed by any group of people or any human authority, but by Jesus Christ himself and by God the Father, who raised Jesus from the dead" (NLT). Apostles were distinguished leaders who were sent to spread the gospel.

---

1. Fiedler, "Gender Equality," 19–36.

The Apostle Junia

Romans 16:7 reads, "Greet Andronicus and Junia, my fellow Jews, who were in prison with me. They were highly respected among the apostles and became followers of Christ before I did" (NLT). Junia was a distinguished member of the apostles who served side by side with Andronicus. However, some scholars have debated that Junia was not a woman but a man; "the esteemed apostle Junia," as stated by Belleville, becomes the masculine "Junias."[2] To change the woman's name Junia, to Junias, a man's name, is to disregard the fact that women can be leaders in Christian ministry. Translations such as the NKJV, NRSV, ESV, and NLT, however, stand steadfast in their rendering of *Iounian* as the feminine form of Junia. Both the Bishop of Constantinople and John Chrysostom had no problems affirming that Junia was an exceptional woman leader.

One way to read Romans 16:7 is to understand that Junia came to know the Lord Jesus before Paul did. Kathryn Riss thought Junia came to know the Lord "a few years after the Resurrection of Christ" and concluded she was "one of the earliest converts to Christianity."[3] Junia must have performed very well in many of the roles of apostleship as she was praised and referred to by Paul as an outstanding apostle. Junia was not only known in church but also outside the church, according to Riss. This suggests that Junia was a key woman leader, given a high level of responsibility.

Prophets

Acts 2:18 tell us, "In those days I will pour out my Spirit even on my servants—men and women alike—and they will prophesy" (NLT). Prophecy provides guidance and instruction. First Corinthians 14:3 reads, "But one who prophesies strengthens others, encourages them, and comforts them" (NLT). Hence, a prophet had a key role in building others up for the Lord. The Bible does not make a distinction regarding who should prophesy. "Men and women alike" can prophesy (Act 2:18). In 1 Corinthians 14:31–32, we read, "In this way, all who prophesy will have a turn to speak, one after the other, so that everyone will learn and be encouraged. Remember that people who prophesy are in control of their spirit and can take turns" (NLT). "All" is an inclusive word that includes both genders.

---

2. See Riss, "Women's Ministries."
3. Ibid.

Anna

Anna was a prophetess and daughter of Phanuel of the tribe of Asher. She was a very old woman who had lived with her husband for only seven years before he died; from that time, she had lived as a widow. Not much of the husband is written anywhere in the Bible. Anna, 84 years old, never left the temple; she spent most of her time worshipping God day and night, fasting and praying (Luke 2:38). She knew that, although she was old, God still had work for her to do. She prepared herself spiritually as she spent most of her time in prayer and fasting. Anna waited expectantly to see the child everyone talked about who would rescue Jerusalem (Luke 2:38). She had received insight into things that are hidden to ordinary people. She was able to quickly recognize that Mary and Joseph were holding in their hands the savior of the world.

Anna is a model for us. After her husband died, she occupied herself with the work of the church. We learn from her that a spouse's death does not spell the end of the surviving spouse's life or ministry. In fact, God can use a widow or widower greatly. Ladies who have lost their loved ones can serve the church as leaders. Moreover, we must overcome the habit of looking at single women suspiciously and overlooking them for church offices. This practice of ignoring single women must be discouraged to prevent the church from missing out on vital ministries. Instead, the best way for the church to steward these gifts is to support women and include them as the opportunities for service arise.

Philip's Daughters

Philip of Caesarea had four unmarried daughters. Acts 21:8–9 unequivocally states that these unmarried women were prophets. Linda Bellville states, "Luke's reference to Philip's daughters is brief. No other commentary was necessary, undoubtedly because women prophets were well established as church leaders."[4] These four daughters are not named although they were active in the church. They must have played an important role to be referred to as prophetesses, who led people by instructing them in the word of God. Herbert Lockyer states, "The church will never know how much it owes to its unknown, consecrated women."[5] As the leaders of the early church, the lives of the four daughters of Philip of Caesarea challenge denominations and churches that do not allow women to preach.

---

4. Belleville, "Women Leaders," 123.
5. Lockyer, *All the Women*, 244.

Evangelists

Evangelists are those people who serve as preachers of the gospel and play a crucial role in leading others to Christ. Ephesians 4:11 lists evangelists among the foundational gifts Christ gave to the church, which includes apostles, prophets, evangelists, pastors, and teachers. These are the gifts referred to as the five-fold ministries of the church, which are basic and essential for church planting and growth. It is important to note that these gifts were inclusive of both genders. Kenya possesses some great women evangelists who carry on the legacy of the early church.

Euodia and Syntyche

Euodia and Syntyche are two women in the church in Philippi who worked hard with Paul in evangelism. In Philippians 4:2–3, Paul encourages these two church leaders to settle their differences. Eshetu Abate notes, "These two women had a commendable witness for the Lord in the past, but now they needed help."[6] Paul referred to their partnership in the gospel as "a friendship of equals."[7] In other words, Paul did not regard them as lesser partners, but acknowledged that they worked alongside his confidant Clement and other unnamed co-workers. Although Euodia and Syntyche were experiencing some conflict, the difficulty did not cause Paul to be dismissive of his colleagues; he still thought highly of them and gives us a positive example to follow. Women and men can and should work hand in hand to advance the kingdom of God here on Earth.

Samaritan Woman

We encounter the Samaritan woman in John 4. Although her name is not mentioned in the Bible, she is perhaps one of the best-known women in the Gospels. After Jesus' conversation with her, asking her for water and telling her about life, the Samaritan woman was astonished. After she left the well, she told other Samaritans about her encounter with Jesus and became an evangelist. John 4:39 tells us, "Many of the Samaritans from that city believed in him because of the woman's testimony, 'He [Jesus] told me everything I have ever done'" (NRSV). This Samaritan woman advanced the kingdom of God simply by telling others what she had seen and heard. She

---

6. Adeyemo, *Africa Bible Commentary*, 1473.
7. Gonzalez-Tejera, "Hispanic America," 136.

was not shy but spoke the message, and many men and women came to hear what she had learned. What a great encouragement for women to know they can be used by God in such a simple yet profound way.

Deacons

The office of deacon was appointed in the New Testament as a caring ministry of the church. The deacons were appointed to do the work of benevolence, including visiting the sick and the bereaved. It is an office of service. The diaconal ministry was established in Acts 6 in order to free the apostles to spend more time in teaching the word and in prayer. Consequently, the deacons would administer the distribution of food and foster unity.

Deacons were selected based on certain qualifications. For example, they had to be of good reputation, manage their families well, and not be new believers. First Timothy 3:10 states, "Before they are appointed as deacons, let them be closely examined. If they pass the test, then let them serve as deacons" (NLT). No doubt, the office of deacon had to be held by people of integrity because it was a leadership role.

Phoebe

Phoebe was a notable leader in the church, who Paul recognized as a servant or a deacon in the church of Cenchrea and a special help to himself (Rom 16:1–2). The apostle Paul also highly recommended Phoebe to the church in Rome and asked that she be received with honor and helped in any way she required. Phoebe was a teacher who stood by the people and did more for others. She indeed was a true servant and leader. She might have become a senior pastor in our contemporary world. Herbert Lockyer refers her as "one of the forerunners of the vast army of women who have rendered such royal service to Christ and His church."[8] Nevertheless, there are some denominations in Kenya that will not ordain women to serve as deaconesses.

Women as Pastors-Teachers

The pastor/teacher ministry is one of the fundamentals of a healthy church. The role of the pastor/teacher is to encourage the maturity of believers in Christ. Consequently, the pastor/teacher is expected to teach, to admonish, to be an example, and to nurture people as they grow in Christ. The pastor/

---

8. Lockyer, *All the Women.*

teacher plays a crucial role in the leadership of the church. The New Testament depicts several women in the role of pastor/teacher.

Priscilla

Acts 18:24–26 (NIV) reads,

> Meanwhile a Jew named Apollos, a native of Alexandria, came to Ephesus. He was a learned man, with a thorough knowledge of the Scriptures. He had been instructed in the way of the Lord, and he spoke with great fervor and taught about Jesus accurately, though he knew only the baptism of John. He began to speak boldly in the synagogue. When Priscilla and Aquila heard him, they invited him to their home and explained to him the way of God more adequately.

In the above verses, we see that this couple knew the Scriptures well and were able to help the bold preacher Apollos who knew some of the Scriptures but not all. Apollos was "competent in the Scriptures" (v. 24, ESV), but his problem was that he only knew about John's baptism, not about the good news of Jesus Christ—so Priscilla and Aquila privately instructed him. The Scriptures help us to see the teaching ministry of Priscilla, who is mentioned together with her husband Aquila six times. They worked together as husband and wife. They travelled everywhere and ministered with Paul. Together, they served as missionaries and co-workers who risked their lives for Paul. They were great partners in the ministry and were recognized and respected in the New Testament.

It is remarkable that, when the couple is described in Acts 18 as instructing Apollos, Priscilla's name is listed first. As Belleville observes,

> As in our "Mr. and Mrs." nomenclature, the Roman husband's name typically appeared first. When New Testament writers refer to their occupation as tentmakers and to "their house," the order is "Aquila and Priscilla" (Acts 18:2; 1 Cor. 16:19). But when ministry is in view, the order is "Priscilla and Aquila" (Acts 18:18; Rom 16:3; cf., 2 Tim. 4:19).[9]

This would suggest that Priscilla took the lead in teaching the word, while Aquila took the lead in tent-making and in the home. The prominence of Priscilla's name suggests that she was a key pastor/teacher in their home church (Rom 16:5). Priscilla, a woman, was able to instruct men, such as Apollos, to be more effective in the ministry of the church.

---

9. Belleville, "Women Leaders," 112.

Priscilla and Aquila's ministry helps us to see biblical equity. She is encouraged to use her gifts, and her ministry did not make Aquila less of a man. They worked as partners. It would be so good to see this reality practiced in Africa. In many Christian organizations, when a woman is a member of the board of directors, she is normally expected to take minutes and serve tea. Equity says both genders are equally qualified to serve tea.

Business Woman

In the book of Proverbs, we learn of a virtuous woman (Prov 31:21–31). She had great responsibilities, provided clothing and food for the family and her servants, managed the estate, taught, and worked with her hands. Her husband was well esteemed in the community. This woman was referred to as a virtuous wife. In the New Testament, we find women who were in business and used by God. This affirms that certain women are called into business by God, a growing trend in Kenya, and should be encouraged by the church. At the same time, as Christians we need to overcome our double standard of calling a woman who is firm, overbearing, and a man who is firm, a strong leader.

Lydia

Lydia is introduced in Acts as a merchant of expensive purple clothing who listened to Paul preach (Acts 16:12–15, 40). After Lydia opened her heart to receive the Lord, she was a changed person. She devoted herself to her new-found faith and was eager to invest her money and time in the missionaries. She persuaded Paul and his company—and later Paul and Silas after they were released from prison—to stay with her in her spacious house. A committed Christian, a rich business woman, a generous person, and a servant of the Lord, she led by example. We can learn from this industrious woman that the church needs to be supported equally by men and women.

Women Who Were Community Administrators

Several women accompanied Jesus throughout his ministry, exercising their gift of administration and seeking his welfare by anointing, providing, and cooking for him. While their service allowed Jesus to concentrate on his ministry, they were no less leaders in their own right. Some of these women's names are mentioned in the Bible; others are not. Luke 8:2b–3 reads, "Mary (called Magdalene) from whom seven demons had come out; Joanna the wife of Chuza, the manager of Herod's household; Susanna; and many others. These women were helping to support them out of their own means." These women led by contributing toward the ministry in order to reach many for Christ.

Mary Magdalene

Mary of Magdala had seven demons that were cast from her by Jesus (Luke 8:2). After her deliverance, Mary became one of his most faithful followers. She, along with other women, contributed financially to Jesus and his disciples' ministry. Mary followed Jesus on his way to the cross. Mary and other women stood at the trial of Jesus, and she was there when he was crucified. She was a very dedicated and committed follower of the Lord Jesus Christ.

It is worth noting that Mary was also the first to know Christ had risen. When she visited the tomb, she discovered that Christ was not there. Seeing her crying at the tomb, Jesus spoke to her and entrusted her with the first post-Resurrection message to give to his disciples. John 20:18 says, "Mary Magdalene found the disciples and told them, 'I have seen the Lord!'" (NLT). Women can learn that they can spearhead a ministry just like men. What we need are men and women who are dedicated and committed to the course of Christ. Both genders can work together in gratitude for what God has commissioned them to do.

Mary of Bethany

Mary of Bethany had a sister Martha and a brother Lazarus who was raised from the dead by Jesus. The family was close friends with Jesus. However, Mary was different from Martha. Lockyer writes of Mary that she was "a woman who cultivated deep, spiritual, inner thoughts, and who was busier internally than she was externally."[10] Mary sat at the feet of Jesus to learn more about the kingdom of heaven while Martha was busy preparing food in the kitchen. Martha complained about her sister to Jesus, who told her, "There is one thing worth being concerned about. Mary has discovered it, and it will not be taken away from her" (Luke 10:42, NLT). Mary was commended by Jesus because she had chosen to learn spiritual things.

Their brother Lazarus fell sick and died. When Jesus visited them, Mary informed him, "Lord, if only you had been here, my brother would

---

10. Lockyer, *All the Women*, 104.

not have died" (John 11:32, NLT). This moved Jesus so that he even wept and went to raise Lazarus from the dead. Mary also did a remarkable act before Jesus was crucified. Mary anointed Jesus with costly perfume that Judas felt could have been sold and given to the poor. Jesus, again, defended and commended Mary. In front of everyone present, he reprimanded Judas and said, "Leave her alone. She did this in preparation for my burial" (John 12:7, NLT). We can learn from Mary's leadership to do the right thing at the right time.

Martha

Martha was a practical person who thrived in serving Jesus. Martha was hospitable and received Jesus in her home (John 11:20, 30). She went out of the mourning house to meet Jesus and told him that if he had been there, her brother would not have died. But Jesus assured her that her brother was going to rise again (John 11:23). Martha served Jesus but complained about her sister Mary who sat at Jesus' feet learning. Jesus rebuked her, suggesting that her outward activities hindered her spiritual development. Martha witnessed how Jesus resurrected her brother. She loved Jesus and served him. She used her spiritual gift of serving and was able to feed the disciples. We can learn from Martha to utilize our spiritual gifts for the betterment of the ministry whether we are men or women.

In some cases where women are the administrators, they have to work twice as hard as men, or even more, to be valued. Moreover, women are generally paid less than men and do not bargain for raises or promotions as confidently as men would. Women need to rise up above cultural barriers and assert themselves. This would include having more women in the boardrooms to contribute to decisions and to add perspectives that would otherwise be ignored in our churches and society. Women deserve to be recognized as administrators.

Joanna, Susanna, Mary, the Mother of James, and Other Women

The women who followed Jesus in his ministry contributed from their resources to support Jesus and his disciples. These women witnessed the death of Jesus, the empty tomb, and the Resurrection. They were also the first to proclaim that the Lord had risen from the dead. Perhaps Joanna and Susanna were named because of their leadership in the group (Luke 8:2–3).

It is significant that it was the women who were first at the tomb after the Resurrection. When they brought their report to the apostles that the tomb was empty, the apostles did not believe them. However, Peter ran to the tomb to verify what he had heard and found that the women had spoken the truth. The question lingers: if a man had reported about the Resurrection of Jesus, would Peter still have gone to check? Challenges were there and are still here. However, as God's children, we need to work together and trust one another. Yet, repeatedly, women who work closely with men are suspected of having ulterior motives. This should not be so if the women are of God.

Nympha

Nympha was from Laodicea, and she had a church in her house. Paul gave his greetings and named her as one of those who were believers in the Lord. It is important to note that Nympha may have been the leader of her house church. Paul's greetings in Colossians 4:15 also included sisters: "Please give my greetings to our brothers and sisters at Laodicea, and to Nympha and the church that meets in her house" (NLT).

Apphia

Apphia was mentioned in Philemon 1:1–2 in Paul's greetings. He said, "I am writing to Philemon, our beloved co-worker, and to our sister Apphia, and to our fellow soldier Archippus, and to the church that meets in your house" (NLT). Paul mentioned Apphia's name—a lady among other people who were not named. We can only speculate that she was a leader.

Eunice and Lois

These two women are mentioned together in 2 Timothy 1:5, "I remember your genuine faith, for you share the faith that first filled your grandmother Lois and your mother, Eunice. And I know that same faith continues strong in you" (NLT). Here Paul was referring to Timothy. These two women influenced Timothy to be what he was. Lois discipled Eunice, and Eunice in turn passed on the faith to her son Timothy. These women help us to see the role of Christian parenting in the home. They were leaders who taught what they knew to their children and their children's children.

Mary, the Mother of John Mark, and Rhoda

Mary, mother of John Mark, hosted believers in her house (Acts 12:12). The Bible states, "Many were gathered for prayer" (NLT). It is remarkable that when Peter realized that he was freed from jail, he went to the house of Mary, the mother of John Mark. This is not a small thing; there were many homes, but he chose Mary's. We can speculate that Mary was a respected leader of the church. Mary also had a servant girl, Rhoda, who served Mary and the people who came to worship in her house, and she was astonished to see Peter knocking at the door.

Mary, the Mother of Jesus

Mary, the mother of Jesus, is the woman who was honored above all other women in the world. Mary became the mother of Jesus Christ our Savior. Mary came from a humble family in Nazareth, and her life was interrupted by a visit from the angel Gabriel who told her that she was to bear a son from the Holy Spirit. Mary, being a virgin, could not understand what was happening. She was engaged to marry Joseph and was anticipating her wedding.

Nevertheless, Mary was quick to respond affirmatively without asking Joseph. Her question was "But how can this happen? I am a virgin" (Luke 1:34, NLT). However, she was convinced that God was able to do anything and that nothing was impossible with him, demonstrating her knowledge of the Bible. Her response to the angel was submissive and full of faith. She was ready to serve, despite any shame that went with the stigma of being pregnant without being married. She was not afraid to be ridiculed, nor was she worried about losing her fiancé. She said, "I am the Lord's servant. May everything you have said about me come true" (Luke 1:38, NLT).

Mary's story is told in all the Gospels. We know that Mary witnessed her son growing, serving, and being crucified, buried, and raised from the grave. She witnessed the joys and the suffering of her son in all his phases of life. She experienced giving birth in the manger, receiving special visitors, and witnessing the miracles her son performed. She also gave birth to other children. Mary was a leader who remained strong despite all the storms of life. This is a lesson for our churches: despite ridicule, men and women need to trust God and do what he wants them to do. By doing this, we will each fulfill God's purpose for our lives.

CONCLUSION

This chapter has profiled women in the New Testament who came from different circumstances and roles. These women were apostles, prophetesses, evangelists, deaconesses, pastors/teachers, business women, community administrators, and other leaders. They led incredible, exemplary ministries and also worked closely with men. The churches in Africa and the world can "take a leaf" out of the New Testament, giving women the freedom to model the roles women played in the early church and to work together with men without being intimidated or inhibited in ministry. Biblical gender equity, simply put, means that women and men can serve side by side, utilizing the gifts God has given them in the fear of our Lord Jesus Christ.

Chapter 9

Biblical Equity and the Meaning of Servant Leadership

—Aída Besançon Spencer

THESE DAYS, AFTER FOUR decades of ordained ministry, when I hear the expression, "servant leadership," I have mixed feelings. At times, I have seen the term used to paint a superficial coat of approval to any kind of leadership, including one that appears self-aggrandizing. For example, leaders doing oppressive acts have said they are doing it for *our* good. I have seen the term work the other way as well, as a blanket criticism of an already-humble leadership. She or he is not sufficiently a *servant* leader because (s)he is not doing what *we* want done! "Servant" and "leader" appear to be oxymorons or opposite titles that do not fit together. Are you the servant, *or* are you the leader? What is the relation between authority and servanthood? Moreover, if men become *servant* leaders, everyone is impressed, but if women act as servant leaders, that is simply evidence they know their place. For example, if the male pastor in a traditional church cleans the church dishes, the parishioners will be impressed. But, if a female pastor does them, the parishioners or even the pastor herself will feel this act is expected of her and, therefore, is demeaning. How, then, can we have equity between male and female church leaders if their actions are routinely interpreted and valued differently?

How, thus, can we define "servant leadership"? The concept in the church, of course, goes back to Jesus Christ and his own teachings on leadership. I would like to summarize his explanations in Mark 9–10 and then define "servant leadership" by developing the principles Jesus exhibited and taught in the Gospel of Mark. I will also illustrate the concept by using key female and male biblical leaders and a contemporary example. We learn that servant leadership entails serving others by serving God.

JESUS' EXPLANATIONS OF SERVANT LEADERSHIP

The key passage on servant leadership occurs in Mark 10:42–45. Jesus and his followers are en route to Jerusalem, where Jesus warns the twelve disciples that, when he finally reaches there, he will be betrayed by the religious leaders of his time and then mocked, condemned, and killed by the Romans. But, at the end, Jesus will rise from the dead (10:32–34). James and John miss his whole point. They are planning for Jesus' glorious reign and want the second and third positions of authority next to Jesus'. When the other ten disciples find out that James and John have been secretly jockeying for prestige and power positions for themselves, they become angry with them. Jesus calls all twelve to his side and says,

> You know that the ones being recognized as ruling among the Gentiles overpower them and their great ones exercise authority over them, but not thus among you, rather whoever may wish to become great among you will be your servant, and whoever may wish among you to be first will be slave of all; for even the Son of Humanity did not come to be served but to serve and to give his life a ransom for many. (Mark 10:42–45)[1]

Many ancient examples exist of the ways Gentiles would usurp positions of power. For instance, almost every Roman emperor, including Augustus, took over power, not by vote, but by overpowering their opponents. They did not rule to serve the people but to gain power, money, and prestige. Jesus told his disciples not to lead as these did, but to gain prestige with God by serving others, following the example of Jesus himself. As God incarnate, Jesus could expect homage and worship and all the earth to serve him. But, instead, he came to Earth to become the very price of humanity's freedom.

The discussion recorded in Mark 10:35–45 between James, John, the other disciples, and Jesus about leadership was not the first one recorded in the Gospel. The disciples had earlier been disputing about who was the greatest among them (Mark 9:33–34). Jesus in Capernaum introduces the same principle to the twelve that he will develop later:

---

1. Unless otherwise indicated, all Scripture translations are by the author.

> "If any wishes to be first, he or she will be last of all and a servant of all," and, having taken a little child, he stood the child in their midst and having embraced the child, he said to them: "Whoever these little children may welcome in my name, welcomes *me*, and whoever may welcome me, welcomes not me but the One having sent me." (Mark 9:35–37)

Jesus reiterates the importance of genuine humility and service. By embracing the child, Jesus identifies the child with himself and with God the Father. Leaders are to have a child-like quality, including an innocence, a purity, a humility (e.g., Matt 18:3–6), a spontaneous affection toward people, and a love of life (e.g., Matt 11:16–17). Jesus also uses children as examples of the type of faith needed to enter God's reign (Mark 10:13–15). A *paidion* could refer to a newborn or a twelve-year-old child.[2] They can be children playing songs in the public square (Luke 7:32). *Paidion* can also be a term of endearment for adults (John 21:5). Simplicity can be profound. My husband, Rev. Dr. William David Spencer, relates to me several illustrative stories from his own life. As a small child, one summer day, feeling happy, he was skipping along in the small city of his childhood when he saw an elderly man attempting to cross a street. He skipped over and gave the man a hand to help balance him as he crossed the avenue. Having crossed the street, the senior tried to give the little boy a dollar (which was a lot at that time) as a way to thank him. But, Bill said, "No, no, no," moving on and waving his hand because he had already been rewarded by being able to help another. Years later, when Bill was in high school, he approached a busy traffic corner. This time, in the midst of a crowd of adults, a young child reached up his hand toward Bill so that the child could himself be helped by Bill to cross the street. Bill was so moved that he wrote a poem to commemorate the event, which he remembers even now:

> Out of the masses, a little child came to me,
> He held out his hand,
> I helped him cross the street,
> Me, out of the masses.

The child gave Bill an identity by choosing him as his servant. The event became an opportunity of grace for the child and for Bill.

Another event I am told happened when I was a little girl and my family traveled from my home country of the Dominican Republic to the neighboring island of Puerto Rico. As I entered a room with many people listening to Latin music playing, I immediately began to dance. (They played

---

2. Mark 5:39–40, 42; Luke 1:59; John 16:21.

a tune, and I danced [e.g., Matt 11:17].) As an adult, I would never have such courage, but as a little child, I could respond spontaneously to the music without embarrassment.

"Many who are first will be last and the last first" (Mark 10:31). The little forgotten missionary woman who spent her life cleaning lepers' wounds and ushering lepers gently into God's presence will be first while the famous televangelist with his own Learjet riding around in a chauffeured car will be least, Bill suggests.

SERVANT LEADERSHIP AS ILLUSTRATED BY JESUS

How better can we capture "servant leadership" than to describe the principles of leading exhibited and taught by Jesus himself in this same Gospel of Mark? The many things we can learn can be grouped into four larger categories: attributes of traditional leadership, communal aspects of leadership, methodologies, and practices.

I. Attributes of a traditional godly leader include having a sense of one's mission and authority when using one's spiritual gift(s).

As one might expect, for a "leader," Jesus had a clear sense of his own *mission*, which he maintained despite outside pressure and criticism:

He came to give his life as a ransom (10:45);

Obedient to the Holy Spirit, Jesus preached God's good news: since God's kingdom has approached, it is time to repent and believe (1:12, 14–15).

Jesus received continuing pressure dissuading him from his mission—from Simon and the other disciples,[3] from his own family and neighbors, from religious educators and leaders of his time,[4] even from witnesses of his potential and actualized healing powers (5:15–17, 40), as well as from Gentile soldiers and rulers (10:33–34; 14:65), criminals, and larger crowds (15:29–30, 32).

Jesus spoke with *authority* when he educated and preached in a regular fashion in synagogues, in homes, outside, in the temple,[5]

---

3. Mark 1:36–38; 14:10, 66–72; 16:8.

4. Mark 3:21–35; 6:2–5; 7:5–9; 8:11; 10:2; 11:18; 12:12–13; 14:1, 10–11, 55; 15:10, 31–32.

5. Teaching occurred in Mark 1:21–22, 27; 2:2, 13; 4:1; 6:2–3, 6; 10:1; 11:27–28; 12:35.

as he forgave sins (2:10–11), healed,[6] and did other miraculous acts (4:39). He did not simply quote other religious leaders, but his actions and teachings were based on God's written and direct oral revelation (1:22; 12:26, 32–37). He will return in judgment (13:26; 14:62). Jesus offered himself as a model for his disciples. Applying Jesus' example to ourselves, we may consider Jesus' extensive acts as his exercising of his spiritual gifts. We, too, have been given spiritual gifts. Thus, we can conclude that we as servant leaders should have a sense of our own mission and should use our spiritual gifts with authority. Having a regular schedule of activities is a good idea. If our master had critics, we should not be surprised if we too have critics.

However, Jesus is the head of his "body," the church, the source of our life (Eph 4:15–16). We, on the other hand, need help from the rest of the body of believers to discern our mission and the mission of our churches and institutions. We need to make sure that our mission is indeed God-approved, as was Jesus' (Mark 1:11; 9:7), and is not simply our own mission.

If anyone should have aggrandized himself, it should have been Jesus, who was God incarnate (14:61–62). But, even being God, Jesus did not simply flaunt himself and his powers (10:17–18). He warned the evil spirits not to shout out he was the Son of God (3:11–12), he visited Tyre and Galilee secretly (7:24; 9:30), he healed without advertising his success (7:36), and he told his disciples not to promote his transfiguration (9:5–9). But, he accepted genuine welcome and recognition (11:8–10). Being genuinely great, as Jesus encourages, should not entail self-aggrandizement for one's own sake. But, a time may come when we, as messengers of the Lord, are welcomed too.

II. As a servant leader, Jesus was *communal*, which is surprising as well.

Who better than Jesus to do a job by himself? But, he did not. Yet, how many times do we as leaders want to do the work all by ourselves, as we may put it, "so it can be done well"? Jesus called a group of disciples to join his mission.[7] As his own mission was criticized, so would the disciples' mission be criticized by some, but welcomed by others. Being Jesus' disciple had a cost, such as leaving one's occupation or enduring the possible abandonment by family (1:20; 10:28–30). The Christian family had precedence over the blood family (3:31–35). The mission had several levels: one was simply to be with Jesus (3:14),

---

6. Healing and deliverance occurred in, e.g., Mark 1:27, 31, 34, 41; 7:25–30; 8:22–25. See also note 14.

7. Mark 1:17; 2:14; 3:16–19.

another was to do supportive tasks,[8] and a third was to proclaim the message, heal the sick, and cast out demons.[9] Jesus trained his disciples and gave them subsidiary authority (3:15). He individualized the tasks and opportunities (5:37; 9:2). Training by Jesus included regular teaching (9:31; 10:23–27), personal explanation, correction, warning, and repetition.[10] Often the disciples did not understand, but Jesus did not abandon them (e.g., 6:52). After completing tasks, the disciples reported what happened (6:30). Jesus also personally helped them when difficulties were great (6:48–50). Jesus' training of his disciples was extensive, intensive, and personal. It demonstrated a *servant* leadership by its focus on others.

Jesus' leadership also showed his communal and servant actions by being supportive of other ministries than his own. For example, the delivered man from Gerasenes wanted to join Jesus in his travels, but Jesus sent him home to share the good news of the Lord's healing with his own household. He shared the good news all the way home (5:18–20). When John wanted to prohibit the person who was casting out demons in Jesus' name, but separate from the Twelve, Jesus would not let John stop him (9:38–41).

III. Jesus used a variety of *methodologies* as a servant leader.

He followed *prescribed legal systems,* but was *not limited by contemporary conventions.* For example, he sent the healed leper to a priest, as prescribed by Old Testament law (1:40–44). In contrast, he did not follow the rabbinic laws on fasting and ritual cleanliness (2:18–19; 7:2–8). He followed the intent of Old Testament laws, but not necessarily the contemporary interpretations, such as on the Sabbath.[11]

Jesus repeatedly had the disciples work in *pairs* (6:7; 11:1; 14:13). This same technique was continued in the early church. For example, Barnabas and Saul both are commissioned by the Lord and then sent off together by the church at Antioch (Acts 13:1–3). By sending workers in pairs, Jesus provided for the workers to care for, teach, and encourage each other. This methodology itself was a type of service for the disciples, as well as a means to improve the quality of the proclamation. Even Jesus wanted support from his coworkers as he prepared himself to endure the ordeal of crucifixion (Mark 14:32–41).

8. Mark 3:9; 6:53; 8:6.
9. Mark 3:14–15; 6:12–13.
10. Mark 4:34; 8:14–21; 9:28–29; 10:9–12, 32; 13:1–5, 9–13; 14:4–9.
11. Mark 2:27—3:5. See also Spencer, "Seven Principles," 121–33.

Jesus' mission could not be measured by the number of converts because listeners were given *freedom to respond* or not respond. He taught everyone to have the ears to listen by becoming receptive to his message (4:1–25). Without receptivity, even Jesus could do few miracles (6:4–6). The pious rich young man who was told to sell his many possessions and give them to the poor was given the freedom to go away sad, even though Jesus loved him dearly (10:17–22). Jesus encouraged his disciples to begin with a little, even the smallest of seeds, a mustard seed (4:30–32).

Once, my husband and I went on a trip to Israel. We had hoped for years to be able to go, and that was permitted by a grant. However, the rich education we received was marred by the demanding schedule we were given: morning and afternoon travel followed by evening lectures. We became so exhausted that we could hardly concentrate. If God created the world in six days and rested on the seventh, could we do less? Jesus, God incarnate, also saw the importance of *rest* for his disciples: "Come, you yourselves by yourselves to a deserted place and rest for a little" (6:31). People who serve others also need to serve themselves if they are to love others as they love themselves (12:33).

Another aspect of servant methodology is making sure one's workers are *rewarded* now, as they will be in the future (13:27). Those who provided spiritual enrichment were to receive physical enrichment (Mark 6:8–10; 1 Cor 9:11; Gal 6:6). This practice is also crucial for long-term ministry. Years ago, when Bill and I taught in Jamaica, we were told how some of the missionaries received financial support from their home countries. When the new Jamaican Christians wanted to support them as well, in consideration of their near poverty, the missionaries told them not to donate since "God's grace would take care of their needs." For them, God's grace was mediated by their donors. When the missionaries returned to their homelands, leaving the church leadership to the charge of the newly trained converts, the Jamaican leaders sought financial support from their compatriots. Sadly, their parishioners repeated to them what they were told; they could wait for "God's grace to take care of them." Thus, they suffered greatly financially. A seminarian told us how he preached a full week revival, spending his own money for gasoline and using his work hours to prepare his sermons. Each night the church leadership took in large offerings, but at the end of the week, they kept all the money, sharing none of it with the seminarian. Instead, they gave him a used book. Jesus, in contrast, taught that the worker is worthy of his wages (Matt 10:10; Luke 10:7).

By looking simply at the Gospel of Mark, we can learn several helpful methodologies for servant leaders: follow the traditional systems but do not be limited by them, have workers work in groups of at least two, give people the freedom to respond, allow for times of rest, and reward workers.

IV. Finally, as a servant leader, Jesus did or taught numerous helpful practices or attributes: compassion for all, patience, flexibility, truthfulness, faith, and prayer.

Jesus had *compassion* on the needy because he was *concerned for everyone*: women, men, girls, boys, children, Jews and Gentiles, and those of low[12] and great reputation and wealth. He had gut-level compassion for the leper, the hungry and confused crowd, and the wealthy young man.[13] He healed many.[14] He saw and rewarded the faith of a group of friends willing to lower their paralyzed friend down through the roof (2:3–5). He was willing to eat with despised tax collectors and sinners in order to bring them to wholeness (2:15–17). Even his opponents recognized Jesus' reputation as not being partial to anyone, but truthfully teaching God's way (12:13–14).

Part of compassion includes *patience*. Patience is needed for the advance of God's reign, even as patience is needed for growing harvests (4:26–29). Even healing sometimes can require patience (8:22–25). *Flexibility* is also helpful. When Jairus asked Jesus to heal his daughter, he may have been dismayed by Jesus' delay to assist the hemorrhaging woman, but Jesus did not hurry his encounters with needy people (5:22–42). When Jesus saw the crowd without a caring "shepherd," he stopped to teach them (6:34).

Jesus' flexibility and compassion did not undercut his promotion of the *truth* to all. He was concerned always to uphold God's priorities and principles, even if such actions entailed costs.[15] He affirmed those who were close to the truth, but critiqued those who oppressed and deceived others (12:34, 38–40; 14:18). In addition, as the faithful God, Jesus encouraged *faith* in God's power.[16] He encouraged *prayer*, even as he himself prayed alone and with others.[17]

---

12. E.g., Mark 10:15; 12:43.
13. *Splagchnizomai, splagchnon. agapaō*: Mark 1:40–41; 6:34; 8:2–3; 10:21.
14. Mark 1:21–26, 31, 40–42; 3:3–5; 5:34, 41–42; 8:22–25; 10:47–48.
15. Mark 8:33; 9:42–48; 11:15–17; 12:29–31.
16. Mark 5:36; 6:37; 11:22.
17. Mark 1:35; 6:46; 11:24; 14:32–39.

In conclusion, Jesus may have said he was a "servant" and "slave of all," yet, because his commission was from God the Father, he was, first of all, a servant of God, not of humans. God saw and served human need, which was the need for a ransom because of human sin. God did not fulfill all human wants. Jesus, too, gives us humans a commission: to proclaim God's good news. However, not all humans are interested in focusing on satisfying their needs; many simply seek their wants. Jesus' disciples are not slaves of other humans, doomed to complete every request. Rather, they are slaves of others in so far as they are serving God who wants the best for all humans. Often God's commission also includes limitations. Not only rest, but also our knowledge limits us (10:40).

Every servant is on the same plane. We are all commissioned, women as well as men. All workers are paid the same at the end of the day (Matt 20:1–16). When we lose family, new family may be restored, but we do not receive merit pay from God. Thus, we need to allow equal space and recognition in the church to all of God's workers.

EXAMPLES OF SERVANT LEADERSHIP

We have been examining the perfect example of servant leadership: Jesus himself. We saw that Jesus had some attributes of traditional godly leadership by having a clear sense of his mission and authority. He served others by being communal, working with others. His concept of servant leadership affected his methodologies and attributes.

The Bible also offers other examples of servant leaders. One effective example is the team of Deborah and Barak (Judg 4–5). Deborah lived in Israel during a period of great evil, yet she was able resolutely to lead her people in a manner pleasing to God. As a prophet and a judge, she held court under the Palm of Deborah, available to her people. Her commission as a judge was to remind the Israelites of the mighty things the Lord had done for Israel so they could worship and serve the Lord who brought them out of Egypt (Judg 2:10–11; 3:7–9), to settle disputes (4:5), and to rescue them from their enemies (2:16–18). God was to be their Ruler, rather than a human ruler who would oppress the people (1 Sam 8:7, 10–18). Deborah was comfortable with the authority the Lord gave her to lead the people to obey God. Although she was married, she regularly worked in her spiritual and political tasks as prophet and judge. She had authority over the military and sent for Barak and appointed him to his military tasks (Judg 4:6–7). Barak was communal. He refused to do his task alone without Deborah and, of course, without his army (Judg 4:8, 10). Interpreters today are sometimes unsure whether Barak did right in insisting that Deborah march with the army. As a result, a woman received the glory of killing the commander of the Canaanite army, Sisera (Judg 4:9, 17–22). Nevertheless, Barak made sure the goal was accomplished: Sisera and his army were defeated. Moreover, in the song that follows in Judges 5, Deborah and Barak are joined together as victors:

> On that day Deborah and Barak son of Abinoam sang this song (5:1);
>
> Wake up, Deborah, wake up! Wake up, wake up, and sing a song!
>
> Arise, Barak! Lead your captives away, son of Abinoam! (5:12);
>
> The princes of Issachar were with Deborah and Barak (5:15, NLT).

Deborah, too, is praised as a "mother of Israel" (5:7). Barak is praised as well as a leader in battle and remembered for his faith (Judg 5:15; Heb 11:1, 32). All the tribes who participated are praised (Judg 5:14–15, 18). And, "most blessed of women is Jael," who is also praised (5:24–27). Nevertheless, all participants give ultimate victory to the Lord (4:14; 5:4–5, 11). Everyone who loves the Lord arises "like the sun which becomes mighty" (5:31). In terms of praise, Deborah and Barak received equity as servant leaders. They each followed their commission from God, but they did it together. Together, they were praised at the end. Deborah had compassion on Barak. She was flexible. Barak could have gone on his own to fight. But, when he asked for her to come, she marched with him. After the battle, they rested as they co-wrote the psalm of thanksgiving. In their psalm, they rewarded everyone who participated by praising their faith and heroism. Nevertheless, they were also truthful, reminding their listeners of those tribes who did not participate because of indecision and the perspective of Sisera's mother (5:15–17, 28–30). Faith in God was, of course, critical for all participants because it was God who commanded the entire venture (4:6–7). Deborah and Barak served the people by serving God. They were true servant leaders.

Another example of a servant leader is Priscilla Ngendo Mereka of Kenya. The Rev. Dr. Lawrence P. K. Mbagara, a Presbyterian minister and organizing pastor of Gateway Presbyterian Church of Boston, Massachusetts, USA, who is originally from Kenya, has highly recommended her as an outstanding model. He gives his personal testimony:

> Priscilla Ngendo Mereka (*Nyina wa Ndungu*—as addressed in the Kikuyu language tradition) served the church and her

community as a teacher, elder in the church, community leader, first leader of the Women's Guild of her denomination, and, finally, leader in the church locally, nationally, and internationally.

Priscilla was born in Ngenda Mission Hospital in the Kiambu District, now the Gatundu District, Central Province in Kenya, Africa. Her parents were among the first converts to Christianity in that mission area, well-known as Gachugu's Family. She went to a missionary school usually known for having the children of Christians in the 1940s. She was trained as an elementary school teacher and taught at several primary schools before she married Nelson Mereka Ndungu. Both were blessed with children like their firstborn son Ndungu Mereka, who today lives in Nairobi North and is a member of Evergreen Presbyterian Church in Milimani Presbytery in Nairobi.

Priscilla Ngendo Mereka lived in Muranga District in Central Kenya in a village known as Naaro. Her husband was also a teacher, and they lived together, and they were coffee farmers and had domestic animals like cows, goats, and sheep.

In the 1960s, the Presbyterian Church of East Africa (P.C.E.A.) was growing very fast as a major denomination in the East African Region. At that time, the church was dealing with serious issues of transition from cultural values to Christianity and education. Some traditional practices were a phenomenon all Christian churches in the region had to handle, causing major hindrances to education, especially to young girls. As a family issue, girls were expected to marry and have children rather than be educated. Family was seen as more important than education and Christian faith and its values.

Both Priscilla and her husband Nelson were ordained elders in Naaro, Muranga, and Thika Presbyteries. By then, teachers and church elders were also community leaders in their areas. Women members in the P.C.E.A. grew fast, and they became the majority in the church.

The General Assembly of the P.C.E.A. in 1968 decided to recruit a woman to be full-time personnel for the entire denomination, and the General Secretary, Rev. Dr. John G. Gatu, was mandated to organize the recruitment process. Mrs. Priscilla Ngendo Mereka became the first full-time woman to lead the entire denomination in the well-known Women's Guild.

I came to know Mrs. Mereka between December 10th and 21st in 1969. She was one of the facilitators of a youth camp in P.C.E.A. Kambui Mission Station, where I was a participant as a youth member and a high school student. Her brother, Titus Wainaina Gachugu, and I were friends, and we led young people from Ngenda Parish. The camp was a Presbyterian camp that had between 500 and 600 participants, all young people. This was my first contact with Mrs. Mereka and I found her with these talents:

A. She was a very smart woman and well dressed.

B. She was a very good speaker and communicator.

C. She had a wonderful voice.

D. She had very good, insightful stories.

E. She sang very well with a great voice.

Finally, she was a very good teacher compared to other teachers in primary and secondary schools that I had attended before.

Mrs. Ngendo Mereka travelled all over East Africa teaching and organizing women groups in parishes and presbyteries within the P.C.E.A. She was involved in leadership in communities locally and nationally. She helped eradicate female genital mutilations (FGM) in her teaching on a healthy approach to sexual issues. She was also a pastoral worker and trained many groups of women to be capable wives to an extent that men demanded in conferences to be taught by Priscilla Ngendo Mereka. She was a woman of integrity in church life (*mutumia ngatha*).

Among her most noble involvements are that she was a member of the National Council of Churches in Kenya, all Africa Conference of churches, World Council of Churches, the World Alliance of Reformed churches, and the Federation of Women of Africa movements.

She joined Professor Wangari Mathai in the worldwide Green Belt Movement to deal with the environmental programs in Kenya, Africa, and the world. She was the chairperson of the Kenyan Greenbelt Council and African Chapter. She was also involved with many school boards in the management of education in Kenya.

My memories and testimonies continue from when I joined her in the General Assembly offices as the secretary of training and personnel development of the church. She was wise and communicated wisely to others like me.

The Woman's Guild in the P.C.E.A. Church is known as her child and has grown to be a major department of the Presbyterian Church of East Africa. One cannot think of P.C.E.A. without thinking of these women of the church.

> Priscilla Ngendo Mereka is a servant leader to be remembered in the history of the Presbyterian Church of East Africa.
>
> The late Mrs. Mereka is survived by eight Woman's Guild organizers sharing the role she played singlehandedly. She was truly a woman servant leader of Kenya and Africa.
>
> Thanks be to God who gave us a leader like Mrs. Priscilla Ngendo Mereka!

This great woman had a clear sense of her mission, authoritatively used her spiritual gifts, persevered, and was concerned for all. She was given power and authority by her church and used these opportunities humbly to serve others by serving God.

CONCLUSION

As we minister today and seek to be servant leaders as modeled and taught by Jesus in the Gospel of Mark, we, too, should serve our people by serving God. We need to avoid potential misapplications of two extremes: the overly authoritarian and the overly communal model. On the one hand, we want to avoid aggrandizing ourselves, using our authority to promote our own interests and needs and prestige, becoming like secular leaders who overpower others in order to gain power. Our authority then becomes ourselves, not God's revelation. We lead by ourselves without training others. We seek our own reward. We reach our goal any way possible and ignore truthful criticism. We set up a system convenient only to ourselves, inflexible, not compassionate, and impatient to all. Truth becomes a hatchet to destroy our enemies. We work only on our own projects. Our prayer is merely a pretense to move others to agree with our own preconceived goals.

On the other hand, if we are overly communal, we may aggrandize others, ignoring the authority God has given us to use our gifts, avoiding all public promotion. We then become like children who are overpowered by adults. We are communal, training others who work in pairs. We give others freedom to respond. We are compassionate, patient, and flexible. But, we are under-rewarded. We only use prescribed ways. We avoid all criticism and truth-telling. Working with others sometimes dilutes our own projects. Our authority then becomes others' approval. We serve others' wants, not their genuine needs. We have no regular system. Our prayer, though, leads us only to hear and obey the desires of others, not necessarily the desires of God.

Instead, the model of Jesus illustrates the teaching of Jesus. A balance needs to be made as leaders serve people by serving God. Yes, we have authority and should be allowed some freedom as we use our spiritual gifts to enrich others. We need to seek out God's mission for our own lives. But, service and mission are also communal endeavors. We need a group to advance God's reign. We need compassion, patience, and flexibility as we train others to obey God and advance God's mission. Truth and love need to be balanced together as equal leaders, hand in hand. We also should work within established systems, but not be limited by contemporary conventions or unsympathetic criticism. We should encourage others, but not force them. We should work for God's approval, but welcome reward and recognition when deserved. Prayer is a means to listen to God as well as become sensitive to others. Humbly, we need to listen to God's word as our authority. Pressure is always a problem, and one important solution is resting while relying on God to sustain the world. Our goal is to work with others as each of us in our unique way serves God. And, in the process, may we all rise up and become mighty together, illuminating the world through God's leading.

PART III

Transformation in Africa as Gender Equity Is Practiced

Chapter 10

Women Leaders Rising Up
Two Case Studies in West Africa

—*Martine Audéoud*

>Were I a persuasive female voice,
>That could travel the wide world through,
>I would fly on the beams of the morning light,
>And speak to men with a gentle might,
>And tell them to be true;
>I would fly, I would fly, o'er land and sea,
>Where'er a human heart might be,
>Telling a tale or singing a song
>In praise of the right, in blame of the wrong.
>Were I a consoling female voice,
>I'd fly on the wings of air;
>The homes of sorrow and guilt I'd seek,
>And calm and truthful words I'd speak,
>To save them from despair;
>I would fly, I would fly, o'er the guarded town,
>And drop, like the beautiful sunlight, down
>Into the hearts of suffering men,
>And teach them to look up again.

PHOEBE PALMER WROTE THOSE lines in 1858 in her book *The Promise of the Father*[1] as a transition to introduce the powerful witness of one of her female friends, a professor of religion, who found complete freedom in her relationships by opening up to a powerful relationship with God the Father, his Son the Redeemer, and the Holy Ghost. The purpose of this intimate relationship that she had developed was to stand up for justice and to be a beam of hope for those suffering and in despair.

Closer to us, Faith Mambura Ngunjiri quotes one of her friends, Ms. Kaara, "The courage comes from the spirit within . . . who empowers her to be what I am . . . the spirit gives her the capacity to pursue the truth without illusion. The spirit emboldens her within the parameters of my Christian faith to seek liberation until I die . . ."[2] This Kenyan female Christian leader had a burning desire for truth to be unfolded in the community around her. What's more, she was ready to stand up for truth and the development of just and peaceful African communities.

A century and a half separates these two women. Oceans separate these two women. However, they have integrated the empowerment that each African female Christian leader can experience under the guidance of the Holy Spirit to stand up with courage for truth and justice in order to develop *shalom* communities around them.

The short biographies of two West-African female leaders that follow—the first living in Burkina Faso, and the second in Côte d'Ivoire—will encourage each reader to be open to the leading of the Holy Spirit. He will lead you to far more than what you could have anticipated, to speak up for those without voices, and to contribute to showing forth Christ's *shalom* kingdom in the communities entrusted to you.

These two leaders are from West-African countries that lag behind in many of the references of the social institutions and gender index for their individual countries. The rate of female illiteracy is still very high in both countries, with Côte d'Ivoire's rate increasing to reach close to that of Burkina Faso.[3] In the area of political life, Côte d'Ivoire seems to provide a stronger legislative support to women than Burkina Faso.[4] For example, two years ago, Côte d'Ivoire promulgated a law allowing both spouses to be considered as co-heads of the family for the first time in the country's

---

1. Palmer, *The Promise*, 174.

2. Ngunjiri, "Lessons in Spiritual Leadership."

3. See, for instance, comparative data at http://knoema.fr/WBHNPStats2015Jan/health-nutrition-and-population-statistics-world-bank-january-2015?tsId=1090070, accessed in June 2015.

4. See, for instance, http://genderindex.org/country/burkina-faso and http://genderindex.org/country/cote-do39ivoire, accessed in June 2015.

history. However, a major gap between the legal framework and the actual practices are evidenced in both countries, especially due to the cohabitation of both the legal and the traditional frameworks governing society. The scope of this chapter will not allow further comments. However, the reader is able to check the references in the footnotes and thus recognize the very challenging environment in which female leaders, and especially Christian female leaders, are called to model out a *shalom* leadership in the church and in the world.

JOANNA

"Spiritual leadership is a thing of the Spirit and is conferred by God alone. When His searching eye alights on a man who has qualified, He anoints him with His Spirit and separates him to his distinctive ministry. . ."[5] This affirmation fits well with Joanna's personal life, which summarizes her desire to serve God and others.

Joanna was an adolescent in Burkina Faso when she had her real encounter with the calling of the Lord. In the work that follows, through the different stages of her life, Joanna is one of those whom God in his grace uses to do his work because of her willingness to be shaped.

The Influence of a Mother

Joanna's mother was a simple but hardworking woman. She was also very attentive to her children. She knew how to support her children.

Joanna's mother had multiple pregnancies with eleven living children. Very early in her life, her mother said, "Do everything to succeed in your studies; try to get yourself a job before getting married." Because of economic reasons and lack of education, she found herself "stuck" in her marriage, often feeling like the mere slave of her father's will. Her life represented what a great majority of African women have to live through. The only way to change was education and financial independence. Joanna found herself in a situation where, as Chantal Kalisa writes, "Stories affirm the survival of not only the storyteller but also the listeners, who 'survive because they have learned from the story.' In the context of violence, storytelling derives heavily from what Dori Laub calls 'the imperative to tell,' especially after a traumatic event."[6] Joanna, however, did not wait to have a job before she

---

5. Sanders, *Spiritual Leadership*, 18–19.
6. Kalisa, *Violence*.

got married. Perhaps she was not quite as convinced as her mother was of the need for financial independence, or she had not really grasped her sufferings.

Joanna is the second of eleven children, the eldest of seven daughters, and was nearly swept away by measles early in her life. Thanks to the perseverance of a courageous and hardworking mother, she survived. Her mother was thus her first role model as a strong female leader. She did not give up on her young daughter in spite of her poor physical condition but persevered, creatively trying to find the ways and means to get her to a healthier level. Thus, early on, she taught Joanna a very valuable lesson on the necessity to creatively care for those who are the weakest and most despised in a society that cherishes maleness and strength. Although women are generally considered as the weaker members in the African community, mothers are usually the pillar of their families and their communities.[7] Their strength and creativity enable them to find ways to unselfishly serve their family and community members in so many ways. Joanna's mother was such a woman.

A Father on Duty

Joanna's father was a Republican Guard, and his duties and assignments took the family to various cities and villages in Burkina Faso. Joanna doesn't talk much about her father except to state that her parents always made an effort to educate their children in the word of God and laid a strong biblical foundation in the children at a very early age. However, as a child, she discovered the benefits of traveling to different places and interacting with ethnic groups other than her own *Mossi* group, learning languages such as Dioula and Gulmantchéma. Joanna's exposure to a variety of cultural and ethnic practices highly impacted her views and apprehension of cultural differences. At a very early age, Joanna learned about different ways of living and thinking, which prepared her to later have an incarnational perspective regarding communities that were different from her own.

School Education: The Experience in a Boarding School

One night, when she had some discipline issues at her Catholic girls' high school, two of her classmates talked to her, and she was convicted of her

---

7. A very powerful example of this can be found in Kilunga Fatuma Kongo's text, *Femmes et Paix*, where the role of women in the construction of peace in this community is very vividly described.

wrongdoing. From that night on, God used her two friends to bring Joanna back on track; he changed her behavior and all those who had known her before were amazed at the transformation that had taken place in her life. The positive leadership of her classmates had a definitive impact on her life and turned it around. This is a vivid illustration of what Betty Mould Iddrisou observed in an article entitled "10 Things about African Women's Leadership":

> Women leaders and politicians need the support of their sisters, mothers, grandmothers, aunts, and classmates and cannot thrive without their active and vocal support. Women are generally thought of as not being supportive of each other, and the experience of many women leaders shows this to be a harsh reality. It takes a lot of inner strength and a thick skin.[8]

When Joanna wanted to stop her studies to go to Bible school, church elders advised her to continue her studies. They had visions for her that stretched far beyond the common expectations of her Burkinabe context; they anticipated her future and her impact on God's people. This visionary aspect of leadership heavily influenced her as she later realized how God-sent this advice had been. She often wonders, "Do I have such a visionary outlook and impact on the young people that I am called to coach or serve at this present time?"

Married Life

Joanna married a pastor, and together they had three children. The experience of living with her mother, somehow, helped her in her marriage as a wife and a mother. Although her husband was not as violent as her father was, she faced a variety of challenges in her own marriage. Searching the Scriptures for how to best handle difficult situations, she persevered in prayer and meditation of the word for encouragement and the ability to support her spouse. After thirty-four years of married life, the greatest lesson she learned was that "the prosperous couple is the couple that agrees together." When one is able, despite one's differences to listen and focus on the essentials, God makes the couple prosper and blesses what belongs to them and what they do. Such harmony does not necessarily mean agreeing with the opinion of the partner but knowing how to create the peace and serenity required for the intervention of God in spite of divergent viewpoints. This is such a contrast to the traditional African or Burkinabe view

---

8. Iddrisou, "10 Things."

of the husband's role, which is an authoritarian role where the wife has no say in major decisions and often serves as a servant or slave to her husband. Joanna and her husband had the privilege of understanding early on the necessity of focusing on God himself as the center of their marriage, instead of the husband focusing mainly on having his needs met. As a mother, the sense of sacrifice always animated Joanna; she did everything in her power for the success of the children that God had given them. As the Domestic Violence Taskforce acknowledges, "We realize that our Christian perspective comes from a variety of sources taught to us, modeled for us, or gleaned from our own reading. The Bible and tradition are the main sources, but are we clear as to the specific source of our beliefs and attitudes?"[9] Joanna kept teaching her children to make the Bible their reference book for all aspects of their lives. Today, by the grace of God, all her children are still following the Lord, attend church regularly, and have succeeded in their studies.

Leadership in Her Professional Life: Intellectual Pursuit

Besides having obtained an MA in Modern Literature at the University of Ouagadougou, Joanna was able later on to do theological studies in England for two years and enroll in leadership development programs that provided her with the conceptual framework to exercise her leadership in the various organizations that she felt called to develop and lead. Throughout these educational endeavors, there were people or groups of people who believed in her, encouraged her, and told her that she could make it happen. They stood by her as she was facing a variety of challenges to move up in her education.

Joanna's hunger for further training and her need for intellectual freedom was part of what she felt that her mother had yearned for. This acknowledges what Lufuluvhi Maria Mudimeli discussed in her doctoral dissertation[10] regarding the need for higher education for African women. More specifically, Joanna believed higher education could empower many women for leadership in the church just as it did for her.

Professional Experiences

When Joanna completed her studies at the University of Ouagadougou, she asked to be a teacher of the French Protestant College in Ouagadougou,

---

9. Domestic Violence Task Force, *The Church and Domestic Violence*. Referenced in Van Dyk, "The Voices of Women," 61.

10. Mudimeli, "The Impact."

inspired by the influence of missionaries who taught her when she was young. Her teachers had not only practiced their profession, but had also seized the opportunity to be good witnesses of Christ in all areas of their lives. Convinced that their example has allowed her to know the Lord and remain faithful to him, she is committed not only to teaching intellectual knowledge but also to sharing the gospel with students of her classes.

During the course of the next thirteen years, Joanna's professional capacity increased enormously. She founded *The Contact Magazine* and became the director of publication. She was appointed chief executive officer of Radio Gospel Development (RED), a position she held for the next eleven years. She was elected the president of the National Association of Audio-Visual Communications of Burkina Faso, the consortium of all private radio stations in Burkina. Eventually, she resigned as CEO of RED and founded the Christian Action Association, All for Solidarity (ACTS Ministry), a ministry that shows God's love in tangible ways to orphans and widows who have been affected by poverty and the AIDS pandemic—the most vulnerable individuals in Burkina Faso. They are the forgotten ones.

Some ministries that ACTS provides include an orphanage, a preschool through secondary education for 800 village children, vocational training for orphans, and a meal program for students and orphans. Through a medical center, it provides healthcare for the community and disaster relief for poor village families. The women's cooperative programs reach 9,000 women; and they sponsor adult literacy programs for women as well as evangelistic outreach ministries to rural communities. It has been a real joy for Joanna to develop and serve these communities of the poorest, leading them to experience a small part of the divine *shalom*, which we are called to extend here on Earth. The Burkinabe government recognized her contributions several times throughout these years.

Since January 2014, Joanna has served as executive secretary of the Pan-African Christian Women Alliance (PACWA),[11] a movement that seeks to empower Christian women to reach to the full potential that God desires them to have. She feels a strong call as a female leader to encourage other Christian African women throughout the African continent to grow and be empowered. As a female leader, she realized that once she moved on with her life and enjoyed her husband's blessing, there was almost no limit to the areas of leadership she could be called to. All her previous professional and educational experiences seemed to converge for her in a powerful way so that she could serve Christian women throughout the African continent.

---

11. See http://www.aeafrica.org/commissions/pan.htm.

God made her aware that, as a female Christian leader, she was not a prisoner of her past or her ethnic and cultural background. God used her past to build his glory in her life and in his sovereignty equipped her to become a Christian female role model for African women. Because of who she is in Christ, she can speak to and serve the youngest child, while meeting the next day with some of the most important rulers of this world. The intimacy of her relationship with God has moved her to a nearly constant attitude of praise and adoration. As Joanna says, "*He is worthy of my praise and worship!*"

A story of another woman shows how God has raised up a woman leader in another West-African country, Côte d'Ivoire (Ivory Coast). Pierrette is another doctoral student who stands out in her determination to serve the Lord at all costs.

PIERRETTE

Spiritual Growth

Every leader has a background, a past that fixes her present and determines her future. Thus the leader who refuses, despises, or even ignores her past is like the blind person Jesus describes. "Can a blind man lead a blind man? Will they not both fall into a pit?" (Luke 6:39, RSV). To avoid suffering the same fate of the blind following the blind spoken of by the Lord, Pierrette has willingly taken time to scrutinize her past (pre-conversion and conversion) and to reflect on her current situation (post-conversion) with a view to anticipating her future with the Lord, the servant leader above all others.

Born in the 1960s, Pierrette had a turbulent childhood and adolescence, due particularly to the loss of her father at age three. Later, she was negatively influenced by non-Christian friends. The consequences and effects of these past years remained with her, as "bad company corrupts good character" (1 Cor 15:33). She was then adopted by her stepfather, who introduced her to a new life, a Christian family and different disciplines. Within her new family, meditation of the word, prayer, praise, and personal evangelism were part of everyday life.

However, although she was a Sunday school member from the age of five and a member of the young adult group in the Methodist Christian community of Yopougon SICOGI in Abidjan, she led a double life. Her parents engaged in constant quarrels and gave little attention to their children; eventually, they divorced, and Pierrette went to live with her mother. Later, to enroll in high school, she was separated from her mother. During her first year of high school, she was attracted by the family spirit of some of her classmates who brought her into their gang. She learned karate to defend herself against other groups from the ghetto that sowed terror. Under the pressure of gang members, Pierrette started to smoke, drink, assault people, and miss school. She lived this double life for several years, a thug during the week and a Christian on Saturdays and Sundays. Although she lived this life of shame, the seed of the word of God kept germinating in her heart. She grew increasingly thirsty and hungry for God. This life became unsustainable; she was the laughingstock of her friends from the ghetto to whom she tried to share her faith in Jesus Christ. Their mockery made her aware of her state of misery.

However, it was impossible for Pierrette to stop smoking and drinking. She would manage to stop for one or two weeks, and then her habit would flare up again. This vicious cycle kept getting worse, and she wanted not only to be no longer a slave to these vices but also to stop being the subject of the mockery of her friends from the ghetto. She was able to convince her parents to help her transfer schools and bring her back to her mother, a decision that changed the course of her life. Back home, because her mother had managed to work through the failure of her marriage and made a fresh start, Pierrette had her full attention. Her mother was very strict with her daughter and controlled her friendships. Her mother gave firm instructions to one of the church youth members to lead Pierrette to all the youth activities of the church. Pierrette submitted to all the restrictions with a lot of resentment until the day she gratefully was ready to accept Jesus Christ as her Lord and Savior.

Story of Conversion

One day, her church youth group organized a day of fasting and prayer. During the program, the speaker spoke of the heavenly Jerusalem in Revelation 22:1–2. The speaker said the only way to go there was to invite Jesus Christ into one's heart. As he preached, Pierrette's desire to be in the presence of the Lord was gradually growing. At the end of the message, when the speaker made an altar call, Pierrette sensed a struggle between a desire to accept Jesus as her Savior and a desire to resist. Then she was delivered from the struggle—at which point she stopped smoking and drinking. The following year, she chose to preach and participate in additional activities in the youth group and the choir. Little by little, over several years of perseverance, abnegation, and studies, Pierrette became a minister of God in the

Christian community that had simultaneously witnessed her growth, the Methodist Church. She was ordained as a pastor in that church in 2003.

Pierrette credits her female predecessors in the Methodist Church for paving the way for women like her to move to become female Christian ministers. Although the Methodist Church only granted a limited form of ordination to women in 1911, the leadership of women in the Methodist Church dated back to Susanna Wesley (1669–1742)[12] and has developed throughout the growth of this church movement. It was only in 1974 that women could be fully ordained in the Methodist Church.[13] In Africa, the process has been a bit slower with the first African woman ordained in Côte d'Ivoire in 1994.[14]

Pierrette is now working on a doctoral degree at the Faculty of Evangelical Theology of the Christian Alliance (FATEAC). Although God had originally educated her at the beginning of her life, sin and evil company had distorted Pierrette. The love of the Lord Jesus Christ transformed her and remodeled her as a servant leader. Indeed, God has made of a turbulent childhood and a challenging youth an adult who, after passing between the hands of the potter in the home of the potter (Jer 18:1–12), became a vessel of honor for the glory of the transformational leader above all, Jesus Christ of Nazareth. The history of her spiritual development leads us to review the circumstances and people that helped shape her, including family and economic, political, and religious factors.

People Who Have Influenced Her

The Lord has used many people to forge her personality. The first of all these people was her mother. This woman of character has impacted her life through a very rigorous education. Sometimes Pierrette wondered if her mother was her birth mother as she was so harsh at times. Her mother, however, had faced her share of trials and challenges and reflected on these experiences with her daughter. Consequently, they developed an intimacy that was crucial to Pierrette's growth in incarnational leadership and emotional intelligence. Laura A. Davis asserts that "great leaders aren't just their intellects or brains. They also use their hearts and souls as well as their minds.

---

12. Susanna Wesley was the mother of Charles and John Wesley, the pioneers of the Methodist movement. See, for example, http://xntdnn.azurewebsites.net/gcsrw3/Leadership/WomeninUMChistory.aspx, accessed in June 2015.

13. See website above.

14. According to Pierrette herself.

They understand the power of thoughts and emotions in creating results."[15] Pierrette's leadership was significantly enhanced by understanding how to recognize and acknowledge, reflect on, and manage her emotions and those of the people she was in touch with, and later on, leading. Her ability to recognize the influence of her emotions on how she was interacting with those whom she led as well as the emotions of those whom she led, gave her the capacity to increase exponentially the impact of her leadership in a non-threatening and compassionate way.

Then comes Pierrette's paternal grandmother. She realized later on that Pierrette was leaving the Abouré culture and saw the influence of Anyi culture and language—the language and culture of her stepfather—on Pierrette. Her education at the culinary, medicinal, cultural, and linguistic levels contributed significantly to build Pierrette's identity as an Abouré African woman. Thus, Pierrette became culturally knowledgeable in two different ethnic groups. Through the experience with her paternal grandmother, she started to understand the value and richness of cross-cultural interactions—which significantly increased as she moved on with her pastoral calling to the point of crossing borders and oceans. She never forgot who she was, while espousing, appreciating, and learning from the diverse cultural settings to which she was later exposed.

As she moved into her doctoral program in transformational leadership, Pierrette had several professors as role models in leadership styles from servant leadership to incarnational leadership to prophetic leadership.

Transformational Leadership Aspects—Areas of Growth and Sources of Satisfaction

The eight basic foundational perspectives of transformational leadership that consolidated the success of Pierrette's personal transformation are vocational leadership, incarnational leadership, reflective leadership, servant leadership, contextualized leadership, global leadership, *shalom* leadership, and prophetic leadership. There may be many other perspectives. Some remain a source of difficulty for her. If they seem difficult to integrate, she works, by the grace of God, toward integrating them more fully in her life, and that grace fulfills her.

When there is a gap between the need and action, then leadership becomes more than necessary. So why, Pierrette wonders, does she still have trouble saying no to all the requests that come to her? Why does it happen too often that she commits to a mission with euphoria without having

15. Davis, *Emotional Intelligence*.

estimated the pros and cons beforehand? Why can't she do as Nehemiah did, when his nocturnal journey (Neh 2:11–12) made him take the time to assess the situation before taking action? In her desire to become an excellent female leader, it seems to her that she still thinks that the positive aspects of her leadership stem from what she is doing instead of from who she is in Christ. She really wants to focus on finding rest in her identity as a female child of God who does not need to respond to each solicitation in order to find appreciation or give personal meaning to her leadership. She seeks to learn more from Christ who said, "If you remain in me and I in you, you will bear much fruit; apart from me you can do nothing" (John 15:5, NIV).

Furthermore, she sometimes feels that she can please everyone and even encourage partisanship. She wonders why, instead of following the example of Nehemiah, an impartial leader (Neh 5:7) who did not favor the rich over the poor but made a plea to defend the underprivileged, she happens to give in. Pierrette feels that she is still too much influenced by her natural, cultural environment which is highly community oriented and where she has been trained since early childhood to take care of those who are close by and blood relatives. She would like to spend more time reflecting on the parts of her culture of origin that need to be transformed by the Lord's presence and the Holy Spirit in her so that she will be able to exercise a more powerful prophetic leadership in the communities that she serves.

J. Oswald Sanders summarizes the leadership of Nehemiah, saying, "Nehemiah emerges as a man who is vigorous in administration, calm in crisis, fearless in danger, courageous in decision, thorough in organization, disinterested in leadership, persevering in opposition, resolute in the face of threats, vigilant against intrigue—a leader who won and held the full confidence of his followers."[16] Pierrette wants to integrate this kind of leadership. Like Nehemiah, she attempts to be in constant connection with God through a life of prayer. She is full of courage and daring for the salvation of souls, more people- than work-oriented. Her ministry that is focused on God's *shalom* is confirmed by the testimonies of men and women she has assisted during her fourteen years of ministry. She had the grace to be an instrument in the hands of the divine master to make positive changes in the spiritual, social, and economic conditions of some members of our communities.

She feels within her the call for leadership to accomplish some of this transformational work for orphans, children at risk, and widows through her NGO. In terms of incarnational leadership, guided by compassion and empathy, she shares the daily burdens of this segment of society that is

---

16. Sanders, *Spiritual Leadership*, quoted in Liu, "Developing," 58.

often overlooked. She defines herself better as a servant leader. Serving God through the poor in humility has always energized her. As Ziglar says, "Your attitude, not your aptitude, will determine your altitude."[17]

The leader who brings *shalom* to his or her community knows and practices self-sacrifice. This sacrificial offering of herself is copied from the model of Jesus Christ, the servant leader never fully imitated. Pierrette has also made reconciliation the focus of her ministry. At the risk of her life and that of her family members, she visited the city of Bouaké (in the Ivory Coast)[18] many times in 2003 with the objective to bring together the parties at war in the Ivorian crisis. From Abidjan to Paris, from Accra to Lome, she has contributed to the search for peace, the divine *shalom*, because of the love of God and the love of her nation of Côte d'Ivoire. She is a leader who desires to bring God's *shalom* into her environment. Through her activities, she is helping the church to pursue reconciliation between individuals, between individuals and their environment, and between God and individuals. In fact, her life's commitment is to develop the well-being, the abundance, and the integrity of the community and the individuals in her church and in the communities around her. She yearns to develop a prophetic leadership to give a voice for the voiceless (Prov 31:8).

Finally, Pierrette wants to highlight the leadership model that characterizes her. She is *glocal*. She has a clear comprehension of the complexity of the global, pluralistic, urban, economic, and political aspects of today's world, and sees the church as a global church entity that is called to respond to these global challenges. She believes in the future of the body of Christ as a concerted action of all the home churches or local churches who, in their specificities and diversity, contribute to the richness of the global church.

The different perspectives of transformational leadership she has studied led her to see herself in the clear mirror of her realities in order to build a strong leadership through personal transformation and assessment. She lives on this earth to be a servant leader in the full sense of the term in response to the call of the perfect servant leader.

FINAL THOUGHTS

Both Joanna and Pierrette have become, in their respective countries, epitomes of female leaders according to the heart of God. Both of them needed to

17. Ibid.

18. During that decade, the country was separated into two parts, the North and the South. Bouaké was one of the leading cities in the North and thus was in conflict with the South led by the city of Abidjan.

emerge in a society where women who are becoming leaders have innumerable traditional and societal challenges to overcome.

How did they do that? Both of them had a mother who had already paved the way for them and modeled how to overcome life's challenging circumstances and transform them into opportunities. Both of them also were advised wisely by their mothers to move on with their education in order to have a greater panoply of opportunities in life later on with a strong focus on biblical teaching. Both of them had also decided that they would not consider marriage in the traditional way, but dared to develop their marriage relationships within the biblical framework of a working partnership, thus moving ahead of the legislation and the traditions of their countries. The *truth of the word set them free* (see John 8:32), and they both have chosen to believe God's word first and foremost.

We can echo Makanjuola's words: "I wish to state categorically and unequivocally that those factors always used in preventing women leadership in the church in Africa are no longer tenable. If other continents have outlived such prejudices, Africa should stop lagging behind in implementing the divine mandate of giving women the room to display their God-given talents."[19] Will more African women believe in God's mandate on them for the advancement of God's kingdom and step forward to show forth God's glory throughout Africa, and thus throughout the world?

---

19. Makanjuola, "Assessing the Hypotheses," 71–78.

Chapter 11

Biblical Equity Practiced in the Reformed Tradition in Zimbabwe

—*Rangarirai Rutoro and Ester Rutoro*

INTRODUCTION

HUMAN BEINGS ARE MORE inclined toward maximizing personal gains at the expense of other people and other species on Earth. The church today is struggling with a lot of questions which need to be answered. In a world where many questions remain unanswered and many problems crop up every day, people are seeking answers from today's church. In a world that is full of unjust practices, most of which are anchored in culture as well as religion, it is the duty of the church to reexamine itself and offer laudable answers based on biblical teaching so that the world can become a better place in which to live. Among the various challenges that the church has to address is the issue of equity.

EQUITY IN THE ZIMBABWEAN CONTEXT:

The Zimbabwean society is divided into distinct social groups based on class. There are hidden rules that determine class in Zimbabwe. One's economic status determines the class into which a person falls. Crossing the social class boundary is very difficult as the upward movement from one economic class to the other is hindered by several factors.

One of the main obstacles to people's upward movement in social status is corruption, which has affected many sectors of the economy. One case in point includes university graduates. It is difficult in today's socio-economic environment for a student from a poor background without connections to obtain a high-paying job regardless of the graduate's qualifications or intellectual aptitude. Due to corruption and nepotism, the poor are marginalized and endure low-paying jobs while the rich enjoy more lucrative jobs.

Another hindrance to people's progress is poverty. The cost of education is very high, and many ordinary people cannot afford to educate their children. Although the school system does not segregate between schools for the rich and schools for the poor, the fees at certain schools determine who can attend. The schools with lower fees offer limited services and courses. They lack facilities like laboratories which would enable the students to secure jobs in the sciences, which happen to be the highest-paying jobs in the country. Thus, although social inequity is not defined in hard and fast rules, the system itself divides Zimbabwean society into distinct social classes.

The inequities are intensified for women. Gender-based inequities are even more difficult to break than economic inequities because the former are so deeply entrenched in culture and are jealously guarded generation after generation. These deep-seated inequities come in the form of unequal distribution of resources, access to power, and freedom of expression. The church, like the society within which it is embedded, accepts gender-based inequities as a part of culture. Members of the church and the clergy consciously and unconsciously bring their cultural practices into the church, even turning them into rules that have to be followed. Thus, the gender equity problem has crossed socio-cultural boundaries into the church.

It is imperative that we explore equity within the Reformed tradition in Zimbabwe to identify where the church stands in regards to this challenge. This paper will concentrate mainly on the Reformed Church in Zimbabwe as a case study. However, a brief overview of the Church of Central Africa Presbyterian—Harare Synod, will also be provided.

A BIBLICAL PERSPECTIVE ON GENDER EQUITY

The word of God is the whole truth for the church. One of the fundamental principles of faith upon which the Reformed Church in Zimbabwe is anchored is *sola scriptura*, that is, abiding by Scripture alone. It is with this in mind that the church should explore God's word and seek to understand it like the Bereans, who "were more noble than those in Thessalonica, in that they conceived the word with all readiness of mind, and searched the scriptures daily, whether those things were so" (Acts 17:11, KJV). Our argument in this section is based on the *golden rule* in Luke 6:31: "And as ye would that men should do to you, do ye also to them likewise" (KJV).

The above verse shows the perspective of Jesus Christ on social justice and respect for persons. Jesus shows that if equity is to prevail, people should do what they expect other people to do for them. This is applicable to both the inter-class and intra-class equities. It is imperative that everyone views the next person the same way she/he views herself/himself. If the golden rule were followed, then gender-based inequities and social inequities would cease to exist.

The apostle Paul, through the inspiration of the Holy Spirit, shows that before God everyone is equal as God is no respecter of persons (Rom 2:11). It is only because of the Fall that people started to subdue each other and to seek overpower those presumed to be weaker. This truth is further clarified by Paul in his letter to the Galatians where he says, "There is neither Jew nor Greek, there is neither bond nor free, there is neither male nor female: for ye are all one in Christ Jesus" (Gal 3:28, KJV). This is the truth the church should preach and reflects the essence of God's teaching to his people on equity.

To help the church appreciate its biblical role of social transformation, the authors have come up with models which place the church in positions relative to other institutions.

EQUITY IN THE REFORMED TRADITION IN ZIMBABWE

There are several churches in Zimbabwe grounded on the Reformed tradition, namely the Lutheran Church, the Presbyterian Church, the Church of Central Africa Presbytery, and the Reformed Church in Zimbabwe. This chapter will dwell on equity in the Reformed Church in Zimbabwe (RCZ).

The RCZ doctrine is anchored on the Belgic Confession of Faith, the Heidelberg Catechism, and the Cannon of Dort. Based on the Confession of Faith Article 2, which was authored by Guido Du Bres in 1561,[1] the Reformed Church believes that God makes himself known to us by his holy and divine word. Thus, the RCZ is grounded on God's word for all its doctrine and confession. The first part of the Heidelberg Catechism, which is

1. Du Bres, *Doctrinal Standards*, 3.

taught to all RCZ Christians before they are baptized, clearly shows that in the Creation God created people who were supposed to be like him in goodness, but human nature was corrupted by the Fall as we see in Genesis 3. The catechism goes on to say that we need a regeneration of the spirit to regain the original plan of God for humanity. The original plan of God for gender equity is shown in Genesis 1:26–27: "God said, 'Now we will make humans, and they will be like us. We will let them rule the fish, the birds, and all other living creatures.' So God created humans to be like himself; he made men and women" (CEV). Both males and females were created in God's image, and neither was superior to the other, which is the ongoing intention and basis of how men and women are to relate to one another. Based on the above grounds of the Reformed faith, we now turn to the RCZ constitution to analyze to what extent it addresses the issue of equity.

EQUITY IN THE CHURCH OF CENTRAL AFRICA PRESBYTERIAN—THE HARARE SYNOD

The first congregation of the CCAP in Zimbabwe was established in Harare in 1945. Other congregations—Gweru, Bulawayo, Kadoma, Mutare, Kwekwe, Marondera, and Chinhoyi—were later established. These were all under the presbytery of Nkhoma. When the presbytery of Nkhoma became a synod in 1956, Harare became a presbytery under the Nkhoma Synod. On May 1, 1965, the Harare presbytery became a synod. The Nkhoma Synod from which the Harare Synod was founded does not accept women as ordained ministers, elders, or deacons. In his study, Gondwe[2] shows that the attitude toward women's ordination is influenced by the patriarchal nature of the Malawi society. This cultural influence has, in turn, barred the acceptance of women in the Harare Synod as the CCAP in Harare is mainly comprised of descendants from migrant workers from Malawi.

THE HISTORY OF FEMALE EXCLUSION IN ORDAINED MINISTRY IN THE REFORMED CHURCH IN ZIMBABWE

The Reformed Church in Zimbabwe was founded in 1891 by Andrew Andrias Louw, a Dutch Reformed Church missionary from South Africa. From its inception, the church has experienced great transformation in its doctrine concerning the issue of gender. At its inception, it is clear that the founding fathers incorporated western patriarchal philosophy into the

---

2. Gondwe, "The Possible Influence," 58.

doctrine of the church. The wife of the founder of the Reformed Church in Zimbabwe, Mrs. Louw, approached the gender gap in church ministry by "training the wives of African teachers, evangelists, and ministers [on] the way to run a Christian home."[3] A course on women's ministry was taught at the seminary, which aimed at training student pastors' wives the ways to run the Women's League. Such training was not emancipatory, but only deepened the gender disparities between men and women in the church. Ordained ministry remained for a long time a male preserve, with no females occupying positions of leadership in the church. It was only in 1984, ninety-three years after its founding, that the RCZ allowed the election of women as elders, and only in 2002, after Rangarirai Rutoro and Wilbert Runyowa's report entitled, "Resource Development and Women in Leadership Positions in the Reformed Church in Zimbabwe" was served before the General Synod, that women were allowed to be trained as ministers.

In 2007, Rangarirai Rutoro wrote a doctoral thesis on "Lay Leadership Development in the Reformed Church in Zimbabwe," in which special attention was paid to the issue of women. He notes that the "theology in the RCZ needs to interpret the Christian faith tradition in the light of its present realities and also discern what God requires of it."[4] He goes on to say that the inclusion and involvement of women in broader leadership structures will bring transformative development in the church. Nevertheless, glaring shortcomings remain in addressing gender issues in the RCZ. The ordination of women has been accepted, implemented, and is slowly bearing fruit, but much needs to be done within the systems and structures of the RCZ to make it more responsive to gender challenges.

THE REFORMED CHURCH IN THE ZIMBABWE CONSTITUTION

The RCZ has made great strides since the early days, moving from the missionaries' approach to women's roles in the church to a more empowering one of choosing women for positions previously occupied solely by men. On the surface, the constitution of the RCZ does not seem to address the issue of equity explicitly. Nonetheless, a deeper analysis of the constitution shows implicit references to equity. In Section 3 of the creed, it is stated that "the RCZ is founded on the Bible as the Holy and infallible Word of God."[5] This implies that the church is guided by the word of God which clearly ad-

---

3. Van der Merwe, *From Mission Field*, 97.
4. Rutoro, "Lay Leadership Development."
5. RCZ Constitution 2010.1.

dresses the issue of equity. It is pleasing to note that the constitution shows clearly the inclusion of both men and women in the key church offices. This is shown by the use of "he/she" when referring to ministers and elders and deacons/deaconesses. Using more inclusive language, the guide to church worship has replaced *varume ava* (these men) with *vanhu ava* (these people) and *hama idzi* (colleagues).[6]

THE RCZ STRATEGIC PLAN (2011–2015)

According to the RCZ Strategic Plan,[7] reformation is continual and holistic based on new revelations revealed to the believer and to the church through the word of God. This is significant because the convictions through revelation from the word of God are also continual, and the RCZ has sought to continually reexamine its practices through strategic planning. The vision of the RCZ reads that its purpose is "to be a missional and communal church that witnesses the kingdom of God in Jesus Christ bringing transformation to humankind."[8] Three issues stand out in this vision:

- It is a church that preaches the word of God and takes it to the people (a missional church).
- It is a church that serves the community, understanding the real challenges faced in communities so that they can address them in a contextual manner (a communal church).
- It is a church that envisions that it might bring transformation to humanity (a transformational church).

The issue of transformation to humanity is striking in this vision. It shows that the church has set itself to be involved in the rejuvenation of social values degraded through sin. The issue of equity is one such value.

The first part of the RCZ mission statement has great implications for equity. It reads, "We obediently and faithfully witness the Kingdom of God to humankind through: preaching, teaching, and living the Word of God through the inspiration of the Holy Spirit in a holistic and contextual manner."[9] The Strategic Plan shows the church's commitment not just to preaching, but also to teaching and living the word of God. The church has committed itself to be exemplary in deriving everything they do from the word. According to their Strategic Plan, the church has committed itself to

6. RCZ bhuku YoMupiriro 2010, 25, 28.
7. RCZ Strategic Plan 2011–2015, 4.
8. RCZ Strategic Plan 2011, 5.
9. RCZ Strategic Plan 2011–2015, 5.

preach, teach, and live the word in a holistic manner. This implies that the church is determined to look at all facets of humanity—social, economic, political, cultural, physical—and be guided by the Holy Spirit to address issues in each domain as they arise.

INCLUSION OF FEMALES INTO REFORMED CHURCH MINISTRY

The inclusion of females into ordained ministry has been a product of prolonged debate on the acceptability of females into the clergy. Research was undertaken and consultations were done until females were accepted into the clergy.[10] Consequently, since 2005, eleven female ministers and four female evangelists have been admitted into ministry. Out of about 104 ministers within the RCZ, only 11 are females. The disproportionate number of ordained women, in part, can be attributed to the fact that women only entered into ordained ministry, starting about ten years ago. Of greater concern is that, on average, only one female has been enrolled at Murray Theological College per year since 2003.

Low female enrollment and matriculation will result in the poor representation of women in decision-making positions in the church for years to come. Ester Rutoro asserts that "it is not enough simply to let women into positions previously occupied by men; what is needed is also a redefinition of the structures."[11] It is apparent that there is a need to further strengthen the structures of the RCZ to take cognizance of the gender equity dimension. The following sections critically interrogate the areas that need strengthening for the RCZ to address the gender equity issue more effectively.

AREAS THAT NEED STRENGTHENING

According to the Strategic Plan of the RCZ, the church appreciates the need for a transformative agenda in today's world as we reread and reinterpret the Bible. The RCZ admits that "the church is under siege from strong evil spiritual forces" and that "there is lack of religious tolerance and respect for human life/dignity."[12] Notwithstanding, the Strategic Plan fails to identify the current gender and social equity crisis, thus, revealing a glaring gap in the core values of the RCZ.

10. Runyowa and Rutoro, "Resource Development."
11. Rutoro, "Gender Transformation," 162.
12. RCZ Strategic Plan, 4.

Secondly, the church's self-awareness with respect to gender disparities needs to be reflected in the RCZ Constitution. In its present form, this document does not state how the RCZ is to deal with gender equity issues within the church.

Thirdly, gender equity needs to become a factor in critical decision-making boards. In spite of the increase in the number of female ministers, the 2014 General Synod did not come up with a single name of a female clergy candidate to become the moderator. So far, only one female was elected in 2015 to serve in the capacity of synod secretary. The other seven positions are held by men. In addition to the moderature, the major decision-making posts are occupied by men, e.g., the chief internal auditor and his vice, the education secretary and his committee, the treasurer and his vice, the church's finance chairperson, all the chairpersons of the church's presbyteries, and the heads of all the church's high schools. In short, equity in the RCZ in major decision-making posts remains greatly imbalanced.

It is also worth noting that the catechism has no section which prepares new converts to embrace gender equity. New converts are baptized without having been transformed in their mind about gender and equity issues. The socialization of young children is left in the hands of cultural institutions with the church doing very little to prepare her children to value equity. Similarly, gender equity needs to be emphasized in seminaries, where the theological training in RCZ remains skewed in favor of men. There is a distinct lack of women's voices in the training of ministers for the RCZ, an absence which impacts gender perceptions of ministers who engage in theological discourses almost exclusively with men.

CONCLUSION

This chapter has explored the issue of gender in the Reformed Church in Zimbabwe. Although there is evidence that the Reformed Church in Zimbabwe has made significant progress and has been ordaining women ministers for over a decade, there are still plenty of areas that need to be addressed because deep-seated patriarchal attitudes die slowly, especially when they are reinforced by the larger culture. Therefore, the church needs to continue forging ahead in its promotion of gender justice, which begins by shedding light on God's intention for men and women to be equal. It is vital that more people speak up and voice the need for gender equity within the church. Then equitable practices can follow that will lead to the widespread transformation of society.

Chapter 12

Inclusive Leadership in African Instituted Churches in Nigeria

—*Samuel Peni Ango*

INTRODUCTION

RECENT YEARS HAVE WITNESSED increasing focus on gender equity in Christian ministry, though arriving at universal consensus is still a long way from realization. Esther O. Ayandokun and Jonathan Ola Ojo note that, though "some churches in the twenty-first century world are still struggling with whether women should keep silent in the church . . . many churches in Nigeria (and Africa) have overcome this struggle . . . many . . . women get involved in the ministry of the church."[1] There is noticeable increase in awareness of the contradictions of gender disparity. That is why Lis Goddard, in a book made up of a series of email exchanges between her and co-author Clare Hendry, says, "Many lay men and women will be asking the fundamental question about whether or not women could or should have authority in the church as ultimately held within Anglicanism by bishops."[2]

Women have had to speak out persistently for equity in order for the issue to come to the front burner of church and society. As Mercy A. Oduyoye notes about the years just preceding the twenty-first century, "Women

1. Ayandokun and Ojo, "Let Women Be Silent," 314.
2. Goddard and Hendry, *The Gender Agenda*, 21.

in the past decade or so have had to insist that human rights are women's rights as well."[3] She therefore suggests, "The quest for women's rights universally should become the preoccupation of African women and men and especially that of all people of faith."[4] She is very hopeful that "appropriating the mind of Christ, and living in the presence of God will . . . lead to the realization that the vicious cycle of male entitlement and female self-abasement can be transformed into a caring circle."[5] The voices of women, with a little support from men sometimes, have resulted in the phenomenon of feminist theology.[6]

Describing feminist theology as "an advocacy theology concerned with the liberation of women from oppression, guided by the principle of seeking to achieve the full humanity of women,"[7] Ursula King observes the much larger scale of the oppression of women in the Third World, resulting in feminist theology being expressed as liberation theology.[8] Commenting on a compilation of twelve articles by feminist authors in a 2007 publication which were originally presented at "a day-long conference at the Graduate Theological Union (GTU) in Berkley, California, on March 30, 2005, to celebrate the history and work of the Center for Women and Religion at the GTU,"[9] Rosemary Ruether reminisces that "thirty-five years later, the development of feminist reflection in every field of religious studies, such as scripture, theology, church history, pastoral psychology, and ethics, has proliferated in the Christian world."[10] It is in the context of increasing discussion on issues affecting women that this chapter considers biblical equity in African Instituted Churches in the Nigerian context.

AFRICAN INSTITUTED CHURCHES

African Instituted Churches (AICs) have gone by various, similar-sounding appellations such as African Initiated Churches or African Independent Churches. Gideon A. Oshitelu, for instance, refers to them as Aladura (Independent) Churches or Indigenous Churches, which he claims broke away from the orthodox or mission churches such as Anglican Church

3. Oduyoye, "Culture and the Quest," 3.
4. Ibid.
5. Ibid., 7.
6. King, "Introduction," 3–4.
7. Ibid.
8. Ibid.
9. Ruether, "Introduction," 1.
10. Ibid., 3.

Missionary Society (CMS), Methodist or Wesley Church, and the Baptist Mission Society (BMS).[11] He further declares, "The Indigenous or Independent Churches were founded or pioneered in Africa, by Africans and for Africans. They were and are independent of foreign control. They are self-propagating, self-financing, and self-supporting, morally, materially, and spiritually."[12]

In addition, some schisms arose from church crises between 1891 and 1920, including reactions to mission society policies, e.g., the United Native African Church (UNA), the Native Baptist Church (NBC), and the United African Methodist Church (UMA).[13]

Leke Ogunewu lists churches among those he calls the Aladura Christian Tradition in Nigeria as including the Cherubim and Seraphim Society (C&S), Christ Apostolic Church (CAC), the Church of the Lord (Aladura) Worldwide (TCLAW), and the Celestial Church of Christ (CCC), all founded and run by indigenous leadership.[14] Established due to the political need to be free from white-dominated churches, and the religious need to express the founders' spiritual and physical endowments, the independent, indigenous, or initiated churches are also said by Oshitelu to include Christ Apostolic Church (CAC), The Apostolic Church (TAC), the Cherubim and Seraphim Society (C&S), and the Church of the Lord (Aladura).[15]

Engelbert Beyer lists the characteristics of the Aladura Churches as including the importance given to healing through prayer (evaluation and rejection of medicine); value attached to dreams and prophecies; success in life; African forms of prayer, music, and dance; place given to women in their services; smaller churches and congregations; understanding of the Bible; value given to the Old Testament; attitude toward polygamy; importance of doctrine and faith; suffering and the cross of Christ; and protection and the fight against evil powers.[16] According to Beyer, the CAC was founded during the influenza epidemic of 1918. It broke away from the Anglican Church in 1923. It was founded by David Odubanjo, and its greatest prophet was Joseph Ayo Babalola.[17] The Apostolic Church was a revivalist Pentecostal church in union with the British Apostolic Church. In it, among other Bible doctrines with Pentecostal emphasis, monogamy is required for

---

11. Oshitelu, *History of the Aladura*, 1.
12. Ibid.
13. Ibid., 4–20.
14. Ogunewu, "Revitalizing Theological Education," 125.
15. Oshitelu, *History of the Aladura,* 27–101.
16. Beyer, *New Christian Movements,* 14.
17. Ibid., 14–15.

all ministers. At some point, CAC and TAC worked together, but the former broke away from the latter due to disagreement over the use of medicine. Neither church, however, gave much attention to the roles of women.[18]

The Cherubim and Seraphim Society originated in the 1920s due to the outbreak of the bubonic plague and small pox. It was founded by Moses Orimolade Tunolase and Mrs. Abiodun Akinsowon in Lagos in 1925. They opposed traditional medicine and paganism and saw members as equal to the seraphim in heaven.[19] The C&S believe in the Trinity, salvation through Jesus Christ, the holy names of God and the angels found in the sixth through the tenth books of Moses, and the names of Raphael and Solomon. Visions and dreams are interpreted through astrology, clairvoyance, and chiromancy. They accept modern medical treatment and tolerate polygamy.[20]

The Celestial Church of Christ broke from the Methodist Church. It was founded in Port Novo, Benin Republic, in 1947 by Samuel J. B. Oshoffa. It aimed to abolish witchcraft through prayer to Christ. The church has seers and opposes fetish practices, smoking, alcohol, pork, and foods offered to idols. They oppose red or black dresses except for professional use. Male and female members are forbidden to sit side by side in church. Menstruating women must not enter the church until after sanctification. Female members are forbidden from entering the altar area or leading the congregation in worship.[21]

The Church of the Lord (Aladura) was founded by Josiah Olulowo Oshitelu. He separated from the Faith Tabernacle in 1930 and established his church in 1931. In the Church of the Lord (Aladura), polygamy is allowed. Menstruating women must worship at a place set apart. The church believes in healing, revelation, and prophecy, etc.[22] Oshitelu also notes some general characteristics of the Aladura churches as including extemporaneous prayer (some with baptism of the Holy Spirit and speaking in tongues), faith healing (some forbidding the use of medicine), and the use of holy water. Many have faith homes for sustained prayer for those in need who lodge there temporarily. They forbid taking corpses into church. They also include the use of candles, incense, healing services, lively participatory worship, and dynamic liturgies with the use of symbols. They believe in spiritual healing

---

18. Ibid., 16–17.
19. Ibid., 19–20.
20. Ibid., 23.
21. Ibid., 24–27.
22. Ibid., 23–24.

and acts of exorcism. They believe in prayer at mountains and at riversides, oaths, vows, and covenant making, as well as ancestor veneration.[23]

The African Instituted (or Initiated, Independent, or Indigenous) churches have not been left out of the female leadership discussion. This discussion has raged for some time with various nuances.

SOME VIEWS ON FEMALE LEADERSHIP

The subjugation of women in general as well as in church leadership can be linked to the predominant structures of societies around the world. Hope Amolo points out, for instance, that "the socialization processes of many African communities have conditioned men and women into believing that women are unable to perform managerial functions in the labor market. This wrong notion of gender is the filter through which many things are determined even in the church today."[24] Her reaction to this situation is, of course, that "from a biblical point of view, world history, and common sense, it is certain that a woman is man's counterpart rather than his inferior."[25] Both biblical literature and the growing consensus among both men and women the world over, point to the need to abandon the archaic structures that support inequity and embrace equity in life and ministry.

It is the belief of Krajewski and Burke, for instance, that practice has resulted in the predominant view of women as being inferior. Reviewing and commenting on sociological theories of gender inequality, they observe, "Women, spending significantly greater time in household activities than men, negatively affect their earnings . . . the husband contributing significantly less time to household work than his wife," which results in a lower labor participation and less economic success for the woman than the man.[26] They assert on the basis of their review that, "as a result of gender inequality, women have lower wages, lower labor force participation rates, fewer opportunities for job relocation, lower occupational status, and in Japan, lower educational attainment."[27] Obviously, most impressions of female inferiority have deep foundations in cultural practices rather than in the inherent qualities of women. These subjective factors of inequity are definitely evident in the traditional attitudes of most African Initiated Churches.

23. Ibid., 102–108.
24. Amolo, "The Role of Women," 156.
25. Ibid.
26. Krajewski and Burke, "A Brief Commentary," 174.
27. Ibid., 177.

However, African Instituted Churches, as well as other newly established ministries across Nigeria, are becoming more unequivocally supportive of women playing more equitable roles, just as men are doing. It is the view of Mary Oduntaon of the Church of the New Jerusalem that "a woman should head a local church as a pastor because women have every right to be ministers. . . .Both man and woman are complementary to each other, assisting, sharing, loving, caring, procreating, etc."[28] Wilson Badejo of the Four Square Gospel Church also declares unambiguously: "We must change our theology and some of our traditions and affirm with clarity and conviction the biblical basis of full participation of women in church ministries. We cannot settle for less if we actually expect the return of our Lord Jesus Christ soon."[29] It is also the view of Allen Tanko of the Eagle Nest Church that "we have scripture's position on the mighty ways in which the Holy Spirit anoints women in both the Old and New Testaments. From the Bible accounts, there is no inequality between man and woman before God."[30] Moreover, looking at the issue of women's silence in Christ Apostolic Church in Nigeria, Dorcas Akintunde declares, "From Jesus' relationship with women, gender discrimination has been abrogated. Let the church reexamine the biblical teachings which are replete with the equality of both men and women in creation and redemption."[31] There is certainly a gradual awakening in the African Instituted Churches to the need for women to take their rightful place in ministry. Such an awakening is in agreement with the trends of thinking in other streams of the body of Christ today. In addition, G. A. Oshitelu explicitly states that, from its inception, the Aladura (Independent) churches have "encourage[d] women in the church ministry. Just as in Yoruba traditional religion, a woman can be the high priest or priestess in traditional shrines. Also, there are many founders, leaders, and prophetesses in the Aladura."[32]

Supporting the views expressed by people in the African Instituted Churches, John Stott points out that "the record of the oppression of women has been so long-standing and widespread that there is a need for reparation by a male-dominated society."[33] In view of Genesis 1:26–28, he argues that "there is no suggestion in the text that either sex is more like God than the

---

28. Oduntaon, "Ordination of Woman," 51.
29. Badejo, "Ordination of Woman," 62.
30. Tanko, "Women in Ministry," 63.
31. Akintunde, "No Longer Be Silent," 97.
32. Oshitelu, *History of the Aladura*, 110.
33. Stott, *Issues Facing Christians Today*, 325.

other, or that either sex is more responsible for the earth than the other."[34] Insisting that the Bible from beginning to end affirms the equality of the sexes, Stott says, "We are equally called to rule the earth, (and) to cooperate with the Creator in the development of its resources for the common good."[35] He therefore advises that in view of God's endowment of women with spiritual gifts and his call for them to use those gifts for the common good, "The Church must recognize God's gifts and calling, must make appropriate spheres of service available to women, and should 'ordain' (that is, commission and authorize) them to exercise their God-given ministry, at least in team situations."[36]

In addition, M. Fehintola Akangbe says, "From the annunciation, conception, crucifixion . . . resurrection, and ascension, women have never been left out. Their role is not that of spectators but that of active participants."[37] Moreover, "They did not play any role subordinate to that of men. They played equal roles all along, if not more [so], than those of men."[38]

It is also in this spirit that John S. Pobee cites the roles of Mary Magdalene and other women who contributed to the ministry of Jesus, especially by their material support, pointing out that women have a role to play today in achieving trust, commitment, and community.[39] Hence, Pobee challenges Christians to "move from prejudice, especially the uninformed ones, and unnecessary and irrelevant strife to enable the story of the New Testament vis-à-vis women to inform our education and life in the community of faith."[40] Women are also expected to take steps to establish their presence in the church, not always waiting for men to give them equality. That is why Debra Fulghum Bruce and Helen Oldacre ask women to consider themselves as children of God with amazing potentials and possibilities and to value the selfless services they render the church, their families, and the community.[41] Women are also to see themselves as part of God's magnificent plan for life, each seeing herself as "not only [as] a survivor . . . [but as one who has] learn[ed] to thrive."[42]

---

34. Ibid., 328.
35. Ibid., 329.
36. Ibid., 353–54.
37. Akangbe, "The Role of Women," 132.
38. Ibid.
39. Pobee, "Biblical Studies and Feminism," 28–29.
40. Ibid., 29.
41. Bruce and Oldacre, *Celebrate the Journey*, 17.
42. Ibid., 30.

There are also cases of complaint against women who "share the national cake with the men by receiving bribes. . . . In their bid to get rich, they become selfish . . . not letting other women get to the level they have attained."[43] In most cases, however, the church is urged to recognize the legitimacy of roles for women. Thus, J. N. K. Mugambi calls for more active roles for women in the church of the future,[44] while Goddard and Hendry say, "single-sex leadership in a church is just not how it should be—whether that is all male or all female . . . Let's really expect God to do great things with our women alongside our men even as Jesus did."[45] How have African Instituted Churches in Nigeria fared in regards to the practice of equity in the church?

THE ROLE OF WOMEN IN THE AFRICAN INSTITUTED CHURCHES IN NIGERIA

Oshitelu describes the hierarchical organization of Cherubim and Seraphim as having two types of ranking for male and female leaders. The male hierarchy includes Baba-Aladura (spiritual father), special apostle, senior apostle, apostle, evangelist, pastor, and teacher (rabbi) in descending order. Female ranks include holy mother, mother-in-Israel, senior lady leader, prophetess, and lady leader.[46] This indicates the recognition of specific leadership roles for women in the Cherubim and Seraphim Society, perhaps because it was jointly founded by a male and female. This recognition is also apparent in the Church of the Lord (Aladura). In both churches, women are encouraged to serve in the ministry of the church, perhaps taking example from Yoruba traditional religion (among whom the Aladura churches were originally established), where women can be the high priest or priestess.[47] Furthermore, Oshitelu points out that there are many founders, leaders, and prophetesses in the Aladura churches, especially in Cherubim and Seraphim and the Church of the Lord Aladura: "Indeed, both Prophet J. O. Oshitelu and Apostle E. O. A. Adejobi resisted the effort to ensure only male ministers of the Church of the Lord (Aladura) between 1950 and 1960."[48] It is obvious that there is no uniform attitude and practice among the African Instituted Churches in Nigeria as regards the role of women in ministry.

43. Tanu, "Prophetess Huldah," 225.
44. Mugambi, "The Future of the Church," 48.
45. Goddard and Hendry, *The Gender Agenda*, 154.
46. Ibid., 58.
47. Ibid., 110.
48. Ibid.

This was further confirmed by interviews conducted with leaders of the African Instituted Churches in Ilorin, Nigeria.

RESULTS OF RESEARCH ON THE POSITIONS OF AFRICAN INSTITUTED CHURCHES IN ILORIN, NIGERIA, ON THE ROLES OF WOMEN IN THE CHURCH

In March 2015, I made contact with leaders of five African Instituted Churches in Ilorin, Nigeria—namely, The Apostolic Church, Nigeria; The Christ Apostolic Church; Ayo-Igbala Cherubim and Seraphim Church; Celestial Church of Christ; and The Church of the Lord, Aladura. I wanted to know if any of them ordain women into the clergy of their church, the scriptural basis for the position of their church on women in the clergy, the main theological or ecclesial argument for their church's position on the ordination of women, and the highest administrative position a woman may hold in their church. I sought to find out if some women have complained about their leadership roles in their church and what specific roles women have agitated to occupy. I also tried to find out if their church's administrative or liturgical literature provides for women in ordained or other leadership roles, whether the administrative or liturgical literature comments on women in ordained or other leadership roles, and what the personal view of the leader interviewed is on the role of women as leaders in the church.[49]

The Apostolic Church, Nigeria

On the ordination of women into the clergy, Pastor (Dr.) C. O. Odewole, the Area Superintendent (Apostle) of The Apostolic Church, Nigeria, in Ilorin, said the authority in The Apostolic Church, Nigeria, does not ordain women to become clergy in the church. On the scriptural basis for the church's position on women ordination, Odewole cited Exodus 28:1–3; Numbers 18:1–7; and Matthew 10:1–4, in which specific instructions were given for the ordination of Aaron and his sons, and Christ sent out twelve male disciples to preach the gospel.

As for the main theological or ecclesial argument for the church's position on the ordination of women, the Apostolic Church leader said there has never been any theological or ecclesial pronouncement on women

---

49. Some of the interviews were conducted using facilitators, so some of the responses were not detailed enough, especially on scriptural, theological, and ecclesial bases for the churches' positions on ordination of women. However, the basic position of each church on ordination of women was obtained.

ordination in the church, but he believes it is "widely known" through Bible teachings that the highest position for women in the church is that of deaconess. Therefore, he said, the highest administrative position a woman might attain in The Apostolic Church is that of deaconess. The Apostolic Church leader claimed women have never complained about their roles in the church. He said further, "Women do not agitate to play any leadership role in the church. It is the authority of the church that will make any one to be either a group leader or a women's movement leader, a secretary or a treasurer for a period of time, as the head of the church will direct."

According to the Apostolic Church leader, the liturgical and administrative literature provides for the role of women. For instance, Tenet number 9 of the church provides for "church government by apostles, prophets, evangelists, pastors, teachers, elders, deacons, and deaconesses (Eph 4:11, 13; Acts 13:3; 14:23); each of these sets of people knows their boundary through teaching. No one will go beyond his or her jurisdiction." He further said that the administrative set up of the church provides for women's ordination, but only to the level of deaconess. Their leadership role is restricted to the women's movement level.

I sought to know the personal opinion of the leader on the ordination of women in the church. Odewole said he believed a thorough search of the Bible would lead to an understanding of the role of women, which presumably supports the exclusion of women from overall leadership.

The Christ Apostolic Church

On the ordination of women, Pastor P. A. Ogunwale, the District Coordinating Council (DCC) Superintendent of the Christ Apostolic Church, domiciled at CAC Oke-Isegun, Taiwo Road, Ilorin, and a member of the General Executive Committee (G.E.C.), said the CAC does not ordain women clergy. On the scriptural basis for the church's position on women's ordination, Ogunwale cited Matthew 10:2–4 and 1 Timothy 2:11–12; 3:1ff. The Timothy passages are, respectively, where Paul commanded women to keep silence and to not teach, and where the position of bishop seems to be limited to men.

As for the main theological or ecclesial argument for the church's position on the ordination of women, the Christ Apostolic Church leader said that, based on teachings from the Bible, none of the elders chosen by Moses was a woman; none of Jesus' apostles was a woman; Paul did not enlist a woman as a bishop; and Paul's doctrine does not allow women to exercise authority over a man. Therefore, the highest ecclesial position attained by a woman in the Christ Apostolic Church is lady-evangelist or prophetess. The Christ Apostolic Church leader claimed no women have complained about their leadership roles in the church, nor have they agitated to play any specific roles.

The Christ Apostolic Church leader said that the position of the church on the ordination of women is supported by the church's liturgical and administrative literature. I sought to know the personal opinion of the leader on the ordination of women in the church. Ogunwale said the CAC seems to be fair to women, especially since women could be made church matrons, ordained as deaconesses, and allowed to freely operate as lady-evangelists and prophetesses.

Ayo-Igbala Cherubim and Seraphim Church

In his turn, Special Apostle T. A. Kayodeof Ayo-Igbala Cherubim and Seraphim Church in Ilorin, who described his position in the church hierarchy as "founder," said the church ordains women into the position of clergy. The leader of the Cherubim and Seraphim Church cited the example of Deborah in Judges 4 and 5 as the reason for his church's ordination of women. As for the main theological or ecclesial argument for the church's position on the ordination of women, the simple reason given by the Cherubim and Seraphim leader is that God used many women in the Bible to fulfill his mandate.

The highest position that can be attained by women in the Cherubim and Seraphim Church is supreme head. While the Cherubim and Seraphim leader claimed women have never complained about their roles in the church, he says they have agitated to be women's leader and to preach. Whereas the leader of the Cherubim and Seraphim Church said the church's literature provides for the ordination of women, the Draft Constitution of the Cherubim and Seraphim Movement Church Worldwide 2014, available to me, uses male-centric language and only provides for "The Spiritual Father," though women's leadership and female spiritual workers are specifically mentioned.[50] I sought to know the personal opinion of the leader on the ordination of women in the church. Kayode said he believed women are always committed to the tasks assigned to them, presumably justifying their ordination.

---

50. *Cherubim and Seraphim Movement*, 28–29.

The Celestial Church of Christ

As for the Celestial Church of Christ, Superior Evangelist S. O. Olusoga (JP), who is the number one leader in Ilorin, said his church does not ordain women into the clergy. Paradoxically, the leader of the Celestial Church of Christ also cited the example of Deborah in Judges 4 and 5, not explaining how this prohibits the ordination of women. Perhaps he meant that Deborah was subject to her husband, Lapidoth. As for the main theological or ecclesial argument for the church's position on the ordination of women, the Celestial Church of Christ leader cited 1 Corinthians (he wasn't sure of the chapter and verse, but probably meant 14:34) where Paul said women should keep silence in the church as the reason why women should not have any authority in the church. This is an indication that some leaders do not even study the Bible too diligently before taking or maintaining a stand on the exclusion of women from ordination. In any case, the highest position to be attained by women in the Celestial Church of Christ is Sunday school or children church teacher. The Celestial Church of Christ leader says women have complained about their leadership roles and want to be preaching from the pulpit and leading prayer.

The leader of the Celestial Church of Christ also said the liturgical and administrative literature provides for and comments on the ordination of women. A publication on the symbols on the altar of the Celestial Church of Christ by Emmanuel Adgoke, a supreme evangelist with the church, is conspicuously silent on any role for women.[51] I sought to know the personal opinion of the leader on the ordination of women in the church. The Celestial Church of Christ leader held unto the declaration of Paul in the First Epistle to the Corinthians that women should remain silent in the church.

The Church of the Lord (Aladura)

The Church of the Lord (Aladura) in Ilorin was led by Venerable Israel Okewale. He was the Diocesan Head of Kwara Diocese, as well as Minister in Charge of Kwara State Headquarters in Ilorin. He said his church ordains women into the clergy. In fact, at the time of my interview with him, his wife was a minister and prophetess in charge of another branch. Women perform equal ministerial functions as men. While not citing any specific scriptures, Venerable Okewale pointed out that God created women equal to men; he made them in his image, male and female. He also said Jesus had women disciples and made no pronouncement against them.

---

51. Adegoke, *Celestial Church*.

As for the main theological or ecclesial argument for the church's position on the ordination of women, the leader of the Church of the Lord (Aladura) said the church has no theological or ecclesial arguments on the matter, since they depend on the word of the Lord for every appointment. It is what the Lord says to them during prayer that they do, including whom to appoint to any position. In the Church of the Lord (Aladura), women have attained to all ecclesial positions, but no woman has ever been primate. The leader said there is no particular reason for this. The appointments of all primates, so far, have come about by listening to the Holy Spirit, and only men have so far been appointed. If the Holy Spirit directs the appointment of a woman as primate, the church would obey.

In the Church of the Lord (Aladura), women have neither complained about their leadership roles, nor have they agitated for any specific roles. The leader of the Church of the Lord (Aladura) says the church's literature provides for the role of women, citing the church's 2015 Calendar.[52] I sought to know the personal opinion of the leader on the ordination of women in the church. Okewale said there is nothing wrong with women's ordination because whatever God says is to be obeyed, implying that God supports women's ordination; that is why he instructs the Church of the Lord (Aladura) through the Holy Spirit to ordain them. Moreover, he said, women sometimes perform better than men.

It appears that the Church of the Lord (Aladura) is the most progressive of the African Instituted Churches on the issue of the ordination of women, followed by the Cherubim and Seraphim Church.

A FEMALE VIEW OF GENDER EQUITY IN THE AFRICAN INSTITUTED CHURCHES

The late Dorcas Olubanke Akintunde was a fierce advocate for women's rights in Africa, and was posthumously celebrated by the (Nigerian) National Association for Biblical Studies, Western Zone, by dedicating a conference and the publication of the proceedings to her.[53] In her writings, she gives some attention to the plight of women in the Aladura churches.[54] She sees no difference between the socio-cultural background of African women and the women in Aladura churches in Nigeria. Both among the Yoruba, where the Aladura churches were mainly founded, and among the Aladura churches

---

52. The Church of the Lord (Aladura), *Churchman Calendar,* 35th Issue, 2015, lists all ordained ministers, which includes women in all ranks except primate.

53. Adegbite, *Biblical Studies and Feminism.*

54. Akintunde, *The Ministry of Women.*

themselves, women are regarded as inferior to men. However, women play important priestly roles in traditional society. The Aladura churches depend on Scripture and unwritten cultural traditions for their position on women, and this explains the general silence of their literature on the issue. "The church leaders believe that the subordination of women to men was a dictum of natural law, and therefore, divinely intended."[55]

Contrary to claims by some church leaders, Akintunde asserts that women spoke against exclusion in the CAC in 1943, complaining to prophet Babalola, who encouraged the inclusion of women in church affairs, yet "in Christ Apostolic Church, women are not ordained as pastors, though some women possess the gift of prophecy and true vision in line with God's word."[56] According to Akintunde's listing, from president to five levels of superintendent cadre and evangelist cadre, followed by pastors and evangelists, women function at the ninth level down the hierarchy of CAC: "Since the inception of the Christ Apostolic Church, there has been the President of the Mission at the top of the hierarchy, followed by the General Evangelist, General Superintendent, the Assistant General Superintendent, and District Superintendents. These are closely followed by the Pastors, Evangelists, and Lady Evangelists. In none of the topmost hierarchy could women be represented."[57] Though Akintunde makes the same claim against the Church of the Lord (Aladura), a chart she presents shows women at the second and third levels of the hierarchy.[58]

Akintunde points out that in the Celestial Church of Christ, women are not allowed in the altar area, no matter their rank, and menstruating women are not allowed in the church without cleansing rituals.[59] Generally, among the Aladura, Akintunde claims, women do not officiate at baptismals, weddings, naming and Holy Communion services, nor at dedications of children, buildings, or church properties.[60] However, in the CAC, they may interpret during sermons and read lessons on special occasions, while prophetesses or female evangelists may function under male leadership. Men lead at CAC conferences for ordained ministers' wives, though the wife of the president may speak on women-related issues.[61]

55. Ibid.
56. Ibid., 115.
57. Ibid., 116.
58. Ibid.
59. Ibid., 117.
60. Ibid., 118.
61. Ibid.

Akintunde argues that women are more numerous in religious activities. They spread the gospel, especially among women and girls; they sing, serve as deaconesses, as Sunday school teachers, in social ministry, and prison ministry, especially to female prisoners.[62] She therefore laments that "a lot of talents in women are either lost or remain untapped and unnoticed because of the limitations set upon women."[63] She calls for a change of attitude and exhorts women to challenge "the patriarchal definition of womanhood and admit the fact that their subordination is not the will of God or the intention of Jesus."[64]

The late Dorcas Akintunde's views help us to see very clearly that the subjugation of women in the ministries of the African Instituted Churches, as well as in other denominations, have no sustainable justification. It has already been seen that some of the African Instituted Churches, like the Church of the Lord (Aladura) and the Cherubim and Seraphim Church, have given some leadership roles to women, though not at the highest level. These are indications of greater possibilities. Many Pentecostal and some mainline evangelical churches like the Baptist Church are also beginning to ordain women. I believe that the body of Christ will benefit tremendously if many more churches open their ministries to the ordination of women so as to harness their natural zeal, passion, and commitment so that those churches may begin to experience exponential growth.

CONCLUSION

The situation of women among the African Instituted Churches in Nigeria is by no means a uniform one. While the majority of them still relegate women to the background of ministerial leadership, citing scriptural and cultural or natural reasons—or no reasons at all—a few have consistently given women prominent leadership roles, including leading congregations as senior ministers. Prominent among such churches is the Church of the Lord (Aladura). Every church tradition points to some scriptural basis for their position on women, the most negative being Paul's apparent directives for women to be silent and not to teach in the church. However, it would seem best in these end times for the African Instituted Churches to allow for greater equity so that the Church in Africa may more efficiently and fully fulfill her mandate of evangelizing a dying world.

---

62. Ibid., 120–127.
63. Ibid., 142.
64. Ibid., 144.

Chapter 13

The Experience of Women Leaders in the Presbyterian Church of Nigeria

—Miracle Ajah

INTRODUCTION

AGAINST ALL ODDS, FROM the pre-colonial era to the present, a good number of Nigerian women have exhibited undeniable leadership qualities. In Nigeria's pre-colonial history, Queen Amina of Zaria led an army and drove out invaders from Zaria. Through selfless leadership and sacrifice, Moremi of Ile-Ife secured the future of her people and land.[1] During Nigeria's colonial era, prominent women leaders like Funmilayo Ransome Kuti, a crusader and challenger of despotic leaders, led Egba women in protest against taxation; Margaret Ekpo, a prominent civil rights activist, spearheaded the Aba women's riot against taxation; and Hajia Gambo Sawaba championed the cause of the oppressed in Northern Nigeria.[2] In recent times, the contributions of women in governance like Okonjo Iweala (finance minister and coordinator of the economy) and Dora Akunyili (the director of the National Agency for Food and Drug Administration and Control—NAFDAC) stand out.

The United Nations Development Program (UNDP), in its 2005 Human Development Report, however, listed some examples to show that in

1. Olufade, "Nigerian Women," 161.
2. Ibid.

spite of the considerable progress in developing women's capacities, women and men still live in an unequal world. Scholars hold divergent views on the issue of gender inclusivity in leadership. Whereas gender traditionalists posit that the Bible clearly mandates male authority over women and adhere strictly to the prohibition of women in Christian leadership, Evangelical egalitarianism or biblical equality believes that gender, in and of itself, neither privileges nor disqualifies a believer's calling to ministry, nor does it differentiate the biblical authority to be exercised by men and women. A third view, the complementarian view, contends that even though men and women are equal in the sight of God, they have different and distinct roles which set them apart in their spiritual authority.[3]

This chapter argues that leadership in society should be measured by the contributions of the leader and not by his/her gender. Scripture does not extend authority to men just because they are male. Rather, leadership and service are products of God's gifting, one's intimacy with God, and one's moral choices. Adopting a narrative approach and the content analysis of relevant materials, this study examines the contributions of some women leaders in the Presbyterian Church of Nigeria, the challenges facing women leadership, and the recommendation of appropriate policy interventions that would enhance gender inclusivity in the light of biblical equity. It is expected that religious leaders, theologians, educators, politicians, leaders of industries, and students will find this work very useful.

CLARIFICATION OF TERMS

Biblical Equity

The word *equity* is synonymous with uprightness, justice, and fairness. The International Standard Bible Encyclopedia (ISBE) describes equity as the spirit of the law behind the letter; justice is the application of the spirit of equity; honesty is the general, everyday use of justice or fairness, equity being the abstract ideal. The Court of Equity overrides the Court of Common Law, deciding not upon terms, but upon the spirit of the deed.[4] In this paper, biblical equity stresses the understanding that humanity was created to have equal prerogatives and privileges. When Genesis 1:26–27 states that God created man and woman in his own image, it provides humanity with a solid basis for self-worth. Human worth is not based on gender, possessions, achievements, physical attractiveness, or public acclaim, but on

---

3. Groothuis, *Good News*, 3–5.
4. Bromiley, *The International Standard Bible Encyclopedia*, s.v., "equity."

bearing the image of God. God made both man and woman in his image. Neither gender is made more in the image of God than the other. From the beginning, the Bible places both man and woman at the pinnacle of God's creation. Neither sex is exalted above the other, nor is any depreciated. This is biblical equity.

Gender Inclusivity

Inclusivity refers to the fact or policy of not excluding members or participants on the grounds of gender, race, class, sexuality, or disability, etc. This paper presents a model for gender inclusivity in organizations that, if followed, can create an enabling climate for inclusion and growth. This model looks at the various phases of gender inclusion and the corresponding metrics. It is revealed that, while some progress has been made in the proportion of women in entry-level and middle management roles in leadership, there is still a lack of representation of women across all positions and clearly fewer women than men in senior levels within many churches and organizations. This paper takes a holistic approach to the issue of gender inclusivity and proposes a multi-dimensional framework involving an ecosystem that includes individuals, the organization, the social environment, the church, and the government in order to achieve increased levels of integration and the ensuing benefits. It also proposes a set of recommendations to help effect the transformation from inclusivity to total empowerment from the context of each of the stakeholders.[5]

The Presbyterian Church of Nigeria

The Presbyterian Church of Nigeria (PCN) was founded in 1846 by United Presbyterian Church of Scotland missionaries led by the Rev. Hope Masterton Waddell. It bore the name Church of Scotland Mission until 1952 when it was renamed as the Presbyterian Church of Nigeria. In 1987, the General Assembly was constituted with two synods; presently it has nine synods, with over 50 presbyteries and 1000 congregations. It has missions in Benin Republic, Togo, Mali, and Burkina Faso. The church runs two degree-awarding theological institutions: the Hugh Goldie Lay/Theological Training Institution Arochukwu, and Essien Ukpabio Presbyterian Theological College, Itu. PCN is at the verge of inaugurating a new University, Hope Waddell University, at Okagwe Ohafia. It is a member of World Council

---

5. NASSCOM Mercer, "Gender Inclusivity."

of Churches, the All Africa Church Conference, the Christian Council of Nigeria, the World Communion of Reformed Churches, and the Reformed Ecumenical Council of Nigeria. For decades now, PCN has ordained female elders and ministers, serving in different leadership positions.[6]

PERSPECTIVES ON WOMEN

Scholars hold divergent views on the issues of gender inclusivity and women leadership. This section summarizes the three major views on the status of women—namely, the traditional patriarchal view; the egalitarian view; and the complementarian view.

The Traditional Patriarchal View

The biblical world or Jewish environment was openly discriminatory regarding women. Women were regarded as incapable of bearing witness. They remained excluded from essential religious tasks and the religious feasts, neither could they study the Torah nor participate in the sanctuary service. Women were obliged to observe purification rituals with respect to menstruation and the birth of children. For the Jews, the birth of a female was a misfortune. The Rabbi Simeon said, "All are happy when a male births, but all are unhappy when a female births." In addition, the Rabbi Jicaq states, "When a male births, he brings peace to the world [sic], he brings the bread in his hands, but when a female births, nothing is coming with her." According to Rabbi Jehuda (second century AD), Jews should recite the following prayer every day:[7]

> Praised be God, that he did not create me as a *goy* (gentile)! Praised, that he did not create me as a woman! Praised, that he did not create me as an ignorant person![8]

Much controversy has been sparked by St. Paul's message related to women in Christian leadership. This is exacerbated by the divergent gender positions attributed to Paul based on different readings of his texts on women, leadership, and gender. Paul's instructions to women in 1 Timothy 2:8–15 and in 1 Corinthians 14:34–35 to be silent and to refrain from teaching are considered by some to be the most objectionable words in the Protestant

---

6. Kalu, *A Century and Half,* 56.
7. Kasomo, "The Role of Women," 126–39.
8. Ibid.

canon.[9] There are polarized views across the Evangelical continuum on the issue of gender inclusivity. Some scholars argue that this prohibition "not to speak," also interpreted as "not to teach" and further interpreted as "not to specifically teach men," is valid in perpetuity and therefore binding for women today. Scholars holding this position argue that the church should not be swayed by the current liberal zeitgeist, which they contend is no different from that of the liberal New Testament Corinthian culture.[10]

This core text in Timothy appears to contradict the Magna Carta message of Paul in Galatians 3:28 and his other epistles where he is passionately asserting the liberating power of the work of Christ. This work of Christ results in equality—removing the inequity between Jew and Gentile, man and woman, slave and free. This is the most noteworthy strength of Paul's message but is not found explicitly in the Timothy text. Galatians 3:26–28 (NIV) reads,

> So in Christ Jesus you are all children of God through faith, for all of you who were baptized into Christ have clothed yourselves with Christ. There is neither Jew nor Gentile, neither slave nor free, neither male nor female, for you are all one in Christ Jesus.[11]

Several theoretical explanations have been given as the underlying reasons and causes of the marginalization of women. One of these theories is the biological determinant theory. The scholars in this school of thought argue that the roles of men and women are biologically or genetically determined, that there are fundamental and psychological differences between males and females in society, and that this difference makes male supremacy and patriarchy inevitable. According to scholars such as Lionel Tiger and Robin Fox, in comparison with women, men are more aggressive and dominant; they, therefore, monopolize positions of power. Women, on the other hand, are programmed by their genes to reproduce and care for children. They conclude that any attempt to abolish gender roles will go against nature. However, as Ilori points out, the biological determinant theory does not provide a convincing explanation of the subjugation of women in society.[12] While females are obviously biologically different from males, the assumption that nature is responsible for holding women in servitude is wrong. In some cultures in Nigeria, the agricultural sector is dominated by

---

9. Arumugam, "An Evaluation," 2.
10. Ibid.
11. Ibid.
12. Ilori, "Time Allocation," 112.

women while men are mostly involved in petty trading. In metropolitan Lagos, for instance, the commercial load carriers are mostly women who are physically strong enough to carry heavy loads even in advanced pregnancy states.[13]

Next is the cultural determinant theory which postulates that culture rather than biology is responsible for the relegated positions of women. The argument here is that culture determines the appropriate forms of behaviors for both sexes as well as those from society to society. Oyekanmi opines that biological characteristics do not bar women from particular occupations; rather, the mother role is a cultural constraint and a validating myth for the "domestic oppression of women." For instance, in African society, the popular belief is that men are superior to women. Women are brought up in this conventional way, and they in turn bring up their children in the same way. Until recently, the male child was believed to be more beneficial to the family; consequently, there is a preference for male education.[14]

The Egalitarian View

Evangelical egalitarians generally take an opposite view to the traditional patriarchal view. Craig Keener states, "The Bible permits women's ministry under normal circumstances and prohibited it only under exceptional circumstances." He presents Scripture passages that support women as prophetesses, judges, female apostles, and women who shared in Paul's ministry of the gospel. In his response to Scriptures that appear to prohibit women in ministry, such as 1 Corinthians 14:34–35 and 1 Timothy 2:11–14, Keener suggests that these passages addressed specific situations and concludes that they do not, therefore, contradict other passages in favor of women's ministry.[15] Linda Belleville of North Park Theological Seminary also argues for an egalitarian view of women in the church. She contends that the difference between complementarians and egalitarians is a "different understanding of the created order of male and female." Belleville views the "divine intent" of Genesis to be "that of partnership, a co-dominion over the earth . . . Dominion of one over the other . . . is gender dysfunction, not gender normalcy."[16]

Deborah Menken Gill argues in support of the egalitarian view from the perspectives of the nature of Jesus' ministry practice, his teaching

---

13. Fapohunda, "Women Emancipation," 21.
14. Ibid.
15. Kerr, "Women in the Emerging Church," 144.
16. Ibid.

manner, and his doctrinal content.[17] From the ministry practice of Jesus, Gill opines that while Jesus' contemporaries regarded women as sex objects, he treated them as persons (Luke 7:36–50; 11:27–28; John 8:2–11). His ministry was directed to male and female alike while preaching; performing miracles, healings, and deliverances; and raising the dead (Matt. 8:1–15). Though Palestinian social customs strongly disapproved of men conversing with women, Jesus interacted with them personally even when they were strangers or despised people (Matt. 9:18–26; Luke 10:38–42). He balanced the parables with male and female activities so that both genders would receive the message (Luke 13:19–21; 15:3–10; 18:1–14; Matt. 25:1–30). Jesus' doctrinal content was egalitarian in tone. No instructions in Jesus' theology applied only to women. He explained that there are no sexual distinctions in eternity. He did not confine women's role to the domestic sphere—cooking, serving, and feeding (Luke 10:38–42)—but he himself frequently served others. Jesus came to cancel the consequences of sin, to reverse the effects of the Fall, and to put right side up a world whose values were upside down.[18]

Galatians 3:26–28 is one of the strongest texts in support of biblical equality and is consistent with Paul's overall theology of liberty in Christ. What makes this so remarkable is that Paul is addressing religious status and hierarchy, which are now broken down in the New Covenant. Why did it have to take Christ's death to eradicate these social barriers of discrimination when, in fact, salvation was available to the Gentile, slaves, and women in the Old Covenant too? The distinguishing feature is the claim that Paul so earnestly makes: in Christ, all are one. Social barriers and privileges do not apply anymore in the New Covenant. To be of Jewish heritage, of free status, or of the male gender is no longer a privileged precondition to becoming an equal member in the body of Christ through baptism.[19]

The Complementarian View

In advocating for the complementarian view, the Council on Biblical Manhood and Womanhood sets forth the teachings of the Bible about the complementary differences between men and women as essential for obedience to Scripture and for the health of the family and the Church.[20] Complementarian Thomas Schreiner of the Southern Baptist Theological Seminary states that he understands Scripture to "forbid women from

17. Gill, "The Liberated Woman," 1–9.
18. Ibid.
19. Arumugam, "An Evaluation," 4.
20. *The Journal for Biblical Manhood and Womanhood*.

teaching and exercising authority over a man," according to 1 Timothy 2:12. Furthermore, he maintains that the different and distinct roles for men and women were established in Genesis 1—3, as well as marriage and ministry texts such as 1 Timothy 2:11–14, 1 Corinthians 11:2–16, and 14:33b–36.[21]

Many complementarians argue that women should serve in the church in many capacities but not in positions such as head pastor. While Schreiner observes, for example, that women did serve as deacons in the New Testament church, he believes that the deacons of the early church fulfilled a different role than deacons in many modern churches (i.e., he maintains that there were elders or overseers to govern and deacons for support positions, whereas today many deacons serve as members of the governing board of a church). Further, Schreiner concludes that complementarians should "celebrate and advocate" women serving in ministry roles other than that of head pastor or those in which they would exercise authority over men.[22]

The review of different perspectives on women has shown that the traditional patriarchal view was exclusivist with regard to women's participation in leadership or any major role above the men. But there were no clear reasons why men are so privileged, except their being created first in the Creation narrative (Gen 2). The contention of the egalitarian view that men and women were created as image bearers of the living God brings a distinctive and vital witness of faith into a world where Christ observed that "the harvest is ready and the laborers are few" (Luke 10:2). It is not helpful to read isolated Pauline texts that are used to enforce a patriarchal dominance in the church which is contrary to the overarching message of unity, mutuality in ministry, and equality in Christ. The complementarian view towed a middle course between the traditional patriarchal and the egalitarian views. They agreed with the egalitarians that men and women were created equal, but differed in their placement of men over women in leadership roles. This study proposes that leadership in society and the church should be measured by the contributions of the leader, and not by his/her gender. Scripture does not extend authority to men just because they are male. Rather, leadership and service are products of God's gifting, one's intimacy with God, and one's moral choices.

SOME WOMEN LEADERS IN PCN

This section summarizes the contributions of some women leaders in the Presbyterian Church of Nigeria, who have distinguished themselves in

21. Kerr, "Women in the Emerging Church," 143.
22. Ibid.

leading one aspect of ministry or the other, thereby adding value to the life and witness of the Presbyterian Church of Nigeria. The leaders discussed here do not represent the whole spectrum of women leadership in PCN; they are microcosms of the bigger picture, and the author was privileged to witness their contributions and interact with some of them. The selected leaders include Mary Mitchel Slessor, Mgbeke George Okore, Christian Jireh, and Jessie Fubara-Manuel.

Mary Mitchel Slessor

Mary Mitchel Slessor was a female Scottish missionary who labored in Nigeria from 1876 to 1915. Different reputable scholars have written about her, including Ogbu Kalu, James Buchan, and Carol Christian and Gladys Plummer.[23] She led in the advancement of the gospel and demonstrated a deep-rooted commitment to social activism, including her determination to rescue twins and orphans—sometimes even adopting and raising the children as her own. She strove to make life better for women in general, especially in setting up vocational training schools for them. She promoted the advancement of education, which she also used as a missionary tool; participated in settling disputes, whether as an agent of the British government or on an informal, personal basis; and brought a semblance of order to communities in a time of social and political upheaval.[24]

According to Ogbu Kalu, "Slessor represents a genre of missionary presence which rejected the social and spatial boundaries created by the 'ark syndrome' in missionary attitude."[25] In Calabar, she was a catalyst that challenged the mission to change emphasis, to become a sending body rather than a mostly stationary body, a practice the mission's converts had been urging for some years. She garnered support from younger mission colleagues in addition to being admired by British colonial personnel and the people of the districts where she lived and worked.[26]

Mary Slessor's importance in the history of the development of the church in Africa cannot be denied. She is remembered by some and venerated in both Scotland and southeastern Nigeria. In 2000, she was chosen as one of the millennium persons of Calabar, the place she began her witness. She is honored in the area with statues, each a likeness of Slessor holding

23. See Kalu, *A Century and Half*; Buchan, *The Expendable Mary Slessor*; and Christian and Plummer, *God and One Redhead*.

24. Hardage, "The Legacy," 114.

25. Ibid, 115.

26. Ibid.

twin babies. A hospital, churches, and schools are named after her. In Scotland, a ten-pound note bears her picture. Queen Elizabeth laid a wreath at her grave in Calabar in 1956. The museum in Dundee displays stained glass windows that depict events from her life. PCN and the Church of Scotland hosted a centenary memorial/celebration of her death in early 2015. Slessor herself would have shunned such goings on.[27]

Mgbeke George Okore

Mgbeke George Okore was ordained on February 20, 1982, as the first female minister of the Presbyterian Church of Nigeria, and she was inducted to the full charge of St. Stephen's Presbyterian Church, Aba, Abia State. She was the first woman to study with men at Trinity Union Theological College, Umuahia (an institution jointly owned by Anglican, Methodist, and Presbyterian Churches). In her biography, it is reported that her male colleagues at Trinity College did not make her feel welcome. They could not figure out why she was there and wondered why a church would want to ordain a woman as a minister over men. But, interestingly, at her ordination and induction ceremony, the same students turned up *en masse* in solidarity with her.[28]

Okore's ordination did not come on a platter of gold because PCN was using her as a test case for women in ministry. She distinguished herself by holding many leadership positions inside and outside of the church. She was the principal of Hugh Goldie Lay/Theological Training Institution, Arochukwu; clerk of different Courts of the Church; chairperson of the Board of Christian Education, PCN; and consultant for the African Women of the member churches of World Alliance and Reformed Churches (WARC); etc.[29] According to the Reverend Benebo F. Fubara-Manuel, "Ministry for women in Nigeria has not been the same since she came in. She has not only given to women's ministry the respectability and dignity that it requires, but has also encouraged a good number of women to join the holy ministry."[30] Mgbeke Okore is fondly remembered for her stance on women in ministry. She continuously challenged the exclusion of women in positions of leadership and decision-making. Today, women in PCN are eligible for all church offices and, together with their male counterparts, can perform all the functions in leadership and decision-making.

27. Ibid., 117.
28. Okore, *Women in the Church Ministry*, 37.
29. Ibid., 39.
30. Ibid., 41.

Christian Jireh

The Reverend Christian Jireh, born on September 29, 1957, to the Nsemo family in Calabar, Cross River State, Nigeria, attended Edgerly Memorial Secondary School and holds a Bachelor of Arts degree from the University of Calabar. After her National Youth Service in Enugu state in 1984/85, she proceeded to Trinity College, Umuahia, for training in theology and ministry. Jireh was ordained into the Ministry of Word and Sacrament of the Presbyterian Church of Nigeria in 1989, where she served fulltime for over twenty years, before proceeding to an itinerant prayer and evangelism ministry, which she leads.

Her dynamism and pragmatism in ministry distinguished her in the Synod of the West (Lagos), where she served most of the time. She was so active and resourceful most people forgot that she was a woman. Everyone, both male and female, cherished her ministry. She became the pastor of Festac PCN when they were still worshipping in a temporary site at the CCN facility in Festac Town. Through her doggedness, zeal, and persuasion, the church relocated to their permanent site across the canal. With the church building incomplete, the congregation worshipped under canopies and trees. During her four-year tenure, she completed a cathedral-like church building on their permanent site, which became one of the finest and biggest church buildings in Festac. At best, Christian Jireh should be described as a passionate church builder and revivalist because she repeated the same feat in other parishes where she was posted. PCN Cathedral Apapa is associated with her, including Rehoboth Hall (a large edifice) at Lagos Presbyterian Church, Yaba. She held several key positions in the synod, including that of presbytery moderator of Lagos West and synod coordinator for prayer and evangelism.

Christian Jireh is also "addicted" to prayer; she could hold your hands anywhere or any time to pray in the face of challenges or difficulties. On one occasion, she was part of a team on a trip to pioneer a Presbyterian church in Cotonou, Benin Republic, and none of the team members had a passport, let alone a visa. When the Benin immigration officers were threatening to deny them entry into their country, she quickly stepped aside and held hands with the synod moderator, Rev. Miracle Ajah, to pray for God's intervention. Swiftly, one of the immigration officers came back to inform the team that their head had approved their entry in the country.

Christian Jireh is a founding partner to many remarkable prayer and evangelism initiatives in the PCN and the nation. Some of them include Ministers Prayer Network; International Ministers' prayer conference led by Dr. Mosy Madugba; All Presbyterian Conference (APC) and regional synods; the monthly prayer forum for ministers in the Synod of the West and Lagos West Presbytery; and the directorate of missions in the Presbyterian Church of Nigeria. Jireh believes that the essence of the church is missions; every PCN member is supposed to be a soul-winner, and every PCN parish should be able to open new churches every year. In order to achieve these objectives, the church should strive to be self-sustaining, not just depending on offerings, but having investments like petrol stations and farm projects that help fund the church. Also, she advocates that elders or committed, experienced members should be allowed to open and pastor new churches for the PCN; the current trend of depending on ordained ministry is not enough. Uppermost in her interpersonal relationships with fellow ministers is the promotion of ministers' welfare. She was part of the group that championed the enhancement of the salaries and allowances of the moderator of the General Assembly and other principal officers.

Currently, Jireh is pursuing her strong passion for world evangelization through mobilizing nations for prayer and various forms of evangelism. She strongly believes that the best way to evangelize the society is through the family, for this is how God intended it to be from the beginning (Gen 1:26–28). She also believes that the earth belongs to God and Christians must handle the earth with jealousy as their Father's property. Christianity must therefore influence the nations unto good governance and high moral standards in society and a total Christ-like life for the saint wherever they are. She also believes unequivocally that the church is in need of God-centered revolutions as in the days of Martin Luther. It is not the big cathedral or the big auditorium that produce the salvation but Christ who is available anywhere, even under the tree (John 4:15–24). In as much as attention should be given to the physical building, the building up of the body of Christ should be paramount.

Jessie Fubara-Manuel

Jessie Fubara-Manuel is the author of the book, *Giver of Life, Hear Our Cries!*[31] The book details stories of the desperation and hope of African women and men as they confront the issues of eco-justice, gender-justice, and discrimination and marginalization on account of disability, etc. The book is also packed with vivid descriptions and insightful analysis.[32] But what the book captures is just the tip of the iceberg of the leadership qualities and contributions of Jessie Fubara-Manuel. As a writer, resource per-

31. Fubara-Manuel, *Giver of Life*.
32. Ibid.

son, passionate coordinator of Care Ministry, and a program leader of the World Council of Churches, Jessie is married to a former principal clerk of the General Assembly of the Presbyterian Church of Nigeria, Rev. Dr. Ben F. Fubara-Manuel. Some of her contributions in the church, which have distinguished her, are summarized in this study under the following headings: the Education Assistance Fund, the Care Ministry, Ministry among the Deaf, and Supporting Hands.

The Education Assistance Fund was an initiative that mobilized funds to pay poor students' exam fees, to provide basic library books for primary and secondary schools, and to organize seminars for children on proper reading habits, preparing for examinations, and choosing a profession. Jessie recounted how she was motivated to initiate the project. Her son's friend could not pay for his external exams because his parents were poor, and Jessie came to know of it by chance because of the mood of the child when he was visiting their home. She felt the boy would probably drop out of school or lose a year if nothing was done to help. She also wondered how many other children in her congregation were in a similar state. The Education Assistance Fund initiative, which started at PCN Ehere Model Parish Aba, blossomed and has given succor to numerous kids in the church.[33]

The Care Ministry coordinated by Jessie targeted the aged, the physically challenged, and the terminally ill. According to her, many people think that taking their aged and weak parents or relations to church will be an inconvenience, a distraction to the Spirit's move, or perhaps an embarrassment to them. They are kept at home, shut in and silenced, which is another form of exclusion and oppression. But, Jessie argued, "If we could not bring them to church, we could take church to them." The Care Ministry bridged the gap by visiting those who were sick, aged, paralyzed, or disabled. Holy Communion was also extended to them after service each time it was held in the church. With this simple project, lives were transformed and families testified to happy times with relatives who had given up on life.[34]

Ministry among the Deaf and Supporting Hands were among the various initiatives which were birthed through a compassion and burden to see disabled people receive the gospel and share in *koinonia*. A person with any kind of hearing impairment can receive some sort of reprieve in communication if the person can read and write. But when a person is completely illiterate, the situation becomes very different when it comes to communication. Jessie observed that, initially, they excluded the deaf and dumb in their care coverage because they were no sign language facilities in the town,

33. Email communication with Jessie Fubara-Manuel, 29 April 2015.
34. Fubara-Manuel, *Giver of Life*.

which was a painful decision for her team. But through divine providence, when they moved their ministry to Mary Slessor Memorial Church, Port Harcourt, various doors opened for them. Therefore, they began the Deaf Ministry of the Presbyterian Church in Nigeria. This initiative partners with various international networks for the deaf like the DOOR International—Africa (Deaf Opportunity Outreach)—in alleviating the plights of the deaf and dumb in Nigeria. Jessie was appointed the coordinator for the Nigeria Translation Project to translate the Bible into the sign language of the deaf in Nigeria. Since the inception of the Nigeria Translation Project in 2013, it has sponsored two different teams of over 16 persons from Nigeria for a four-year Bible translation course and practical translation of the Bible into Nigerian sign language. These timely initiatives and Supporting Hands are ongoing.[35]

CHALLENGES FACING WOMEN LEADERSHIP IN PCN

The challenges facing women leadership in the Presbyterian Church of Nigeria is not much different from other experiences in the African context shaped by traditional stereotypes against women. In 2014, a consultative forum and capacity-building workshop organized for different resource persons and leaders in PCN at Hugh Goldie Lay/Theological Training Institution, Arochukwu, came up with a communiqué that identified the following areas in which gender discrimination and marginalization against women is noticeable in the church:[36]

1. Posting: Male ministers are preferred over their female counterparts by different parishes.

2. Guest speakers: Female ministers are rarely used as guest speakers in workshops and conferences.

3. Leadership position: key leadership positions in PCN among the clergy, elders, and laity are dominated by men.

4. Wife battering has remained recurrent in different homes.

5. Disrespect and lack of cooperation with female leaders from their male counterparts have been disheartening.[37]

---

35. Email communication with Jessie Fubara-Manuel, 29 April 2015.

36. PCN 2014, "Gender Issues in the Church," Leadership Workshop Group Discussion; www.societyforacademicexcellence.com, accessed in April 2015.

37. Ibid.

Apart from the observations of the consultative forum, other factors militating against women leadership in PCN include the notion that patriarchal institutions tend to push women back into the private sphere. Cultural and religious socialization persists that consider Nigerian women as subordinates and men as their superiors. For instance, most mainline churches in Nigeria, such as the Anglican Church and the Roman Catholic Church, still limit women in certain leadership roles, especially where the priesthood and leading men are concerned. This mentality affects Presbyterians who share ecumenical fraternity with them. In most African cultures, women are not supposed to lead men, let alone make decisions that affect communities and nations. Ngunjiri was right when she observed that "African women have been missing in the history of the continent for a long time, due to the incessant patriarchal structures that relegate their leadership activities to oblivion."[38]

The owning of property by women in the African traditional context still looks absurd, and this affects Presbyterian men. Most men would rather that their names be written on landed property or assets than that of their wives or female children. To make matters worse, the repressive nature of socialization leads women to oppress women, and the lack of self-esteem exhibited by most women only adds to their marginalization. Most women involved in ordained ministry in PCN find it difficult to accept certain postings that take them away from their husbands, and the church has limited vacancies to post such female ministers.

Women's leadership in the PCN is caught in the bigger web of gender marginalization in the nation. Notwithstanding the 30 percent minimum threshold in decision-making for women recommended in the UNDP 1995 Human Development Report, the average female representation in politics is less than 5 percent in the country, and many of the women nominated are not elected. Although they are active in community affairs, women also are not adequately represented, except where conscious efforts have been made to establish a quota for them. Women's representation in the judicial system has improved through the growth in numbers of new female lawyers, magistrates, and judges, but the proportions still tend to be low. Despite the presence of some women in judicial and parliamentary systems and in top ministerial and decision-making positions, their low numbers hamper their effectiveness in initiating change for women. Agomor observes that women's representation at the highest levels of decision-making in public service was 4.3 percent in 2002.[39]

---

38. Musekura, "African Women," 55.
39. Okoyeuzu, "Shaping the Nigerian Economy," 17.

OVERCOMING THE CHALLENGES

Lessons abound from the testimonies of some of the women leaders in PCN selected in this study. The first lesson is that emergence in leadership positions requires perseverance and commitment. The four women, Mary Slessor, Mgbeke George Okore, Christian Jireh, and Jessie Fubara-Manuel, share in common a deep-rooted passion for their ministries and an unrelenting pursuit of them. Second, participation is the beginning point of winning. Just as fire exists by burning, so leadership functions by participation and making a contribution. Third, individual competence is important. The women leaders in PCN were gifted differently; each had a passion for a different aspect of human needs, and they excelled in meeting those needs. Their contributions flowed from within them; they were not trying to copy anyone. Finally, they recognized those in the margin and aligned themselves with them. They saw a forest and treated it as a harvest; no wonder great testimonies followed them. Their leadership qualities have become a framework of operation for women's leadership in PCN and beyond.

In an attempt to proffer solutions to the numerous challenges facing women leadership in PCN, the consultative forum that met at Hugh Goldie Institution recommended that aggressive education for gender equality should be sustained for men and women in every sphere. It posited that through education, a perverted mentality and biased mindset could be corrected, as touching on their complementary roles in the society. They also pleaded that the PCN leadership should sensitize others to the need for capacity building and character/integrity development of both men and women; that gender issues should be viewed as dynamic, not always dwelling in the archaic patriarchal era; and that PCN should stand against barbaric cultural practices against widows in society.[40]

United Nations agencies such as the UN Development Fund for Women (UNIFEM), the International Research and Training Institute for the Advancement of Women (INSTRAW), and the UN Development Program (UNDP) support gender awareness training for policy-makers, provide technical assistance, and build strong gender components into their own programming and projects.[41] Similarly, the Commonwealth Secretariat has commissioned several studies on gender and economic policy-making and applies a gender perspective to analyze the effectiveness of governmental policies and public services. The World Bank also emphasizes the

---

40. PCN forum, Hugh Goldie Institution, 2014.

41. *United Nations General Assembly Session 31* (1976), Resolution 133, A/RES/31/133.

developmental costs of ignoring women and denying them access to key resources, urging countries to draw up gender action plans.[42]

By 2007, the Nigerian government had enunciated a Seven Point Agenda, a policy document which was followed by Vision 2020 in 2010. All of these initiatives include efforts to address the gender gap, gender equality, and women's empowerment. The measures to be adopted to achieve these goals included: ensuring equitable representation of women in all aspects of governance; pursuing, where feasible, an affirmative action of proportionate representation of not less than 30 percent; establishing scholarship schemes at the secondary and tertiary levels in order to expand educational opportunities for female students where necessary; and expanding a program on non-formal education through sustained advocacy education (e.g., adult and vocational education to cater to women beyond school age).[43]

CONCLUSION AND RECOMMENDATIONS

As discussed in this study, challenges abound that hinder women's participation in leadership in PCN and beyond. Everyone interested in promoting biblical equity and gender inclusivity in leadership must work toward overcoming the challenges facing women. In addition, an aggressive education for gender equality should be sustained in the Presbyterian Church of Nigeria.

Furthermore, the church is encouraged to adopt and implement the National Policy on Women, which was constituted in 2000.[44] This policy aims at ensuring that the principles and provision of equal rights, obligations, opportunities before the law, and non-discrimination against any citizen is enforced. This policy thrust covers equity, social order, social well-being, resource allocation, economic growth, and efficiency, which is summarized as follows:[45]

a. Promote the welfare of women in general.

b. Promote the full utilization of women in the development of human resources and bring about their acceptance.

c. Work toward total elimination of all social and cultural practices tending to discriminate against and dehumanize womanhood.

42. Okoyeuzu, "Shaping the Nigerian Economy," 19.
43. Ibid., 21.
44. Olufade, "Nigerian Women," 167.
45. Ibid.

d. Devise ways and means of encouraging self-reliance in women.

e. Conduct research and formulate plans to improve the status of women and attain policy objectives in relation to women.[46]

---

46. Ibid.

Chapter 14

Practicing Biblical Equity in African Society

—*John Peter Bwire*

INTRODUCTORY BACKGROUND

THIS STUDY EXAMINES BIBLICAL equity within an African cultural context by analyzing data from different writers and experiences in practical life. It also examines current and past experiences of gender inequality in African society, progress that has been made since the post-colonial period in the 1960s, biblical teachings of equity to be practiced, and a set of recommendations for best practices among leaders with respect to gender equity in Africa.

At a societal level, we will examine gender relations in employment, education, and marriage within the African public sphere in general and, more specifically, within my constituency of Funyula in Busia County, Kenya, with occasional references to other contexts. Even though there have been significant gender equity changes in African society, much still needs to be done, beginning with the transformation, through the word of God, of individual mentalities as well as inherent cultural practices.

First, some terms and concepts must be explained as used in this work.[1] According to Timothy Njoya, terms such as *gender balance, affirma-*

---

1. Anne Cranny et al., *Gender Studies*, 1–4.

tive action, and *mainstreaming* do not proclaim the humanity, dignity, and sovereignty of women and men as enshrined in the Bible.² To be clear in our meanings and to be gender sensitive, there is a need to conceptualize certain terms in this chapter. Suzanne Staggenborg defines *gender* as "arrangements that are socially determined, while sex refers to biologically determined characteristics such as women's bearing children."³ Gender is about social and cultural choices and roles. Gender not only resides in individuals, but also in organizations and institutions within society. Therefore, we also need to look at widespread cultural assumptions embedded in our institutions, individual attitudes, and behaviors.

Laura Kramer says that *gender* refers to the physical categories or the totality of meanings that are attached to the sexes within a particular social system; thus, *gender system* is a system of meaning differentiation linked to the sexes through social arrangements. Issues of gender equity are embedded in our social systems; therefore, we need to understand social patterns—from daily interactions in our families to social structures. Kramer defines a *social institution* as "a constellation of activities and ideas that addresses a major area of human need in a particular society."⁴

Socialization is the process of learning the rules of the social group or culture to which we belong or hope to belong and learning to define ourselves and others within that setting. Through socialization, we internalize, or accept as correct, the rules and definitions of the social group. An *institution* is "a set of relationships and/or practices which are expressions of mainstream social values and beliefs."⁵ *Patriarchy* is a social system within which maleness and masculinity confer a privileged position of power and authority: where man is the self to which woman is the other. Traditions worldwide have been excluding women from positions of power and authority except where it works for the good of men or the whole social system.

---

2. Equity has to aim at giving dignity, humanity, and equal opportunity to all in a male dominated society. This then is the basis of biblical practice in the society. From Njoya, *The Crisis*, 93.

3. Staggenborg, *Gender, Family*, 2.

4. The particular content of socialization is influenced by cultural variations related to the region in which we live with regard to race, ethnicity, etc. Socialization is a social control of gender roles, especially where biological sex is related to life opportunities. For a long time, combat roles were only meant for men. Some socialized titles (e.g., chairman and commander in chief) control who should occupy those offices. In this way, socialization imposes values and societal norms on individuals. Those who accept them gain from opportunity structures, rights, rewards, and limits within those arrangements. See Kramer, *The Sociology of Gender*, 7.

5. Ibid.

A *role* is the set of responsibilities, privileges, and obligations that are connected to a particular social position or status. The following determines role expectations: class, ethnicity, and religion. Having defined some operational concepts and terms in this chapter, the following section discusses inequalities in African society.

BIBLICAL INEQUALITY PRACTICES IN AFRICAN SOCIETY: PAST AND PRESENT

After independence in most African countries, the agenda was to lament inequality in society.[6] A decade ago, the lamentation moved to women's empowerment, feminist theologies, gender mainstreaming, advocacy, and finally to analyzing women's milestones. In the twenty-first century, the focus should be on equal gender participation at societal levels and in dialogue. As we reflect on past achievements and set future goals, the agenda should be to maintain what has been achieved so far and to bring both men and women to reason together using Christian principles of equity as enshrined in the Bible.

The biblical equity message is never preached in a vacuum, but to a people in a context (Africa) with a political culture and social and economic practices, some of which are barriers to biblical equity. While progress is being made, patriarchy still influences most activities and choices made in society. We will consider the following areas where inequality in African society persists: attitudes, mentalities, traditions, relationships, education, and politics.

African traditional culture has been the common obstacle and the cause of gender inequity. The perpetuation of inequalities in society begins early in life. For example, how young people are prepared for life impacts their worldview and perspective of equity. There can be a profound difference between the socialization of youth who grew up in a traditional context without going to Sunday school and missionary-sponsored schools and those who did. Most traditional initiation ceremonies among the Bukusu, Kisii, and Maasai have not adopted gender equity in the way young people who are brought up in the church do. From birth, boys are still taken through traditional physical and mental rituals to toughen them to become warriors, fighters, overcomers, dominators, and even despisers of women. During initiation ceremonies like circumcision, which girls in most communities do not undergo, boys are taught to maintain their composure. For example, within the Bukusu Luyha subtribe, boys are hardened not to cry

---

6. Waliggo, *Struggle for Equality*.

while being circumcised. However painful the process might be, no conventional medicine is used. To treat the pain inflicted, bitter herbs are placed on the wounds, and the boys are given bhang or alcohol (though this is not common nowadays).

Traditional initiation practices are geared toward teaching boys to be in control and to gain power and authority. On the other hand, girls are socialized and expected to be humble and obedient to men, never arguing or fighting back. Once married, women are taught to serve their husbands by taking care of the domestic chores and submitting sexually to their husbands' needs and demands. Grown men are not expected to stay in their mothers' homes or even to greet women. In short, they are raised in a culture of disrespect that regards women as uncircumcised or people from another community.

As a result, men deal with boys and fellow men ruthlessly, whereas they deal with girls and women unkindly, like people that are not of their own kind, because women are weak. These trends which are seen as creating "flamed mainliners and masculinities" have gradually been changing, particularly in urban settings.[7] Most Christian parents are advocating for circumcision to be done in hospitals and for initiation to be carried out by churches so that boys are taught Christian values and virtues by church leaders. At the same time, in communities such as the Maasai where girls traditionally undergo circumcision or Female Genital Mutilation (FGM), girls are assembled and taught Christian values to fill the gender void. However, for many communities, the church's appeal to stop FGM is rejected and viewed as a cowardly approach to life.

In traditional Africa, only men owned property. With more women being educated and owning property today, women are relieving some of the stress associated with providing for the family, but at the same time, some men are feeling threatened by these same women. In fact, in my society, men shy away from marrying successful women with power and authority. Men still demand to be recognized by women even when they fail to be responsible. Early marriages of girls to older men and the taking of second wives are still rampant in Nyanza, North Eastern, and Coast provinces in Kenya.

In traditional society, men, not women, became leaders, kings, and chiefs, and they were expected to make all the decisions and policies regarding development. Among the Nandi, women were not even supposed to be heard, let alone to contribute meaningfully in public discourse with men. In

---

7. Njoya, *The Crisis*, 16. Njoya seems to suggest that men in urban settings no longer deal with boys as ruthlessly as do men in rural settings.

the Samia culture of Busia County, if a boy cried, he was warned not to cry like a woman. The family lineage continued through male heirs, although apparently the pattern may differ among the Kikuyu. Dowry payment still presumes that women are men's property. Some women are still married off to men not of their choice, especially among pastoral communities like the Maasai, Somali, Samburu, and some Kalenjin subtribes.

Gendered social life not only affects how people view maleness and femaleness but what kinds of opportunities are available to each. Poverty contributes to hold many women down. For example, in the universities in Kenya, the poor, a disproportionate number of whom are women, cannot afford to take expensive courses and end up taking whatever courses they can afford. Consequently, the majority of those training to be teachers are women, and the majority of those training to be engineers and doctors are men.

Education. In the past, the right to be educated belonged to boys/men even up to the first generation after independence. By contrast, it was a privilege, not a right, for girls to go to school. The second generation of students after independence in the '70s saw girls receive some education, but mainly primary education, and very few went on for secondary education. In Buradi primary school, Busia County, where I went for primary education in the early '80s, only two out of twenty girls in our class managed to join a secondary school, whereas over twenty boys out of thirty nine joined secondary school. Some of the girls in my class got married soon after finishing primary school, others when they reached the age of seventeen. Even with the advent of universal education in Kenya, the twentieth century saw relatively little progress. Those women who do pursue university studies often do so later in life and in parallel programs in the evenings.

Cultural norms and colonial laws. Traditional codes of ethics have continued to uphold unequal norms and are commonly expressed in proverbs, sayings, stories, legends, and myths. African traditional culture has stereotypically portrayed women as weak. For instance, in my culture, a clever boy is compared to his father even if the father is not that clever, while a foolish girl is foolish like her mother. Some of these stereotypes were captured in the famous Churchill comedy in Kenya—from laughable jokes to extreme cases of manifest inequality. The Kenyan Constitution, promulgated in 2010, promises enormous rights of equality.[8] However, the relevant legislation and policy implementations, including affirmative action, have proved difficult to enforce. The efforts to nominate women into positions of leadership have not yet yielded the desired results of equality.

---

8. See chapter 6, article 36 on equality and article 38 on gender.

Religion. African traditional religion was purely a man's affair in the Samia culture of western Kenya. Women could not lead in worship or even attend the sacrifices that occurred deep in the forest. Male elders represented the family and society in religious ceremonies. Women might occasionally join in the dancing and praising of the gods or cry and mourn during times of suffering to appease the gods. The influence of African traditional religious practices remains strong even among African Christians.

Christian leaders in Africa have biblical texts to turn to that can help bolster women's place in the church, but men who are in the majority still choose to interpret the biblical text in a way that demeans women. The Bible affirms the equality of men and women before their Creator, but as of 2015, there are only four women clergy out of over forty priests in Nambale Diocese. All the mainline Protestant churches in Kenya—the Anglican, Methodist, Reformed, and Presbyterian churches—are headed by men. Actually, most decision-making positions are occupied by men, while the choir and other service-oriented ministries are dominated by women. One of the church leaders confessed that it is not profitable to train girls in the ministry because they will eventually marry and join another denomination or diocese that spent nothing on her training. In the Presbyterian Church, lay leaders are called elders, which in turn has led to a protracted debate as to whether women should be called elders or leaders. When will church leaders help transition the community of faith from a place of inequality to equality?

Employment. In my village, where the Samia culture prevails, the first woman gained employment in the nearby town of Busia as a nurse in 1983. Busia is 35 kilometers away from our village, but her husband refused to allow her to stay there. Eventually, she resigned and came home frustrated.

Negative representations in the media. The media portrays women as inferior and often as men's property or mere sex objects. For instance, the use of nude women in advertisement and the marketing of products and services are not only offensive to women but unethical and downright degrading. The use of nude men to advertise products is rare compared to that of women. In music and dance performances, women are clad in costumes that leave them half naked, and they gyrate their bodies in ways aimed to attract men. In films and movies, men act while women appear gratuitously to provide an image of beauty or glamour for the sake of men. Women are seen crying and doing nothing during an attack, while men fight back to protect women and children. Such representations by male directors or producers, whether deliberate or not, is unfair to women. But neither should we go to the opposite extreme and make films that depict women beating up men or where men are tortured. Moviemakers should address inequalities and negative gender representations in society, focusing on issues such as rape, gender violence, domestic slavery among house help, and sex trafficking.

Traditional marriage. In my village, marital affairs and engagements persist in being discriminatory toward women. Negotiations leave out the girl who is to be married. Her opinion rarely counts. For instance, Onyango, my neighbor, only needed to identify a girl. The rest followed automatically. After the parents accepted the dowry payment of two cows and a goat, the girl, Ajiambo, was kidnapped on the way to fetch water and brought to the man's house. Her consent or opinion did not matter. We were young when this incident happened. Today, Ajiambo has been married over thirty years and has eight children. These forced marriages eventually came to be recognized in the church with the couple receiving prayer and a marital certificate. "Come-we-stay" affairs (or common law unions) emanate from this traditional, easy way of getting a wife; after all, the same church that insists on holy matrimony will bless it later. For example, when couples marry under customary marriage, they later go to church for blessing and to get a certificate. Traditionally, in circumstances where a woman could be married off to an old man sometimes forcefully, as a second wife, the woman could do nothing but cry and cry—nothing more. Widows who manage to inherit land and property find it difficult to change the name from the clan or family of their husband and transfer the property to their own name. This is because land belongs to the clan traditionally.

According to the Kenyan Constitution[9] today, marriage is between a man and a woman above 16 years with consent. Eighteen years and older is considered an adult. The law has made forced marriages illegal, as in most African countries, yet the majority of women are still not aware of these legal rights. The law has also addressed matters of inheritance, divorce, widows, custody of children, and property ownership in the family. Five decades after independence, a lot has changed in many countries, and the following section examines some of the changes.

PROGRESS MADE TOWARD PRACTICING BIBLICAL EQUITY IN SOCIETY

The Bible should be the main source of Christian living and lifestyle in society—in private and in public. It is through the Bible that God reveals his nature, wisdom, will, and plan for humanity and salvation. Christianity has already transformed some cultural practices that undermine gender equity.

---

9. *The Constitution of Kenya*, chapter 6, Bill of Rights, article 42.

Pelle Billing has outlined some pillars of biblical equity that have been instrumental in surmounting some of the barriers in Africa:[10]

- Men and women have the same intrinsic value.
- Men and women are equally valuable to society.
- Men and women should have equal opportunities and responsibilities.
- There should be no discrimination on grounds of gender.
- Equity does not mean sameness or uniformity.

The biblical pillars listed above can serve as the foundation for best practices for Christians and help shape the struggle for equity, which is also being advanced by women's commissions, constitutions, gender mainstreaming and gender sensitization, and other frameworks of advocacy. Biblical principles could thereby be used normatively to provide guidelines for establishing a more equitable society. Let us consider the following areas where changes have already been realized.

Equitable gender treatment and access. After Kenya's independence, the social meanings attached to being male or female have been changing, especially in urban areas. Due to forces unleashed through more education, media exposure, modernity, and urbanization, women's career opportunities have increased. Women occupy a range of jobs—from being housewives to being property owners. Christian values are also challenging gender stereotypes and contributing to the uprooting of structural inequality while constructing dynamic, new cultural and social realities. Juliana Claassens emphasizes that equal opportunities mean equality in the workplace, equal work, equal pay, and no discrimination or sexual harassment.[11] In the Anglican fraternity, equity translates into women being able to be ordained priests and consecrated bishops, and in nondenominational churches in Kenya, it means ministries can be led by women, such as Margaret Wanjiru of Glory Ministries.

Constitutional dispensation: The new Constitution in Kenya and in other African countries has brought social, political, and economic transformation in African communities. Today, either spouse can initiate divorce, and women can report sexual harassment at the workplace or bring other cases of gender inequality before a public court of law. Women who are economically independent are discovering greater freedom in making choices about their lives, as compared with those who depend on their husbands as their only source of livelihood. In Kenya, Uganda, Rwanda, and Tanzania,

---

10. Billing, "Defining Gender Equality."
11. Claassens, "Teaching Gender," 152–53.

local administration (chiefs and district or county officers) has been mandated to preside over civil cases of land and marriage during their meetings (called *baraza*) without preferential treatment based on ethnicity. Biblically, the best practice is to initiate dialogue through pastoral means, where each spouse is heard and given a chance to reconcile whenever possible. The clergy and other religious leaders are encouraged to attend such meetings to provide guidance and counsel. In divorce cases, in most communities apart from the Kikuyu, mothers continue to be custodians of children until they attain the age of eighteen years.

Equity in the public sphere. In politics, it is now accepted for women to hold public offices. In East Africa, more than 50 percent of Rwanda's political offices are held by women, while in Kenya, affirmative action is written into the constitution. In Kenya, some government institutions of higher learning and cooperatives are headed by women. Both Kenyatta University (KU) and Jomo Kenyatta University of Agriculture and Technology (JKUAT) are headed by women. Other women occupy ministerial posts in the county and national governments. In some parts of central Kenya, such as Nyeri, women are taking full responsibility where men are indisposed or deemed irresponsible due to unemployment or drunkenness. Positively, some workplaces are adopting policies to accommodate mothers with small infants. For instance, Safaricom Company has even created a private space for mothers to breastfeed.

As part of the biblical mandate, Christians should advocate for a legal framework for gender rights, sensitize society on how to deal with cultural stereotypes against women, and provide a conducive environment for increasing gender participation and implementing resolutions that promote gender equity resolutions. The following institutions must make a concerted effort to overcome the remaining challenges toward biblical equity in society.

a. Government: Political legislation and policy reforms need to level the playing ground for men and women with actionable consequences, and the church must not be left out of this process.

b. Civil organizations and other non-governmental organizations (NGOs): These organizations have a role to partner with the church to educate, train, and sensitize the masses about constitutional reforms, as well as provide biblical teaching on equity through seminars, workshops, and conferences. These educative programs can target youths, women, and men's fellowships, people with disabilities, and other groups within society.

c. Church: The church is responsible to make biblical equity a reality in society by engaging in participatory roles in the public sphere and extending the kingdom of God on Earth through making the gospel relevant to all situations and contexts. These efforts aim at transforming cultural, economic, and religious inequalities in the society. Thus, the church serves not only as the conscience of the nations, but as an agent of transformation, like salt and light in the world (Matt 5:13–14).

BIBLICAL EQUITY TO BE PRACTICED IN AFRICAN SOCIETY

Every culture contains both positive and negative elements. The gospel redeems culture and requires us to evaluate our culture to determine what we need to reject, affirm, or adapt. The question that begs to be answered in this section is how communities should practice the redeeming gospel of equity as it touches on everything from gender relations to economics to worship to institutions, such as governments, law courts, churches, and schools.

Before analyzing the particularities, this study examines some related contextual examples. Laura Kramer argues that issues of gender equity are embedded in our social systems, patterns, and daily interactions in societal structures—areas that change must target.[12] The following section explains some of the ways our practices can bring change in society with respect to biblical equity.

- Regarding the Bible as normative
- Integrating the mission of the church and NGOs to achieve cultural transformation
- Practicing the Great Commission
- Contextualizing the gospel
- Transforming the political and legal systems

Regarding the Bible as normative. The Bible guides decision-making and Christian living. However, the Bible's interpretation and reinterpretation has to be subject to revision so that the truth is comprehensible to all genders. In our generation, leaders in the church and society need to pay greater attention to using gender-sensitive language and embracing a theology that regards women and men equitably. This calls for a transformative model and contextualization of the gospel in Africa.

12. Kramer, *The Sociology of Gender*, 1–2.

Integrating the mission of the church and NGOs to achieve cultural transformation. Practicing biblical equity calls for collaboration between individuals and institutions. Only through a combined, integrated effort can structures as well as individuals be transformed. We need to practice the gospel of social action to overcome cultural barriers and to check inequitable practices and systems. With accountability, people can enjoy fullness of life in harmony with God (John 10:10; Col 3:8–15; Eph 4:13). When people obey the gospel of Christ, it changes their lives as they respond with love toward others (Rom 5:5) and become new creatures in Christ (2 Cor 5:17). The same transforming power of God redeems economic, social, and spiritual systems with all of its sins, inequities, and discrimination.

Practicing the Great Commission. The Great Commission (Matt 28:19) is God's mission in Christ on earth (*Missio Dei*). Loren Mead asserts that believers are partakers in this life-transforming calling.[13] In the Incarnation, God became human, sending his Son to save us and to change us. In the Great Commission, Christ is sending us to all the nations with the gospel of change. Gender equity is one aspect of that transformation, characterized by reoriented relationships and the capacity to make godly and informed choices, leading to character growth, the acceptance of gender differences, and the flourishing of the body of Christ under the reign of the Holy Spirit. Institutions and structures of inequality may change not only by rebuking evil systems but also by nurturing communities where grace and security abound and members intentionally foster Christian values, such as love, honesty, faithfulness, trustworthiness, obedience, and justice. Furthermore, the church can advance God's mission and reign in the world by collaborating with other institutions and NGOs. The church thereby acts as a mediating institution, which is rooted in different cultures, carrying people's worldviews, ideologies, and values on gender. To move from inequality to biblical equity requires integral evangelism and social action.

Equity and reconciliation, practiced and guided by Scripture, must have explicit goals. The following principles can inform the practice of biblical equity:

- Avoid conforming to worldly and cultural practices that oppose the Bible (Rom 12:1–2).

- All are accountable before God for following and not following God's laws (Ezek 11:12).

- Live lives that reflect the kingdom of God and redeemed humanity (1 Thess 3:12–13).

---

13. Mead, *More Than Numbers*.

- Exercise stewardship as God's caretakers, not owners, giving others access to material resources, equity of opportunities, and divine responsibilities.
- Exercise healthy gender relationships (1 Kgs 5:12), characterized by well-being (Gen 37:14), prosperity (Jer 33:6, 9), and upright character (Ps 37:37).
- Preach a liberating gospel of freedom, underscoring self-worth and self-esteem.

Through preaching and training, the church and other institutions should teach individuals and groups practices that focus on the new kingdom of Christ on Earth, which is full of equity, generosity, selflessness, reconciliation, and God's grace and compassion for the vulnerable and underprivileged. There is a need for the church to engage leaders in all sectors of society with the issue of gender equity, facilitating discussions, seminars, conferences, and workshops. The resulting change will not only bring economic, political, and social equity in society, but a spiritual quality of hope and faith in Christ. Thus, biblical equity aims at a holistic change of individuals and institutions.

Contextualizing the gospel. The goal of contextualization is to make the gospel of Christ relevant in the African context. The gospel came to Africa wrapped in the matrix of European civilization. The church in Africa has the task of unwrapping the gospel, a process that involves translating the Bible into local languages, relying on local missionaries, and using indigenous worship materials. The church has to champion and advocate that men and women were created in the image and likeness of God based on Scripture (Gen 1:27).[14]

Christ should be the Lord, the head, and the center of society. Some societies, however, are run by money, so much so, that the one with money is the boss. This phenomenon is common when electing political leaders in Africa. The rich are elected to offices of parliament while the poor never make it. According to Timothy Njoya, when Jesus is the boss, the gospel transforms and enriches the values and virtues attached to human beings and property.[15] Practicing biblical equity, as it pertains to social and economic realities or gender, is a duty and a calling for Christians.

Transforming the political and legal system. Politics and law are structures that should encourage change and maintain order along with the

---

14. "So God created mankind in his own image, in the image of God created them: male and female he created them" (Gen 1:27, NIV).

15. Njoya, *The Crisis*, 175.

church. Both institutions control power arrangements. The role of the government should be to provide policies that will ensure an equitable distribution of resources, employment, and workers' rights, including equal pay, family and medical leave, and working hours. The government shapes the gendering of social life. Government laws should also regulate the behavior of organizations and individuals. Government programs must not discriminate against either gender, and women ought to be included in the processes that bring about political change. The Constitution of Kenya enshrines affirmative action, requiring that 30 percent of every sector of employment, including politics, employ women. The reality is that the policy is hard to implement.

Waliggo, who quotes Luke 4:18–19, claims that Jesus Christ came to free all.[16] Unfortunately, in male-dominated cultures, customs, family hierarchy, society, and religion continue to undermine the God-given rights of women. Women are still victims of oppression and discriminatory laws, often holding insignificant positions in labor and society. They lack opportunities for self-actualization. Waliggo laments the fact that the immense contribution of women in the national economy still goes largely unrecognized. Furthermore, their work in the church and their role in the family as homemakers, wives, and mothers are almost never appreciated.

In spite of growing pressure within our legal framework and from world organizations, the patriarchal worldview persists. Old habits die hard. Cultural components which are embedded in a people's language, knowledge, and beliefs still influence individual behavior and social patterns. Men's authority in the family and in the public sphere, supported by economic and political structures, creates, promotes, and maintains a patriarchal status quo. The decision makers, who are mostly men, continue to make decisions that favor them, as reflected in the Kenyan parliament where men remain in the majority. Simply put, there is no equity for women without equal representation.

Culture at times overrides legal systems and influences behaviors, opportunities, and responsibilities. Political civil wars and turmoil, as well as heinous, corrupt, and fraudulent practices in Kenya, the Democratic Republic of Congo, Nigeria, Sierra Leone, Gabon, Uganda, and Burundi, to name but a few, have challenged Christian values of equity on the continent. It is the Christians who have discriminated against their brothers and sisters, murdering them on the altar of political expediency and negative ethnicity. Some of these countries have Christian majorities, and yet their impact is low—why? Because the Bible has not adequately penetrated into

---

16. Waliggo, *Struggle for Equality*.

people's lives and practices. If Christians were to choose between following political leaders and church leaders, they will choose politicians. The church worldwide continues to be compromised by secularism. But effective practices of biblical equity must reverse this trend. We need to see the Bible as an instrument of transformation affecting all spheres of the society.

RECOMMENDATIONS

Gender equity is not an event; it is a struggle and a journey that men and women must walk together in a patriarchal society. Most scholars that this study has engaged with agree that the level of equity both at the family and societal levels is still low.[17] This study has identified and recommended a participatory model that can be adapted to reduce the levels of inequality in society.

1. *Gender participatory model.* Njoya has identified organizations that have made some strides in fighting for women alone:[18]

   - United Nations Funds for Women (UNIFEM)
   - Collaborative Center for Gender and Development (CCGD)
   - Coalition of Women Against Violence (COVAN)
   - Kenya Anti-Rape organization (KAR)

   These organizations are headed by women as pioneers of the struggle in Kenya. However, gender equity needs a platform where men and women can engage openly on an equally dignified basis. This will help, first, to fight gender-based discrimination of all forms and, second, to identify roots of conflict and violence at the family and public levels, as gender inequity is embedded in our religion, law, customs and traditions, social psyche, attitudes, myths, stereotypes, and language.

   The spirit of fighting back and equipping women to take over positions in male-dominated structures, however, can be counterproductive. Gender equity efforts by women should not aim at fighting men's status in society because this will only escalate into enmity and retaliation. Njoya alludes to the fact that "Kenya and the whole

---

17. See Hendriks, *Men in the Pulpit, Women in the Pew?*, Njoya, *The Crisis*, Waliggo, *Struggle for Equality*, and Staggenborg, *Gender, Family, and Social Movements.*

18. Njoya claims that these bodies have gained a lot for women but ended up rekindling men's aggression. Men have also been forming parallel bodies to fight back. There should be organizations that can bring both to one table to reason together (4-5).

world have been hit by the upsurge of the push for gender equality and equity."[19] He recommends that men must engage women in the struggle; otherwise, a one-sided effort can be detrimental to men. When men have felt threatened by women who have asserted themselves forcefully, the result has been mistrust, violence, and even death. Instead, women who have made it to the top should sacrifice their pride to help carry the burdens of those still struggling. In a spirit of give and take, women can encourage men to dismantle patriarchal systems. There are tremendous advantages to adopting a cooperative spirit, embracing both genders, avoiding physical confrontation, and not resorting to condemnation or demonization of the opposite sex. A participatory model will help to build bridges based on Christian principles of love, equity, and peace as opposed to the cultural and secular power struggles that have been witnessed globally by women's organizations and feminist theology.

The participatory model works in marriage, children-rearing, education, family maintenance, equity in politics, and employment. Equal participation involves both genders communicating frankly, respectfully, and on an equal basis. According to participatory theory, there will be less competitiveness and violence between the genders. Both in private and in public, men and women shall each have a say, be able to dialogue, and have equal access to opportunities and resources.

2. *Paradigm shift*. We need a paradigm shift in gender socialization, decision-making, legal frameworks, and other structures that make opportunities accessible. Instead of depending on politicians and other experts, Christians should weigh their opinions against the Bible. The values of the Bible and Christ must be normative in a believer's life.

3. *Transformative leadership*. Let us advocate for transformative leadership training in church and society. Church leaders must be above reproach, well trained and skilled in church affairs, and possessed of Christ-like qualities. These are the leaders who will drive change, contextualize the gospel, translate the Scriptures, and allow the word to challenge African worldviews of inequality. Perhaps, the millennium development goals (MDGs) can be adapted, not from top to bottom but from bottom to top by governments. This has to be entrenched in national constitutions for effective implementation.

4. *Biblical equity missions and visions*. Programs that target empowering one gender over the other should change tack and avoid counterproductive

---

19. Njoya, *The Crisis*, 4.

results. A holistic, transformative approach to education, training, and Bible study classes at the grassroots, congregational level should be inclusive and focus on human rights. Practicing biblical equity in society means living a lifestyle that resonates with the teaching of Jesus Christ and the calling, first, to be humans and, second, to be male and female co-workers in the same vineyard.

5. *Mentorship and role modeling by leaders.* There are few role models in society. Biblical theology is eschatological and must prepare believers to live harmoniously and equitably here and now, as a transition to eternity. Salvation begins with the ushering in of God's equitable reign here on Earth. This doctrine should be imparted in catechism classes, songs and hymns, sacramental rituals, and church ceremonies. In contrast, inequality should be denounced as a selfish attitude that allocates limited resources and life treasures to an elite few. What will it profit a person to exclude others, gain the whole world, and miss heaven?

CONCLUSION

Examination of the practice of biblical equity in society shows that a lot has changed in Africa and globally. Advocacy for equity has been done through church structures, education, politics, and legal frameworks, among other efforts. Access to equal opportunities and equal representation in leadership, making the Gospel relevant to both men and women, and challenging cultural practices that propagate inequality can be seen as indicators for equality.

On the other hand, even though there is awareness of biblical equity practices, living a life of equity in society is still inadequate. Christians are easily swayed by secular forces and materialistic individual gains against practicing Christian virtues like love, honesty, kindness, prudence, transparency, justice, and love for our neighbor.

Gender equity is a complex enterprise and might require several decades to secure more ground. The adaptation of paradigm shifts and new models like participatory theory should help the church and relevant institutions come together to fight inequalities that still exist. While gender as a social construct has been used to justify men's dominance over women across society, for Christians, biblical teachings with gender-sensitive interpretations can offer a corrective measure and actually push for equity. There have been many positive moves by individuals, churches, and organizations toward equalizing the position of men and women in Kenya and globally through legislation and policy in all spheres of public life. A journey of several kilometers begins with one step, and Africa is on a good course toward biblical equity.

Finally, biblical equity should not impose one culture over other cultures so as to destroy another's identity and dignity. Jesus Christ broke the wall of discrimination and antagonism between men and women. The gospel of reconciliation encourages all people to engage in a life of mutual support and enrichment so that God's glory may expand and fill the earth. We need to move from theories to practice.

Chapter 15

Biblical Equity within African Families

—Judy Mbugua

INTRODUCTION:

A JOKE IS TOLD about a man and his wife that were having an argument about who should brew coffee. The husband told his wife, "You are in charge of the cooking around here, so you should do it." The wife replied, "No, you should do it, and besides, it is *in the Bible* that the man should make coffee." Astonished, the husband replied, "Oh really? Show me, if it truly says so." Without missing a beat, she flipped the pages and showed him in the Bible where it says, *"Hebrews"* (He-brews). Humorous story, indeed, but it raises this question: "What does the Bible say about practicing equity in the family?" As our homes become more equitable, the transforming effect will be felt in our society.

The quality of our actions is a direct function of the quality of our mindset. We are no better than our thoughts. Proverbs 23:7 says, "For as he thinks in his heart, so *is* he" (NKJV). As human beings, we develop our ways to function in society by the process of socialization. The dictionary defines *socialization* as "a continuing process whereby an individual acquires a personal identity and learns the norms, values, behavior, and social skills appropriate to his or her social position."[1]

1. Dictionary.com, s.v., "socialization," http://www.dictionary.com/browse/socialization?s=t, accessed on 12 March 2016.

Gender equity does not imply that women and men are *identical* or have equal competencies, interests, or genetic traits. Rather, it affirms that God designed men and women to complement and benefit one another. The practice of biblical equity within the family is reflected in the quality of relationships between spouses, parents and their children, and siblings. Mutually edifying relationships at these three levels are a product of the practice of biblical equity.

PRACTICING BIBLICAL EQUITY BETWEEN SPOUSES

The first level where individuals in the family exercise equity is between the spouses. The manner in which the husband treats his wife, especially before the children, is the strongest witness to biblical equity or the lack of it. In Africa, it is not uncommon for many a husband to speak spitefully of his wife when a crisis arises. A common example is when a child has failed an examination in school; the child is automatically referred to as *mtoto wa mama* (Mama's child). The converse is true when the child excels; the child becomes "Daddy's child." The Bible tells us how we are to relate to our spouse. We are told, "You husbands must be careful of your wives, being thoughtful of their needs and honoring them . . ." (1 Pet 3:7, TLB). Equity is expressed through honoring the spouse and being thoughtful of the spouse's needs. How a spouse honors his or her spouse will depend on the specific couple, but some practices include the following:

- Assisting in household tasks when the spouse is tired, weary, or unwell.
- Speaking words that build the spouse's self-esteem.
- Deliberately allocating time to know the other's welfare at the end of each day.

The tone of voice with which husbands address their wives reflects the value that they place on her, either as a subordinate partner in the union or as an equal partner of the grace of life. Children learn the value of women through their observation of their father's relationship with their mother.

One area that truly reflects our understanding of biblical equity is in how the husband and wife relate in their finances. We are living in a day wrought with economic challenges that threaten the very fabric of many families. Traditions and culture socialize each spouse into the expected roles in the marital union. Where economic hardship leads to men losing their jobs or earnings, tension arises. The husbands feel frustrated because their traditional role as provider is cut short. Women, on the other hand, out of a need to alleviate the pressure, are engaged in additional income generation.

Studies have shown how certain men have literally abandoned their homes due to debt or inability to provide for their wives. The expectations of both husband and wife need to be transformed by the word, even as we live in places of new demands in the current day. Traditional roles will have to give rise to new ways of adapting to change. The Proverbs 31 woman is illustrative; she is not a traditional, stay-at-home caregiver, as culture would expect. She has been given room to exercise her God-given skills and talents to equally earn for the family's well-being. In fact, the husband feels honored rather than threatened by the wife's income:

> A wife of noble character who can find? She is worth far more than rubies. Her husband has full confidence in her and lacks nothing of value. She brings him good, not harm, all the days of her life. She selects wool and flax and works with eager hands. She is like the merchant ships, bringing her food from afar. She gets up while it is still night; she provides food for her family and portions for her female servants. She considers a field and buys it; out of her earnings she plants a vineyard. (Proverbs 31:10–16, NIV)

The husband of the Proverbs 31 woman made a wise and equity-based choice to release his wife to be the best she could be. She was allowed to purchase lands and develop real estate, and in turn, he watched her make investments and bring home the returns. A traditional African family does not conform to the picture in the text. This is because the Proverbs 31 woman's role is not like the traditional woman's role expected in Africa!

What are some of the lessons we can draw from the passage? First, we learn that the virtuous woman's husband trusts the motives of the wife in her earnings. He trusts that all additional income is not a threat to his status as head of the home; rather, it complements his own efforts. The couple is a good example of an equitable relationship, where the spouses consider each other's income as an addition to the family's funding, filling up where the other lacks. By contrast, for many African families, the wife's income is considered a threat or competition to the husband's position or power. Second, we are shown further that the wife has the backing of her husband to make private investments that result in family growth. She considers a field and buys it; she even travels to seek raw materials for production. That is a sign of an emotionally secure marriage. In the African traditional context, the wife would hardly be allowed to own property, let alone land—the ultimate real estate. Consider the following quotation drawn from a survey of family ownership patterns in a village in Uganda:

> Even if a woman is given a chicken or a goat by her parents, she cannot own it. It belongs to her husband. A wife may work hard and get a chicken. If it lays eggs, they belong to the husband.[2]

When we contrast this example with the Proverbs 31 family, we realize that biblical equity affects our attitudes about property ownership within the marriage and family.

Another, often emotive, topic regarding the spouses' finances is accountability and openness. As far as many African families are concerned, the husband has right to know the wife's income and expenditure, but not vice versa. Biblical equity calls upon us to be "naked and not ashamed"—not only physically, but also financially. Intimacy or transparency as far as incomes and expenditures are concerned is still lacking among many spouses. In several African countries, a woman's husband or brother has access to her bank accounts, providing him with information on her assets—but not vice versa. Such a skewed perspective on family incomes hampers true intimacy and equity as stipulated in the Bible.

One key area that makes or breaks marriages and families is the handling of debt. In many instances, the husband's debts come to be known by the wife either when the auctioneers barge into the home unexpectedly or when creditors show up at the funeral. Yet these debts, whether intentional or not, can be managed with wisdom. Biblical equity in this area calls for the spouses to:

  a. Reveal their individual debts to each other.

  b. Make plans to consistently make payments to reduce the debt.

  c. Make needful life adjustments on monthly expenditures to reduce debt.

  d. Avoid unnecessary indulgences that increase debt.

Consider the following example of a couple whose practice of biblical equity helped them rise from the shackles of debt and save the family.

> Three years ago, my husband and I found ourselves drowning in debt—$80,000 to be exact (and that's not even counting the mortgage). Around that time, coincidentally, our church began offering a financial program. . . . We spent the last $100 from that pay period to sign up. And the rest, they say, is history (or at least, most of our debt is now history). As I write this, over the past three years, we have paid off $66,000 in personal debt. No magic, no quick fixes, no debt consolidation, or bankruptcy filing. Just persistent sacrifice. We have saved ourselves

---

2. Narayan et al., *Voices of the Poor*.

from financial destitution by making a number of simple, small changes in our lives.[3]

From the above example, we learn several lessons:

a. *Acceptance*: The husband and wife jointly owned their responsibility to resolve their debt. The couple agreed that debt had become endemic and needed to be remedied. They refused to live in denial.

b. *Information:* The husband and wife jointly enrolled in a forum to gain wisdom in managing their family debt. For many homes, only one spouse is willing to develop their knowledge base. In most cases, it is usually the wife.

c. *Adjustment*: The husband and wife jointly worked out a plan for debt-reduction, using the information learned at the finance program by the church.

Another major area that either builds or breaks a couple's unity is their handling of in-laws. Often, traditional values can override the mutual affection that was shared leading up to marriage. This is where the husband expects the wife to conform to the expectation of leaving her parents' home and being fully committed to the matrimonial home. Yet, at the same time, he conveniently overlooks the biblical injunction that states:

> "This is it! Adam exclaimed. "She is part of my own bone and flesh! Her name is 'woman' because she was taken out of a man." This explains why a man leaves his father and mother and is joined to his wife in such a way that the two become one person. (Genesis 2:23–24, TLB).

The above text tells us that not only is the wife expected to leave her background to cleave to her spouse, but the husband is also. Yet, in many homes in Africa, the converse is true. The wife is expected to relinquish her allegiance to her birth family, yet the husband maintains strong ties to his birth family. In fact, his mother can regularly come and stay at their home, expecting a high degree of hospitality and honor to be accorded to her by his wife. The mother-in-law and father-in-law can even make certain demands on the wife's behavior and child-bearing decisions. A husband may be pressured to pass on the name of his father or mother, becoming unrelenting until he gets a specific gendered child, without regard for his wife's health or life-vision. Biblical equity calls for the husband to protect his wife from harmful pressures and interference, even if it comes from his

---

3. Ramsey, "33 Proven Ways."

own birth family, and the same is expected of the wife with respect to her husband.

PRACTICING EQUITY BETWEEN PARENTS AND CHILD

Having discussed the practice of biblical equity between spouses, the second level of equity, which is practiced within the family, is between the parent and child. In African tradition, boys are valued more than girls, but this is not a healthy way of promoting harmony. Many families have endured great pain due to the husband's quest to get a male child at the expense of the wife's health. In Africa, it is common to see a family with six or more girls with the youngest child being a boy.

It is the duty of parents, however, to begin a process of transformation by validating the equality of boys and girls in their own home. Change must be slow but deliberate. The tendency for a parent to have a "favorite" child based on gender must be guarded against. It is the parents' role to instill self-worth into each child based solely on the fact that they are God's unique creation, made in his image. The parent can highlight what the psalmist illustrates, "For you created my inmost being; you knit me together in my mother's womb. I praise you because I am fearfully and wonderfully made; your works are wonderful, I know that full well" (Ps 139:13–14, NIV). It is unfathomable what wonders such an understanding would do to a child's self-image when instilled at an early age. Think about the girl who learns that she is special, irrespective of her body image! It would save many from the heartaches of adolescence, seeking an identity by conforming to the world's standards of "the petite girl." Then, instead of feeling like a victim of one's gender, each child feels whole and accepted for who they are.

Biblical equity in our relationship with our children is depicted by granting equal access to education and opportunities for growth to daughters and sons alike. The last decade or so has seen a radical shift from limiting girls from education. The campaign for girl-child education and empowerment is not a new concept in this decade.

In September 2000, 189 countries met in New York City, at the United Nations, to commit themselves to work together to build a safer, more prosperous, and equitable world. Eight specific goals were set, known as the Millennium Development Goals (MDGs). Number three on this list is "promote gender equality and empower women." It further seeks to "eliminate gender disparity in primary and secondary education preferably by 2005, and in all levels of education no later than 2015."[4] The sages of the past

---

4. United Nations, "We Can End Poverty 2015."

simply put it this way: *"Charity begins at home."* Before society can fully enjoy this transformation in establishing equity amongst boys and girls, it must begin in the family with parents spearheading this change. It is time for parents to fully embrace the truth stated in the book of Psalms: "Children are a heritage from the LORD, and the fruit of the womb is a reward" (Ps 127:3, NKJV). We will continually find the value placed on both boys and girls as co-partakers of the blessedness of the kingdom of God. Consider this illustration in Psalm 144:12: "Then our sons in their youth will be like well-nurtured plants, and our daughters will be like pillars carved to adorn a palace" (NIV). In summary, it is the duty of parents to build deliberately the esteem and self-worth of each child, irrespective of their gender, highlighting their differences as assets rather than liabilities.

We also need to note that establishing biblical equity at home is helping the girl and the boy dream big. Behind many successful women in prominent corporate or political circles is a father or mother who believed in them and encouraged them. I am one of them. My father kept prodding me to aim high and expressed how he believed in me. He told me I could make it. Here is where we find some parents prodding boys to excellence in technical and so-called "male-dominated" fields while setting the bar lower for girls. This must not be; we should equally encourage greatness and attainment in both girls and boys, seeing that neither is inferior or less endowed. Girls especially must not believe the lie that "the sciences are not for girls." One more big hurdle we must cross in establishing biblical equity at home is the notion that only the male can have access to or stewardship of the family property or assets. In the traditional setting, the girl has limited access to ownership or control of the land or properties of the family.

Finally, in the quest to transform the society, we must deal with retrogressive attitudes and practices right from home. A good example is the African practice of Female Genital Mutilation (FGM), among many communities. At the root of this is the pretext that a parent fears their daughter may lack a suitor for marriage when of age. By perpetuating a harmful practice, parents are sanctioning the devaluation of the womanhood of their female children.

FGM affects up to 140 million women globally and has such dire consequences as hemorrhage, shock, child-birth complications, fistula, and even death. Is it fair to subject the girl to trauma, simply because she is female, and males want her to fit their mold? The most unfortunate part of the story is that the mothers or aunts of the girls initiate the process of FGM in their families. However, the good news is that if the battle is won at home, it spreads to the community. If fathers will stand up for their daughters, even against the will of the community, the good will eventually overrun the evil.

Consider this inspirational report by a girl whose father stood for what is right; she now spearheads anti-FGM campaigns to help others.

> Female Genital Mutilation is the worst violation a girl can go through. But a girl is told to have it by her mother, and so the women and girls in this part of Kenya consider it normal. My parents did not want us to go through these customs, though. My father was a primary school teacher, you see, so instead he ensured that my sisters and I made it through school, despite unbelievable peer pressure. It came at a cost. My parents' decision was so radical and against tradition that when my father took this stance, his own family excluded him. We were mocked and bullied by other girls. It was very hard, but we believed it was the right thing to do. It was because of going to school that I became interested in women's rights and had the opportunity to work for ActionAid.[5]

The long and short of this account is that parents have the undeniable power to positively reverse the course of events to secure their children's future with equity.

Furthermore, the parents are to practice biblical equity, deliberately shaping their children's mindset on gender issues based on the highest standards, the word of God. No actions can be transformed by mere legislation without the corresponding transformation of mindsets. In particular, parents must be very alert to one of the most potent mind-shaping instrument within their four walls at home, the media. Almost nothing compares to the power of the long-term effects of media on young, formative minds, especially with regard to gender identity. Our childhood heroes often come from popular TV programs. Our concept of beauty and attractiveness is strongly influenced by the so called "beauties" on the screens. Worse still is the fact that the young boys learn that a man's relationship with a woman is based on physical attraction, often resulting in sex (according to soap opera storylines). Boys learn at an early age how to relate to women as "sex objects" from the pictures that have invaded our homes. Parents must fight the misrepresentation of women in popular media, and be vocal about it, even in society. Subsequently, if parents are to win the battle for their children's souls, they must censor what is allowed to shape these young, innocent minds. Four walls, high gates, security systems, and ferocious dogs cannot keep out this heinous criminal of gender inequity targeting the minds of our children. God foresaw the potential harm of messages from the media, so

---

5. Chepkemei, "Fighting FGM."

he commanded his chosen people to be proactive in shaping the children's worldview. He said so in Deuteronomy:

> But be careful. Don't let your heart be deceived so that you turn away from the LORD and serve and worship other gods. . . . So commit yourselves wholeheartedly to these words of mine. . . . Teach them to your children. Talk about them when you are at home and when you are on the road, when you are going to bed and when you are getting up. (Deuteronomy 11:16, 18–19, NLT)

Here, God warns against other influences shaping our minds and the need to implant the word in our lives as a remedy. It is a parental obligation to intervene whenever images or words that disparage the genders are aired on media. Parents should be able to talk to children and give them the correct perspective, not remaining silent and passive as the "TV Nanny" shapes the children into inequity.

Traditional cultures have served as reservoirs, preserving certain mindsets and transmitting these mindsets to successive generations. Whenever such norms contradict the truth of biblical equity, it is the parent's role to deliberately teach the right values, as they point out and refute the misrepresentations. Many inequitable values are transmitted through oral traditions such as cultural sayings, proverbs, or songs. Consider the following examples:

a. Ghanaian proverb: "Like hens, women wait for cocks to crow, announcing the arrival of daylight."

b. Kikuyu sayings: *Cia aka ciitikagio cia rara;* literally, "A woman's report or testimony is not to be believed at first, only after further confirmation at daybreak." *Aka matiri cia ndiiro no cia nyiniko;* literally, "Women have no upright words, but only crooked ones."[6]

These sayings are used to indicate that women keep no secrets and seldom tell the truth. A cursory examination of the two preceding examples shows us why equity seems elusive, even among the well-read. Learning these values at an early age, the boys act them out in their relationships with women henceforth. Consider the first example from Ghana. It depicts a woman as lacking any sense of initiative, including the ability to think for herself. What a disappointing way to depict the co-heirs and joint-regents who rule over the earth! Armed with such a mindset, what men will of their own volition seek the promotion of women to managerial and leadership positions? Culture has already taught them that women only move when

---

6. Muchiri, *Papers on Language and Culture.*

the "cock" crows. At the family level, will a husband really consider his wife's initiatives as valid when his sub-conscious mind tells him "until the cock crows, no business will ever get done"?

The two examples among the Kikuyu are even more dramatic. They state in no uncertain terms that conversation with the woman (wife, mother in-law, etc.) will yield little positive and tangible results. No wonder the husband will not take seriously the discoveries the wife makes about potential investment opportunities. To him, it is just as he was told by the elders, a mere babbling that's to be taken with a pinch of salt. So how many disasters in families could have been averted, if only the man had given regard to his wife's intuitive misgivings about a project that finally failed? Here is an example from the Bible. It is a story about Nabal and Abigail.

In the Old Testament account of David in 1 Samuel 25, we are introduced to a wealthy but mean, coarse man called Nabal and his beautiful and intelligent wife Abigail. At a moment of crisis, Abigail was able to avert impending danger by acting swiftly and wisely. Her husband, who probably imbibed negative views of women like those we have considered above, would never have paid heed to her words, so she acted independently for the welfare of their family. David is portrayed as the opposite of Nabal. By virtue of his godly heart, he listens to Abigail, believes her wisdom, and is himself rescued from acting in destructive and harmful ways. Oh, that our families had more David and Abigails!

PRACTICE OF BIBLICAL EQUITY AMONG SIBLINGS

This is the third level at which biblical equity is practiced on the home front. How siblings relate with each other is a reflection of their understanding of each other's worth and value. Nothing impacts our view of our own siblings more than the interaction we observe between our father and mother. What Dad does to Mom informs how boys treat girls. How a father speaks to his wife and what he says about her similarly shapes a boy's understanding of how to address the girls and women in his life. The children's understanding and perception of equity is shaped in different ways every day. Here are a few examples:

   a. Have we trained our sons to willingly clear dishes from the dinner table, just as their sisters do?
   b. Do our sons shirk away from domestic chores with the pretext that their sisters are around to do them?

c. Do we subconsciously program daughters to fear or shirk manual or technical tasks, believing they are supposedly "boys' jobs"?

d. Do we passively watch and say nothing when boys speak roughly to girls, supposing this to be manly, not knowing that it is modeling gender inequity?

Such are the questions to be considered in ensuring sons and daughters relate in ways that truly reflect biblical equity in the home, and thus by extension, in society.

CONCLUSION

From the foregoing discussion, we realize that biblical equity in the family is demonstrated in the quality of relationships between spouses, parents and their children, and among the children themselves. Deliberate steps need to be taken to renew our mindsets to align with a biblical understanding of equity. A mind renewed by the word of God is the key to overcoming the sexism in our socialization and to bringing family and societal transformation.

> Don't copy the behavior and customs of this world, but let God transform you into a new person by changing the way you think. Then you will learn to know God's will for you, which is good and pleasing and perfect. (Romans 12:2, NLT)

Conclusion

—Diphus C. Chemorion and KeumJu Jewel Hyun

INTRODUCTION

IMPLICIT IN THE CULTURAL mandate that God gave humanity at the time of Creation is the call to leadership. Beginning with Adam and Eve, God purposed that leadership be a shared responsibility between men and women. God entrusted the first human couple, and by extension their descendants, with the stewardship of God's creation. Having been created in the image and likeness of God, both men and women are called to exercise leadership in not only managing the wildlife and natural resources that God put at their disposal but also their own human affairs as part of God's creation.

In God's leadership design, men and women stand equal in their stewardship roles. However, in the course of history, after the fall of man into sin, the equity that God instituted was replaced by a hierarchical model derived from Israel's cultural milieu, and the resulting leadership structure made the position of women lower than that of men. The good news is that Jesus restored the original paradigm of leadership that God instituted. Christians are therefore called upon to promote equity in leadership as part of the missionary mandate that Christ gave to his disciples (Matt 28:18–19).

The authors of this book have explored the phenomenon of equity in leadership in the African context from various dimensions, such as African culture and traditional religion, church tradition, and biblical interpretation, as well as contemporary socio-economic and political realities in Africa. The issues presented can be summarized into four main points—namely, obstacles, opportunities, success stories, and the way forward.

OBSTACLES TO EQUITY IN LEADERSHIP

The subject of "Equity in Leadership" is often discussed in contemporary public discourse as a human rights issue. Advocates of gender equity argue that both men and women should have fair access to a full range of opportunities to live to their full potential as human beings. Advocacy for women's rights has received more publicity in the quest for equity because historically the female gender is the most disadvantaged when there is inequality.

Among the factors that have been noted as major obstacles to the realization of equity in leadership are African cultural beliefs and practices. Cultural constructions of gender continue to paint a negative image of the place of women in society. Traditionally, in many African communities, just as in many other parts of the world, power and authority is ascribed to men. The dominance of men over women is exacerbated through folktales, proverbs, taboos, and etiological myths. Children are socialized from the earliest stages of their life to know that the task of leadership belongs to men. Consequently, men hold leadership positions both at family and community levels. Any woman who aspires to leadership positions held by men is usually viewed with much suspicion and is only affirmed after extraordinary performance.

Apart from the effects of negative cultural expectations, women who are interested in public leadership positions also suffer from a hostile sociopolitical environment that serves the interests of patriarchy. This is evident especially in the arena of competitive politics. It is generally thought that politics is a dirty game and not the best career for good women. Testimonies of current female politicians in Kenya reveal that women have to work very hard before they can be elected. Male counterparts will do everything to stop women from clinching elective positions. Most men find it very humiliating to concede defeat to a woman. Therefore, whenever women persist in their campaigns, some men resort to propaganda that taints the morals of women. In other situations, physical confrontation and unwarranted name-calling scare women off from participating in politics. The hostile sociopolitical environment that is experienced in Kenya is also commonly found in other African countries as well as other continents.

Another major factor that works against equity in leadership is misinterpretation of Scripture. In many African Christian denominations, just like those in America, women are barred from performing certain key roles in the church. The most common leadership positions that are not easily granted to women are the positions of church elder and ordained minister. The exclusion of women from the ministry of word and sacrament is often supported by pointing to the first few chapters of Genesis and some sections of the Pauline epistles. But, as it has been pointed out in this book, inequity in leadership does not have a biblical basis. Neither Moses nor Paul advocates for male dominance. On the contrary, when read without cultural bias, the book of Genesis supports the view that men and women should be given equal opportunities in exercising the leadership mandate. Similarly, Paul's commentary on women is often taken out of context to support inequity.

Yet another obstacle to equity in leadership is church tradition in Africa, especially within the mainline churches. Some of the practices carried out as part of church tradition reflect the patriarchal and non-biblical residues of mission churches. In fact, the resistance against women's participation in the ministry of word and sacrament is largely derived from the colonial tendencies of the missionary mother churches.

OPPORTUNITIES FOR EQUITY IN LEADERSHIP

In recent years, many opportunities for promoting equity in leadership have been created. A few examples will suffice to illustrate this point. First, we should note that several African countries have come up with progressive constitutions or policies that promote inclusive leadership. In many democracies, gender equity has been enshrined in the constitution as a way of safeguarding against discrimination of either gender. For example, in the current constitution of Kenya, issues of gender equity are highlighted under the bill of rights in chapter four.[1] In this constitution, women and men are accorded the right to equal treatment, including the right to equal opportunities in political, economic, cultural, and social spheres; all forms of discrimination, including those based on gender considerations, are forbidden. In order to ensure that men and women are included in leadership, the constitution provides for affirmative action which requires that no more than two thirds of members of elective or appointive bodies shall be of the same gender.

The other opportunity that now exists for equity in leadership is the campaign for education of the girl child. In the ancient world, women were considered little more than property. They had no access to education, and their participation in public affairs was very limited. But through the efforts of many pressure groups advocating for the dignity and equality of all human beings, significant progress has been made over the years in restoring the rights of women. Access to education enables women to acquire skills and abilities for doing work that would otherwise be left to men alone on account of their education.

1. *The Constitution*, 7.

SUCCESS STORIES OF EQUITY IN LEADERSHIP

Although the fight for equity in leadership is far from over, there are a number of successes that need to be celebrated. Contrary to cultural dictates that require women to serve men, there are some practical situations where men have been seen at work serving women as they discuss important matters. The number of women who occupy top leadership positions has increased over the last two decades. A good example is the case of Liberia where the current head of state is a woman. The authors of this book have also presented case studies of exemplary women who overcame all obstacles to rise to high positions.

With the constant campaigns to promote equity in leadership, a number of women have become conscious of the need to assert their rights in claiming leadership positions like their male counterparts. More and more women are questioning why women cannot be pastors or leaders of churches. They are also questioning why they should be regarded as less than men. These questions have opened up space for more meaningful engagement in creating awareness for the need to have equity in leadership.

Apart from the works of various pressure groups playing the advocacy role, some organizations have invested in offering transformative education for women leaders with tremendous success. A good example is Matthew 28 Ministries, which has been training women leaders in Kenya since 2006.

The struggle for women's ordination is ongoing in certain denominations. However, through the struggle for equity in church leadership, a number of churches now allow women to be ordained. In the Anglican Church of Kenya, Rev. Lucia Okuthe was the first female clergy to be ordained in 1983. Since then, many other women have been ordained. Other churches in Africa that allow women's ordination include the Reformed Church of Zimbabwe, The Presbyterian Church of Nigeria, and a section of the African Instituted Churches in West Africa, the most prominent of which is the Aladura Church (Church of the Lord). It is, however, notable that although mainline denominations have allowed ordination of women, none of them is headed by a woman.

THE WAY FORWARD FOR EQUITY LEADERSHIP AND MINISTRY IN AFRICA

The quest for equity in leadership is a fight for justice, which must go on until victory is achieved. Several goals must be pursued for total success to be realized. Here we identify four key targets. The first one concerns culture.

As we have noted in our discussions above, structures that bar women from entering into leadership positions are socially constructed through various aspects of culture. In order to reverse this process, there is a need to deconstruct cultural ideas and practices that promote inequality. This can be done by maximizing on progressive aspects of culture that encourage equity in leadership.

Secondly, the struggle for equity needs to start at the family level. In order for biblical equity to be experienced in society, it must first be felt within the family. It needs to be seen in the quality of relationships between family members. It is incumbent upon every Christian family to exercise equity. The husband and the wife must work together as equals and not on the basis of a master-servant relationship.

Thirdly, church leaders and senior pastors need to promote that gender equity be practiced in all aspects of ministry in advancing the kingdom. They need to prioritize biblical teaching on equity and intentionally include it in the church agenda. To do so requires diligence and continual effort in bringing greater awareness of the patriarchal influences and structures that exacerbate equality. Church leaders need to recognize that inequality is a hindrance to the spread of the gospel to every corner of Africa and the world.

Finally, as we have noted throughout this book, the Bible upholds the view that both male and female should hold equal leadership positions in the family, church, and society. There is need to reread and retell Bible stories with a correct interpretation rather than just accepting what has been taught traditionally. Since Jesus restored the leadership structure that was lost at the Fall, it is important that women are given back their leadership role and be allowed to work utilizing their God-given gifts side by side with their male counterparts in any sphere of leadership. By doing so, both men's and women's leadership positions can be appreciated equally and can more effectively fulfill the Great Commission of making disciples of all nations.

To God be the glory!

Bibliography

Adegbite, D. D., et al., eds. *Biblical Studies and Feminism in the African Context: In Honor of the Late Dr. Dorcas Olubanke Akintunde.* Ibadan, Nigeria: NABIS Western Zone, 2012.

Adegoke, Emmanuel. *Celestial Church of Christ: Altar—The Throne of God on Earth.* Ilorin, Nigeria, 2015.

Adeyemo, Tokunboh. *Africa Bible Commentary.* Grand Rapids, MI: Zondervan, 2006.

Akangbe, M. Fehintola. "The Role of Women in the Ministry of Jesus." In *Biblical Studies and Women Issues in Africa: Biblical Studies Series Number 1*, edited by S.O. Abogunrin et al., 113–41. Ibadan, Nigeria: Nigerian Association for Biblical Studies, 2003.

Akintunde, Dorcas O. *The Ministry of Women in Lucan Narratives: A Model for Aladura Churches in Nigeria.* Ibadan, Nigeria: The African Association for the Study of Religion, 2004.

———."No Longer Be Silent: A Critique of Women's Silence in Christ Apostolic Church, Nigeria." In *African Culture and the Quest for Women's Rights*, edited by Dorcas Olu Akintunde, 85–102. Ibadan, Nigeria: Sefer, 2001.

Alder, George. "Give Thanks." In *Redemption and Responsibility: A Few Hours with George Alder*, edited by Mick Bollenbaugh and Garry Tiffin. Eugene, OR: Wipf & Stock, 2000.

Amolo, Hope. "The Role of Women in the New Testament." In *Biblical Studies and Women Issues in Africa: Biblical Studies Series Number 1*, edited by S.O. Abogunrin et al., 113–41. Ibadan, Nigeria: Nigerian Association for Biblical Studies, 2003.

Anglican Church of Kenya. *The Anglican Church of Kenya Constitution.* Nairobi, Kenya: The Anglican Church of Kenya and Uzima, 2002.

Arumugam, Stanley. "An Evaluation of the Theological Message of Paul as It Relates to Gender Inclusivity." In *NTS421: New Testament 4A*. Rivonia: South African Theological Seminary, 2013.

Audéoud, Martine. "Jesus' Approach to Women." In *Faith and Gender Equity: Lesson Plans across the College Curriculum*, edited by C. Jeanne Orjala Serrão and Susie Cunningham Stanley. Eugene, OR: Wipf & Stock, 2007.

Auma-Osolo, Agola. *Why Leaders Fail and Plunge the Innocent into a Sea of Agonies.* Bloomington, IN: Trafford, 2013.

Ayandokun, Esther O. and Ojo, Jonathan Ola. "Let Women Be Silent: Re-Reading 1 Corinthians 14:34–35 in the African Context." In *Biblical Studies and Feminism in* the *African Context: In Honor of the Late Dr. Dorcas Olubanke Akintunde*, edited by D. D. Adegbite et al., 302–19. Ibadan, Nigeria: NABIS Western Zone, 2012.

Badejo, W. A. "Ordination of Woman and Leadership Positions in the Church." In *Woman on the Pulpit*, edited by Simon Itodo Abbas, 54–60. Lagos, Nigeria: Soldiers of the Cross, 2004.

Bailey, Kenneth E. *Paul Through Mediterranean Eyes: Cultural Studies in 1 Corinthians*. Downers Grove, IL: IVP Academic, 2011.

Bauer, Walter, et al., eds. *A Greek-English Lexicon of the New Testament and Other Early Christian Literature*. Chicago, IL: University of Chicago Press, 1979.

Barnes, Grace, and Gwen Dewey. *WILD: Women in Leadership Development*. Harmon Digital, 2013.

Barra, Giovanni. *1,000 Kikuyu Proverbs*. 2nd ed. London: Macmillan, 1960.

Barton, Ruth Haley. *Equal to the Task: Men and Women in Partnership*. Downers Grove, IL: InterVarsity, 1998.

Baskin, Judith Reesa. *Midrashic Women: Formations of the Feminine in Rabbinic Literature*. Hanover, NH: Brandeis University Press, 2002.

Bauckham, Richard. *Gospel Women: Studies of the Named Women in the Gospels*. Grand Rapids, MI: Eerdmans, 2002.

Belleville, Linda L. "Teaching and Usurping Authority: 1 Timothy 2:11–15." In *Discovering Biblical Equality: Complementarity without Hierarchy*, edited by Ronald W. Pierce et al., 205–23. Downers Grove, IL: InterVarsity, 2005.

———. "Women Leaders in the Bible." In *Discovering Biblical Equality: Complementarity without Hierarchy*, edited by Ronald W. Pierce et al., 110–25. Downers Grove, IL: InterVarsity, 2004.

———. *Women Leaders and the Church: Three Crucial Questions*. Grand Rapids, MI: Baker, 2000.

Bellis, Alice Ogden. *Helpmates, Harlots, Heroes: Women's Stories in the Hebrew Bible*. Louisville, KY: Westminster/John Knox, 1994.

Beyer, Engelbert. *New Christian Movements in West Africa*. Ibadan, Nigeria: Sefer, 1997.

Bilezikian, Gilbert. *Beyond Sex Roles: What the Bible Says about a Woman's Place in Church and Family*. Grand Rapids, MI: Baker Academic, 2006.

Billing, Pelle. "Defining Gender Equality"; http:/www.pellebilling com/2009/defining gender equality/.

Bristow, John Temple. *What Paul Really Said about Women: An Apostle's Liberating Views on Equality in Marriage, Leadership, and Love*. San Francisco, CA: HarperSanFrancisco, 1991.

Bromiley, Geoffrey W. *The International Standard Bible Encyclopedia*. Grand Rapids, MI: Eerdmans, 1988.

Bronner, Leila Leah. *From Eve to Esther: Rabbinic Reconstructions of Biblical Women*. Louisville, KY: Westminster/John Knox, 1994.

Bruce, Debra Fulghum, and Ellen Oldacre. *Celebrate the Journey: Discovering God's Vision for Your Life*. St. Louis, MO: Concordia, 2000.

Buchan, James. *The Expendable Mary Slessor*. New York, NY: Seabury, 1981.

Cagnolo, C. *The Akikuyu, Their Customs, Traditions and Folklore*. Nyeri, Kenya: The Mission Printing School, 1933.

Chebet, Dorcas, and Beatrice Cherop. "Gender and Poverty: Rereading Proverbs 3 in Pursuit of Socio-Economic Justice for Women in the Reformed Church of East

Africa." In *Living with Dignity: African Perspectives on Gender Equality*, edited by Elna Mouton et al., 193–218. Stellenbosch: Sun, 2015.
Chemorion, Diphus Chosefu. *Introduction to Christian Worldview: Origins, Meaning, and Perspectives.* Nairobi, Kenya: Nairobi Academic, 2014.
———. "Retelling the Story of Job in Sabaot Worldview." *Journal of Mother Tongue Biblical Hermeneutics* 1.1 (2015) 47–77.
Chepkemei, Dinah. "Fighting FGM in Kenya, a Story of Change"; https://www.actionaid.org.uk/blog/voices/2015/02/03/fgm-a-story-of-change.
Cherubim and Seraphim Movement Church Worldwide Draft Constitution. Kaduna: Cherubim, 2014.
Christian, Carol, and Gladys Plummer. *God and One Redhead: Mary Slessor of Calabar.* London: Hodder & Stoughton, 1970.
"Christianity and Women's Rights." *Universal Declaration of Human Rights;* http://www.heretication.info/_womensrights.html.
Claassens, Juliana M. "Teaching Gender at Stellenbosch University." In *Men in the Pulpit, Women in the Pew?: Addressing Gender Inequality in Africa*, edited by H. Jurgens Hendriks et al., 147–58. Stellenbosch: Sun, 2012.
Cohen, Abraham. *Everyman's Talmud.* New York, NY: Schocken, 1975.
The Constitution of the Republic of Kenya. Nairobi, Kenya: The National Council for Law Reporting with the Authority of the Attorney General, 2010. https://www.kenyaembassy.com/pdfs/the%20constitution%20of%20kenya.pdf.
Cottrell, Jack W. *Gender Roles and the Bible: Creation, the Fall, and Redemption: A Critique of Feminist Biblical Interpretation.* Joplin, MO: College, 1994.
Craig, Kenneth M. *Reading Esther: A Case for the Literary Carnivalesque.* Louisville, KY: Westminster/John Knox, 1995.
Cranny, Anne, et al., eds. *Gender Studies, Terms and Debates.* New York, NY: Palgrave, 2003.
Crawford, Janet, and Michael Kinnamon, eds. *In God's Image: Reflections on Identity, Human Wholeness, and the Authority of Scripture.* Geneva: World Council of Churches, 1983.
Davis, Laura A. *Emotional Intelligence/Personal Growth* (2014); http://www.lauraadavis.com/personal-growth.html.
Diocese of Mount Kenya East. *The Diocese of Mount Kenya East Marches On: Fifth Ordinary Session of the Synod.* Nairobi, Kenya: Diocese of Mr. Kenya East, 1983.
Domestic Violence Task Force. *The Church and Domestic Violence. A Training Package for Clergy and Pastoral Workers. A Joint Project of the Anglican Church and Edith Cowan University.* Perth: Anglican Church Office, 1993.
Du Bres, Guido. *Doctrinal Standards Consisting of the Belgic Confession, the Heidelberg Catechism, and the Canon on Dort*, 1561.
Elliott, Paul M. "'Rightly Dividing the Word of Truth'—What Does It Mean?" http://www.teachingtheword.org/apps/articles/?articleid=66757&columnid=6211.
Epp, Eldon Jay. *Junia: The First Woman Apostle.* Minneapolis: Fortress, 2005.
Evans, Mary J. *Woman in the Bible: An Overview of All the Crucial Passages on Women's Roles.* Downers Grove, IL: InterVarsity, 1984.
Fapohunda, Tinu M. "Women Emancipation for Sustainable Development in Nigeria: Realities and Challenges." *International Journal of Development Studies* 4.4 (2009) 21.

Fielder, Klaus. "Gender Equality in the New Testament: The Care of St. Paul." *Malawi Journal of Biblical Studies* (2003) 19–36.
Fubara-Manuel, Jessie. *Giver of Life, Hear Our Cries!* Geneva: WCC, 2014.
Gill, Deborah Menken. "The Liberated Woman." *Paraclete* 29.2 (1995) 1–9.
Ginzberg, Louis. *The Legend of the Jews*, 7 vols. Philadelphia, PA: Jewish Publication Society of America, 1937.
Goddard, Lis, and Clare Hendry. *The Gender Agenda: Discovering God's Plan for Church Leadership*. Nottingham: InterVarsity, 2010.
Gondwe, Hawkins Chepah Tom. "The Possible Influence of the Crucial Pauline Texts on the Role of Women in the Nkhoma Synod of the Church of Central Africa Presbyterian." MA diss., University of South Africa, 2009.
González-Tejera, Awilda. "Hispanic America—Biblical Equality and United States Latino Churches." *Global Voices on Biblical Equality: Women and Men Serving Together in the Church*, edited by Aída Besançon Spencer et al., 130–49. Eugene, OR: Wipf & Stock, 2008.
Greenleaf, Robert K. *Servant Leadership: A Journey into the Nature of Legitimate Power and Greatness*. New York, NY: Paulist, 1977.
Grenz, Stanley J., and Denise Muir Kjesbo. *Women in the Church: A Biblical Theology of Women in Ministry*. Downers Grove, IL: InterVarsity, 1995.
Griffiths, Valerie. "Romans." In *The IVP Women's Bible Commentary*, edited by Catherine Clark Kroeger and Mary J. Evans. 628–45. Downers Grove, IL: InterVarsity, 2002.
Groothuis, Rebecca. *Good News for Women: A Biblical Picture of Gender Equality*. Grand Rapids, MI: Baker, 1997.
———. "Logical and Theological Problems with Gender Hierarchy." *Priscilla Papers* 14.2 (2000) 3–5.
Hamilton, Laura, et al. "Marital Name Change as a Window into Gender Attitudes." *Gender and Society* 25.2 (April 2011) 145–75.
Hardage, Jeanette. "The Legacy of Mary Slessor, 1848 to 1915." *The International Bulletin of Missionary Research* 6.24 (2002) 114; http://www.dacb.org/stories/nigeria/slessor_mary.html.
Harrison, R. K. *Introduction to the Old Testament*. London: Tyndale, 1969.
Hart, Clive. *Treatise on the Question Do Women Have Souls and Are They Human Beings?: Disputatio Nova: With Translation, Commentary, and Appendices*. Lewiston, NY: Edwin Mellen, 2004; http://mellenpress.com/mellenpress.cfm?bookid=5707&pc=9.
Hassan, Riffat. "Feminism in Islam." In *Feminism and World Religions*, edited by Arvind Sharma and Katherine K. Young, 261–69. Albany, NY: State University of New York Press, 1999.
———. "The Issue of Women-Men Equality in the Islamic Tradition." In *Women and Men's Liberation: Testimonies of Spirit*, edited by Leonard Grob et al., 35–60. New York, NY: Greenwood, 1991.
Héger, Paul. *Women in the Bible, Qumran and Early Rabbinic Literature: Their Status and Role*. Leiden: Brill, 2014.
Hertig, Young Lee. "Introduction: The Yin and Yang Concept." In *Mirrored Reflections: Reframing Biblical Characters*, eds. Young Lee Hertig and Chloe Sun, xv–xxii. Eugene, OR: Wipf & Stock, 2010.
Holbert, John C. *Telling the Whole Story: Reading and Preaching Old Testament Stories*. Eugene, OR: Cascade, 2013.

House, W. "The Speaking of Women and the Prohibition of the Law." *Bibliotheca Sacra* (July–Sept 1988) 301–18.
Hubner, Jamin. "Translating *Authenteo* in 1 Timothy 2:12." *Priscilla Papers* 29.2 (Spring 2015) 19.
Hurley, J. B. "Did Paul Require Veils or the Silence of Women?" *War Time Journals* 35 (1972–73) 19–22.
Hyun, KeumJu. "Mobilizing Women to Follow Jesus Christ and Become Disciple-Makers: A Theology and Practice for Effective Ministry to Women in the 21st-Century Church." DMin diss., Gordon-Conwell Theological Seminary, 2005.
Iddrisou, Betty M. "10 Things about African Women's Leadership" (2012); http://www.pambazuka.net/en/category.php/features/83528.
Ilori, F. D. "Time Allocation of Working Mothers and Its Implication for Fertility in Nigeria." In *A Paper Presented at the International Conference on Research and Teaching Related to Women*. Montreal: Concordia University, 1982.
Jaini, Padmanabh S. *Gender and Salvation: Jaina Debates on the Spiritual Liberation of Women*. Berkeley, CA: University of California Press, 1991.
Jegede, Gabriel Gbenga. "Women and Church Leadership in Yorubaland: The Aladura Experience." *International Journal of Humanities and Social Science* 2.1 (2012).
The Journal for Biblical Manhood and Womanhood: By Women for Women. Louisville, KY: The Council on Biblical Manhood and Womanhood, 2012.
Martyr, Justin. *The First Apology*, edited by John Kaye. Edinburgh: J. Grant, 1912.
Kaimenyi, Catherine, et al. "An Analysis of Affirmative Action: The Two-Thirds Gender Rule in Kenya." *International Journal of Business, Humanities, and Technology* 3.6 (2013) 91–97.
Kalisa, Chantal. *Violence in Francophone African and Caribbean Women's Literature*. Lincoln, NE: University of Nebraska Press, 2009.
Kalu, Ogbu U. *A Century and Half of Presbyterian Witness in Nigeria*. Lagos, Nigeria: Ida-Ivory, 1996.
Kamau, Nyokabi. *Researching AIDS, Sexuality and Gender: Case Studies of Women in Kenyan Universities*. 2nd ed. Limuru, Kenya: Zapf Chancery, 2013.
Kanogo, Tabitha. "Mission Impact on Women in Colonial Kenya." In *Women and Missions: Past and Present Anthropological and Historical Perceptions*, edited by Fiona Bowie et al., 165–86. Oxford: Berg, 1993.
Kasomo, Daniel. "The Role of Women in the Church in Africa." *International Journal of Sociology and Anthropology* 2.6 (2010) 126–39.
Katumbi, C. H. "The Bible, Gender Equality and Teaching Theology in Malawi." In *Men in the Pulpit, Women in the Pew?: Addressing Gender Inequality in Africa*, edited by H. Jurgens Hendriks et al., 104–13. Stellenbosch: Sun, 2012.
Keener, Craig S. *Paul, Women and Wives: Marriage and Women's Ministry in the Letters of Paul*. Peabody, MA: Hendrickson, 1992.
———. *Romans: A New Covenant Commentary*. Eugene, OR: Cascade, 2009.
Keil, Carl F., and Franz Delitzsch. *Commentary on the Old Testament, Volume I, The Pentateuch*. Grand Rapids: MI: Eerdmans, 1986.
Kellerman, Barbara. "Foreword." In *Women as Global Leaders*, edited by Faith Wambura Ngunjiri and Susan R. Madsen. Charlotte, NC: Information Age, 2015.
Kerr, Lauran A. "Women in the Emerging Church." *Reformation Revival Journal* 14.3 (2005) 144.

King, Mignon Ariel, ed. *Extra MoJo! An Anthology of Poetry and Memoir by Black and African-American Women*. New England: Hidden Charm, 2013.

King, Ursula. "Introduction." In *Feminist Theology from the Third World*, edited by Ursula King, 1–20. New York, NY: Orbis, 1994.

Kongo, Kilunga Fatuma. *Femmes et Paix dans la Ville de Bukavu de 1996 à 2006*. Kinshasa, DRC: EDUPC, 2009.

Krajewski, Lorraine A. and Lisa A. Burke. "A Brief Commentary on Gender Inequality Theory—A Sociological Perspective." *Gender Behaviour* 2 (2004).

Kroeger, Richard Clark, and Catherine Clark Kroeger. *I Suffer Not a Woman: Rethinking 1 Timothy 2:11–15 in Light of Ancient Evidence*. Grand Rapids, MI: Baker, 1992.

———. "Pandemonium and Silence in Corinth"; http://www.bibliotecapleyades.net/sumer_anunnaki/reptiles/reptiles11.htm.

LaCelle-Peterson, Kristina. *Liberating Tradition: Women's Identity and Vocation in Christian Perspective*. Grand Rapids, MI: Baker Academic, 2008.

Lambdin, Thomas O. *Introduction to Biblical Hebrew*. London: Longman and Todd, 1973.

Leslie, Julia. "Some Traditional Indian Views on Menstruation and Female Sexuality." In *Sexual Knowledge, Sexual Science: The History of Attitudes to Sexuality*, edited by Roy Porter and Mikuláš Teich, 70–80. Cambridge, Cambridge University Press, 1994.

Lidell, Henry, and Robert Scott, eds. *Greek-English Lexicon*. Oxford: Oxford University Press, 1987.

Liu, Jonathan C. "Developing a Pastoral Leadership Guide in Light of the Biblical Teachings and the Contemporary Management Concepts." PhD diss., Liberty Baptist Theological Seminary, 1995; http://digitalcommons.liberty.edu/cgi/viewcontent.cgi?article=1260&context=doctoral.

Lockyer, Herbert. *All the Women of the Bible*. Grand Rapids, MI: Zondervan, 1992.

Longenecker, Richard N. *New Testament Social Ethics for Today*. Grand Rapids, MI: Eerdmans, 1984.

Lyimo-Mbowe, Hoyce Jacob. *Feminist Expositions of the Old Testament in Africa (Tanzania) in the Context of the Office Held by Deborah in Judges 4 and 5*. Berlin: Logos, 2015.

MacDonald, Margaret Y. *The Pauline Churches: A Socio-Historical Study of Institutionalization in the Pauline and Deutero-Pauline Writings*. Cambridge: Cambridge University Press, 1988.

Makanjuola, Mepaiyeda Solomon. "Assessing the Hypotheses against Women Leadership in African Christianity." *Cross-Cultural Communication* 9.4 (2013) 71–78; http://www.cscanada.net/index.php/ccc/article/viewFile/j.ccc.1923670020130904.3258/5069

Matthews, Ed. "Relationship between the Gospel and Culture: The Continuing Debate." *Journal of Applied Missiology* 1.2 (1990).

Mbiti, John S. *African Religions and Philosophy*. Repr. London: Heinemann, 1985.

———. *Concepts of God in Africa*. London: S.P.C.K., 1970.

McCabe, Elizabeth A. "A Reexamination of Phoebe as a *Diakonos* and *Prostatis*: Exposing the Inaccuracies of English Translations." In *Women in the Biblical World*, edited by Elizabeth A. McCabe, 99–116. Lanham, MD: University Press of America, 2009.

Mead, Loren B. *More Than Numbers: The Ways Churches Grow*. Washington, DC: Alban Institute, 1993.

Meyer, Marvin W. *The Gospels of the Marginalized: The Redemption of Doubting Thomas, Mary Magdalene, and Judas Iscariot in Early Christian Literature*. Eugene, OR: Cascade, 2012.

Miller, C. John. *The Heart of a Servant Leader: Letters from Jack Miller*, edited by Barbara Miller Juliani. Phillipsburg, NJ: P & R, 2004.

Miller, Susan. *Women in Mark's Gospel*. New York, NY: T & T Clark, 2004.

Mishnah Ketubot 7. Sefaria; http://www.sefaria.org/Mishnah_Ketubot.7.6?lang=en&layout=lines&sidebarLang=all.

Moltmann, Jurgen. "Israel's No: Jews and Jesus in an Unredeemed World"; http://www.religion-online.org/showarticle.asp?title=149.

Muchiri, Mary Nyambura. *Papers on Language and Culture: An African Perspective*. Bloomington, IN: AuthorHouse, 2009.

Mudimeli, Lufuluvhi Maria. "The Impact of Religious and Cultural Discourses on the Leadership Development of Women in the Ministry: A Vhusadzi (Womanhood) Perspective." PhD diss., University of South Africa, 2011.

Mugabe, Henry J. "Salvation from an African Perspective." *Indian Journal of Theology* 36.1 (1994) 31–42.

Mugambi, J. N. K. "The Future of the Church and the Church of the Future." In *The Church of Africa: Towards a Theology of Reconstruction*, edited by Jose B. Chipenda et al. Nairobi, Kenya: All Africa Conference of Churches, 1991.

Musekura, Célestin. "African Women in Public Service: Cases for Liberia, Malawi, and Rwanda." PA 6345: Human Resource Management, University of Texas at Dallas, 2011.

Mwaniki, Lydia M. "God's Image or Man's Glory?: A Kenyan Postcolonial Feminist Reading of 1 Corinthians 11:1–16." PhD diss., University of Kwazulu Natal, 2011.

———. "The Impact of the Church on the Development of the Identity of an African Christian Woman: A Case Study of the Anglican Church of Kenya, Diocese of Kirinyaga, 1910–1999." MA diss., University of Natal, Pietermaritzburg, 2000.

Narayan, Deepa, et al. *Voices of the Poor: Can Anyone Hear Us?* New York, NY: Oxford University Press, 2000.

NASSCOM Mercer. "Gender Inclusivity in India: Building Empowered Organizations." New Delhi: NASSCOM International Youth Centre. Gurgaon: Mercer Consulting (India) Pvt. Ltd., 2009; http://survey.nasscom.in/sites/default/files/upload/61812/NASSCOM_Mercer_Gender_Inclusivity_Report.pdf.

Njogu, Kimani, and Elizabeth Orchardson-Mazrui. "Gender Inequality and Women's Rights in the Great Lakes: Can Culture Contribute to Women's Empowerment?"; http://www.unesco.org/new/fileadmin/MULTIMEDIA/HQ/SHS/pdf/Culture-Womens-Empowerment.pdf.

Ngunjiri, Faith Wambura, and E. Ann Christo-Baker. "Breaking the Stained Glass Ceiling: African Women's Leadership in Religious Organizations." *The Journal of Pan African Studies* 5.2 (2012).

Ngunjiri, Faith Mambura. "Lessons in Spiritual Leadership from Kenyan Women." *Journal of Educational Administration* (2010) 755–68; http://www.researchgate.net/profile/Faith_Ngunjiri/publication/254188607_Lessons_in_spiritual_leadership_from_Kenyan_women/links/55096d9c0cf2d7a2812cb229.pdf.

Njoya, Timothy. *The Crisis of Explosive Masculinity*. Nairobi, Kenya: Men for the Equality of Men and Women, 2008.

Nolan, Michael. "Do Women Have Souls? The Story of Three Myths"; http://www.churchinhistory.org/pages/booklets/women-souls-1.htm.

Oduntaon, Mary E. "Ordination of Woman as a Pastor." *Woman on the Pulpit*, edited by Simon Itodo Abbas, 49–51. Lagos, Nigeria: Soldiers of the Cross, 2004.

Oduyoye, Mercy Amba. "Culture and the Quest for Women's Rights." In *African Culture and the Quest for Women's Rights*, edited by Dorcas Olu Akintunde, 1–10. Ibadan, Nigeria: Sefer, 2001.

Ogunewu, Leke. "Revitalizing Theological Education for Efficient Ministerial Training in the Aladura Christian Tradition in Nigeria." In *Indigenization of the Church in Africa: The Nigerian Situation—Essays in Honor of Rev. Dr. E. A. Bamigboye*, edited by Adelani A. Akande et al., 119–50. Ibadan, Nigeria: Baptist, 2012.

Okore, Mgbeke George. *Women in the Church Ministry*. Lagos, Nigeria: JONAI, 2005.

Okoyeuzu, Chinwe R., et al. "Shaping the Nigerian Economy: The Role of Women." *Acta Universitatis Danubius* 8.4 (2012) 15–24.

Okure, Teresa. "Reading from this Place: Some Problems and Prospects." In *Reading from This Place: Social Location and Biblical Interpretation in Global Perspective*, edited by Fernando F. Segovia and Mary Ann Tolbert, 52–66. Minneapolis, MN: Fortress, 1995.

Olufade, Adenike O. "Nigerian Women, Politics and the National Identity Question." *African Educational Research Journal* 1.3 (2013) 161–70.

Omondi, Francis. "Making of Women Bishops in Kenya"; http://www.thinkinganglicans.org.uk/archives/006829.html.

Oshitelu, Gideon A. *History of the Aladura (Independent) Churches 1918–1940: An Interpretation*. Ibadan, Nigeria: Hope, 2007.

Palmer, Phoebe. *The Promise of the Father*; http://wesley.nnu.edu/wesleyctr/books/2401-2500/HDM2485.pdf..

Pausanias, *Description of Greece*, edited by W. H. S. Jones et al. Cambridge, MA: Harvard University Press, 1966–75.

Payne, Philip B. *Man and Woman, One in Christ: An Exegetical and Theological Study of Paul's Letters*. Grand Rapids, MI: Zondervan, 2009.

Philostratus the Elder. *Imagines*. Cambridge, MA: Harvard University Press, 1931.

Phiri, Isabel Apawo. *Women, Presbyterianism, and Patriarchy: Religious Experience of Chewa Women in Central Malawi*. Zomba, Malawi: Kachere Series, 2007.

Pitts, Lovia Joann. *Queen Vashti: Since When Does a Queen Wear Her Royal Crown to a Wild Party?* Bloomington, IN: AuthorHouse, 2012.

Pobee, John S. "Biblical Studies and Feminism in the African Context." In *Biblical Studies and Feminism in the African Context: In Honor of the Late Dr. Dorcas Olubanke Akintunde*, edited by D. D. Adegbite et al., 21–31. Ibadan, Nigeria: NABIS Western Zone, 2012.

Presley, Cora Ann. *Kikuyu Women, the Mau Mau Rebellion, and Social Change in Kenya*. Boulder, CO: Western View, 1992.

Pressler, Carolyn. "Deuteronomy." In *Women's Bible Commentary*, edited by Carol Ann Newsom et al., 88–102. Louisville, KY: Westminster/John Knox, 2012.

Ramsey, Dave, ed. "33 Proven Ways to Reduce Personal Debt"; http://www.becomingminimalist.com/33-proven-ways-to-reduce-personal-debt/.

Rhetor, Alexander. *On the Origins of Rhetoric.* In *Rhetores Graeci,* edited by L. Spender. Leipzig: B.G. Teubner, 1856.

Riss, Kathryn J. "Women's Ministries in the Early Church" (2005); www.Godswordtowomen.org/rissjunia.htm.

Robinson, James M. "On the Origin of the World." In *The Nag Hammadi Library,* rev. 3rd ed. Translated by Hans-Gebhard Bethge and Bentley Layton. Leiden: E. J. Brill, 1988; http://khazarzar.skeptik.net/books/nhl.pdf.

Ruether, Rosemary Radford. "Introduction." In *Feminist Theologies: Legacy and Prospect,* edited by Rosemary Radford Ruether, 1–4. Minneapolis, MN: Fortress, 2007.

———. *Introducing Redemption in Christian Feminism.* Sheffield: Sheffield Academic, 1998.

———. *Women and Redemption: A Theological History.* Rev. ed. Minneapolis, MN: Fortress, 2012.

Runyowa, Wilbert, and Rangarirai Rutoro. "Resource Development and Women in Leadership Positions in the Reformed Church in Zimbabwe." In *Reformed Encounters with Modernity: Perspectives from Three Continents,* edited by H. Jurgens Hendriks, 56–64. Cape Town: International Society for the Study of Reformed Communities, 2001.

Rutoro, Ester. "Gender Transformation and Leadership: On Teaching Gender in Shona Culture." In *Men in the Pulpit, Women in the Pew?: Addressing Gender Inequality in Africa,* edited by H. Jurgens Hendriks et al., 159–69. Stellenbosch: Sun, 2012.

Rutoro, Rangarirai. "Lay Leadership Development in the Reformed Church in Zimbabwe." PhD diss., University of Stellenbosch, 2007.

Sanders, Oswald. *Spiritual Leadership.* Chicago, IL: Moody, 2007.

Schneemelcher, Wilhelm. "The Gospel of the Egyptians." In *New Testament Apocrypha* vol. 1. Louisville, KY: Westminster/John Knox, 1992.

———. "The Gospel of Thomas." In *New Testament Apocrypha* vol. 1. Louisville, KY: Westminster/John Knox, 1992.

Seidman, Naomi. "The Erotic of Sexual Segregation." In *The Passionate Torah: Sex and Judaism,* edited by Danya Ruttenberg, 107–15. New York, NY: New York University Press, 2009.

Sesay, Waithera. *Don't Sleep, African Women: Powerlessness and HIV/AIDS Vulnerability among Kenyan Women.* Pittsburgh, PA: Dorrance, 2011.

———. "Female Bodies: Gender Inequalities, Vulnerability, HIV, and AIDS in Kenya." *Advancing Women in Leadership Journal* 30.17 (2010).

Sharma, Arvind, and Katherine K. Young. *Feminism and World Religions.* Albany, NY: State University of New York Press, 1999.

Silberberg, Naftali. "The Woman's Role in Bringing the Redemption"; http://www.chabad.org/library/moshiach/article_cdo/aid/1128933/jewish/The-Womans-Role.htm#footnoteRef2a1128933.

Smith, J. Stephen. *The History of the Alliance High School.* Nairobi, Kenya: Heinemann Educational, 1973.

Spencer, Aída Besançon. *Beyond the Curse: Women Called to Ministry.* Nashville, TN: T. Nelson, 1985.

———."'Eve at Ephesus' (Should Women Be Ordained as Pastors according to the First Letter to Timothy 2:11–15?)." *Journal of the Evangelical Theological Society* 17 (1974).

Spencer, Aída Besançon et al., eds. *Global Voices on Biblical Equality: Women and Men Serving Together in the Church*. Eugene, OR: Wipf & Stock, 2008.

———. "Seven Principles for the Seventh Day." In *Sunday, Sabbath, and the Weekend: Managing Time in a Global Culture*, edited by Edward O'Flaherty et al. Grand Rapids, MI: Eerdmans, 2010.

Staggenborg, Suzanne. *Gender, Family, and Social Movements*. Thousand Oaks, CA: Pine Forge, 1998.

Steady, Filomina C. *Women and Leadership in West Africa: Mothering the Nation and Humanizing the State*. New York, NY: Palgrave Macmillan, 2011.

Stein, David E. S. "The Grammar of Social Gender in Biblical Hebrew." *Hebrew Studies* 49 (2008) 7–26.

Stephanus, *Thesaurus Graeca Lingaue*, edited by Wilhelm and Ludwig Dindorf. Paris: Didot, 1831–65.

Stott, John. *Issues Facing Christians Today*. 4th ed. Grand Rapids, MI: Zondervan, 2006.

Swidler, Leonard. *Biblical Affirmations of Woman*. Philadelphia, PA: The Westminster, 1979.

Tanko, Allen. "Women in Ministry." In *Woman on the Pulpit*, edited by Simon Itodo Abbas, 61–70. Lagos: Soldiers of the Cross, 2004.

Tanu, Abigail. "Prophetess Huldah as a Principal Strategist of King Josiah's Reform (2 Kings 22:15-20): Lessons for Women in Political and Religious Leadership in Africa." In *Biblical Studies and Feminism in African Context: In Honor of the Late Dr. Dorcas Olubanke Akintunde*, edited by D. D. Adegbite et al., 212–28. Ibadan, Nigeria: NABIS Western Zone, 2012.

Temu, A. J. *British Protestant Missions*. London: Longman, 1972.

Thayer, Joseph Henry, et al., eds. *Thayer's Greek-English Lexicon of the New Testament*. Peabody, MA: Hendrickson, 1996.

Trible, Phyllis. *God and the Rhetoric of Sexuality*. Philadelphia, PA: Fortress, 1978.

———. *Texts of Terror: Literary-Feminist Readings of Biblical Narratives*. Philadelphia, PA: Fortress, 1984.

Tucker, Ruth. *Women in the Maze: Questions and Answers on Biblical Equality*. Downers Grove, IL: InterVarsity, 1992.

United Nations. *United Nations General Assembly Session 31* (1976); http://www.un.org/documents/ga/res/31/ares31.htm.

———. "We Can End Poverty 2015: Millennium Development Goals" (2013); www.un.org/millenniumgoals.

The Untold Story of Ephesus. DVD. Pittsburgh, PA: Listening Takes Heart Productions, 2013.

Van der Merwe, William J. *From Mission Field to Autonomous Church in Zimbabwe*. Transvaal: N.G. Kerkboekhandel, 1981.

Van Dyk, Anna Margaretha. "The Voices of Women and Young People Who Experienced Domestic Violence." MTh thesis, University of South Africa, 2000.

wa Gatumu, Kabiro. "The Authentic Biblical Community: Paul's Perspective on Ethnicity and Gender Relations Vis-à-Vis the African Church." *Sapientia Logos: A Journal of Biblical Research and Interpretation in Africa* 5.2 (2013) 32–76.

Waliggo, John Mary. *Struggle for Equality: Women and Empowerment in Uganda*. Eldoret, Kenya: AMECEA Gaba, 2002.

Waltke, Bruce K. *An Old Testament Theology: An Exegetical, Canonical, and Thematic Approach*. Grand Rapids, MI: Zondervan, 2007.

Wanjohi, Gerald Joseph. *The Wisdom and Philosophy of the Gikuyu Proverbs: The Kihooto World-View.* Nairobi, Kenya: Paulines Publications Africa, 1997.

Weisberg, Dvora E. "Women and Torah Studies in Aggadah." In *Women and Judaism: New Insights and Scholarship,* edited by Fredrick E. Greenspahn, 4–63. New York, NY: New York University Press, 2009.

West, Christopher. *Theology of the Body Explained: A Commentary on John Paul II's "Gospel of the Body."* Boston, MA: Pauline, 2003.

Whitehead, Andrew L. "Gender Ideology and Religion: Does a Masculine Image of God Matter?" *Review of Religious Research* 54.2 (2012) 139–56.

Wiley, Tatha. *Encountering Paul: Understanding the Man and His Message.* Lanham, MD: Rowman & Littlefield, 2010.

Witherington III, Ben. *Women in the Earliest Churches.* Cambridge: Cambridge University Press, 1994.

———. *Women in the Ministry of Jesus: A Study of Jesus' Attitudes to Women and Their Roles as Reflected in His Earthly Life.* Cambridge: Cambridge University Press, 1984.

Scripture Index

GENESIS

	34, 35, 37, 65, 167, 201, 209, 210
1–3	xxv, 32, 34, 41, 169
2–3	35, 49
1	34, 53
2	37, 39, 47, 66, 169
3	39, 47, 142
3:1–8	39n
2:18–25	66
2:18–24	37–39
1:26–27	8, 35–36, 42, 48, 63, 66, 142, 163, 173, 180
1:26–28	36, 48, 52, 66, 158, 163
2:16–17	66
2:23, 24	52, 201
1:26	65, 65n
1:27	10, 14, 25, 27, 48, 78, 91, 191, 191n
1:28	14
2:7	66
2:18	38
2:22	36
2:23	52, 89
2:28	38
3:15	67
3:16	40, 67
3:21	35
5:1–2	52
37:14	191

EXODUS

28:1–3	155
2:23	66n
3:14	35
18:4	38
15:20	46n

NUMBERS

36:1–12	67
27:1–11	67
18:1–7	155
26:33	67
27:7	68
27:8	68

DEUTERONOMY

11:16, 18–19	205
32:18	35
33:7	38
33:29	66n

JOSHUA

17:3–6	67

JUDGES

4–5	117, 157, 158, 215n
5	118
2:10–11; 3:7–9	117
5:15–17, 28–30	118
4:9, 17–22	118
5:1, 7, 12, 15	118
5:14–15, 18	118
5:24–27	118

JUDGES (continued)

5:4–5, 11	118
2:16–18	117
4:8, 10	117
4:4–5	11
4:6–7	117, 118
4:8–9	11
4:4	56n
4:14	118
5:31	118

1 SAMUEL

8	33
25	206
8:7, 10–18	117
12:8	66n

1 KINGS

5:12	191
11:5	35

2 KINGS

5:1–14	68
22:14–20	11
22:23–28	69
5:11	69
5:15	69
5:38	68
22:2	69

1 CHRONICLES

7:15	67

2 CHRONICLES

34	69
34:22–29	11

NEHEMIAH

2:11–12	136
5:7	136

ESTHER

1–2	62
1	62
2	62
7:1–10	11
1:21–22	61
1:12	59
1:19	59, 61
2:14	60

PSALMS

2	33
139:13–14	202
5:2	66n
8:5	10
10:14b	66n
37:37	191
38:22	66n
68:11	93
98:9b	xxiv
99:4	xxiv
127:3	203
139:14	10
144:12	203

PROVERBS

31	199, 200
31:21–31	103
31:10–16	199
2:8–9	xxiv
1:3	xxiv
23:7	197
31:8	137

ISAIAH

18:1–12	134
41:13–14	67, 67n
42:13–14	35
33:6, 9	119
11:4	xxiv
45:19	xxiv
63:16	33

JEREMIAH

18:1–12	134
33:6, 9	191

EZEKIEL

23	33
11:12	190

HOSEA

11:3–4	35

MICAH

3:9	xxiv
6:8	xvii

MATTHEW

25:1–30	168
20:1–16	117
8:1–15	168
9:18–26	168
15:21–28	51
26:6–13	71
10:1–4,	155
18:3–6	111
10:2–4	156
5:13–14	189
11:16–17	111
27:55–56	70
28:18–19	208
28:19–20	xxii
10:10	115
11:17	112
28:19	190

MARK

	112, 116, 121
9–10	109
4:1–25	115
3:21–35	112n
10:35–45	110
6:35–44	51
14:32–41	114
13:1–5, 9–13	114n
8:14–21	114n
2:27—3:5	114n
14:32–39	116n
1:21–26, 31, 40–42	116n
14:10, 66–72	112n
7:2–8	114
9:42–48	116n
14:3–9	71
12:26, 32–37	113
7:25–30	113n
10:17–22	115
14:4–9	114n
1:40–44	114
3:31–35	113
9:5–9	113
10:23–27	114
7:5–9	112n
10:9–12, 32	114n
1:27, 31, 34, 41	113n
3:16–19	113n
6:2–5	112n
6:8–10	115
8:22–25	113n, 116n
9:38–41	114
10:42–45	110
1:12, 14–15	112
5:15–17, 40	112
14:1, 10–11, 55	112n
15:29–30, 32	112
1:36–38	112n, 116
2:3–5	116
2:15–17	116
2:18–19	114
3:3–5	116n
4:30–32	114
5:18–20	114
6:4–6	115
6:48–50	114
10:13–15	111
10:28–30	113
11:8–10	113
11:15–17	116n
12:29–31	116n
1:21–22, 27	112n
5:34, 41–42	116n
5:39–40, 42	111n
6:2–3, 6	112n
15:10, 31–32	112n

MARK (continued)

1:40–41	116n
2:10–11	113
3:11–12	113
3:14–15	114n
6:12–13	114n
8:2–3	116n
9:28–29	114n
10:17–18	113
10:33–34	112
10:47–48	116n
11:27–28	112n
12:12–13	112n
12:13–14	116
14:61–62	113
2:2, 13	112n
1:11	113
1:17	113n
1:20	113
1:22	113
1:35	116n
2:14	113n
3:9	114n
3:14	113
3:15	114
4:1	112n
4:34	114n
4:39	113
5:36	116n
5:37	114
6:7	114
6:30	114
6:31	114
6:34	116n
6:37	116n
6:46	116n
6:52	114
6:53	114n
7:24	113
7:36	113
8:6	114n
8:11	112n
8:33	116n
9:2	114
9:7	113
9:30	113
9:31	114
10:1	112n
10:2	112n
10:21.	116n
10:15	116n
10:31	112
10:40	117
10:45	112
11:1	114
11:18	112n
11:22	116n
11:24	116n
12:33	114
12:35	112n
12:43	116n
13:26	113
13:27	114
14:13	114
14:62	113
14:65	112
16:8	112n

LUKE

7:36–50	51, 168
18:1–14	168
19:1–10	51
15:3–10	168
10:38–42	71, 168
10:39–42	51
8:1–3	70
4:18–19	192
8:2–3	103, 105
11:27–28	168
13:19–21	168
1:34	107
1:38	107
1:59	111n
2:38	99
6:31	141
6:39	132
7:32	111
8:2	104
10:2	169
10:7	115
10:39	71
10:42	104
11:2	34

JOHN

4	100
4:1–42	71
4:15–24	173
8:2–11	168
12:1–8	71
12:1–6	71
21:15–19	72
17:20–23	51
1:12–13	54
11:25–26	71
11:20, 30	105
4:39	100
5:18	66n
8:16	65
8:32	138
10:10	25, 190
11:8b	71
11:11	71
11:23	105
11:27	71
11:32	105
12:7	105
14:26	65
15:5	136
16:21	111n
17:21	xvii
20:18	104
21:5	111

ACTS

6	101
18	73
18:19–26	72
9:36–42	72
12:12–17	72
16:11–15, 40	72, 73, 103
18:24–28	73
19:23–27	3
5:14–16	72
13:1–3	114
18:1–3	72, 73
18:24–26	102
21:8–9	99
17:4, 12	73
1:14	72
2:18	98

5:14	72
8:12	72
10:38	65
12:12	72, 107
13:3	156
14:23	156
17:4	72
17:11	141
17:12	72
17:34	72, 73
18:2	102
18:18	79, 102
18:26	79, 80, 81
19:28	82

ROMANS

	74
16	74, 80
16:1–15	77, 78
8:14–17	54
16:6–7, 12	80
16:1–3	73
16:3–5a	79
12:6–8	86
16:13, 15	80
12:1–2	190
16:1–2	78, 101
2:11	141
5:5	190
12:8	79n
16:1	79
16:3	79, 102
16:5	102
16:7	53, 90, 98, 207
16:11	79n
16:13	81

1 CORINTHIANS

	53
11	89, 93
12.	88
13	93
14	93
11:1–16	17, 77, 87, 93, 169
12:4–11	86
11:17–22	87, 88

1 CORINTHIANS
(continued)

11:2, 4–5	87
3:4–6	73
11:4–5	88
11:8–9	38, 53, 91
11:11–12	52, 53
14:31–32	98
14:34–35	77, 93, 96, 165, 167
1:12	73
9:11	115
11:1	87
11:3	88
11:5	53, 89, 96
11:10	91, 92
11:12	92
11:14	93
11:16	93
11:33	93
14:30	93n
15:10	80
15:33	132
16:19	79n, 102

2 CORINTHIANS

5:18–20	78
3:6	79
5:17	54

GALATIANS

3:2–28	77
3:26–28	54, 77, 78, 166, 168
3:13, 28	52
1:1	97
3:28	Xvii, 12, 51, 53, 54, 78, 96, 141, 166
5:1	52
6:6	115

EPHESIANS

4:15–16	113
4:11, 13	156
4:11	100
4:13	190
5:31	53

6:21	79

PHILIPPIANS

4:2–3	53, 73, 100
1:1	79
2:16	80
2:25	79

COLOSSIANS

3:8–15	190
1:7	79
1:15	89
1:29	80
4:7	79
4:15	73, 106

1 THESSALONIANS

3:12–13	190
4:11–12	84
5:12	79n

2 THESSALONIANS

3:12	84

1 TIMOTHY

	53, 54
1	52n, 84
2	84, 85
2:8–15	165
2:11–15	77, 81, 83
2:12–15	52
2:11–12; 3:1ff	156
3:4–5, 12	79n
1:4, 6–7	82
2:1–2	84
2:11–12	93n
2:11–14	167, 169
3:8, 12	79
1:3–4	86
2:2	84
2:8	84
2:10	84
2:11	83, 84, 86
2:12	85, 86, 169

4:6	79
4:10	80
4:11	86
5:17	79n
6:3	86

2 TIMOTHY

1:5	106
2:15	84
3:17	31
4:19	79, 102

TITUS

3:8, 14	79n

PHILEMON

	73, 79n
1:2	73
1:1–2	106

HEBREWS

11:1, 32	118

REVELATION

22:1–2	133

www.ingramcontent.com/pod-product-compliance
Lightning Source LLC
Chambersburg PA
CBHW050849230426
43667CB00012B/2209